GOD AND OTHER MINDS

A Study of the Rational Justification
of Belief in God

GOD AND
OTHER MINDS

A Study of the Rational Justification
of Belief in God

By Alvin Plantinga

Cornell University Press

ITHACA AND LONDON

First published 1967 by Cornell University Press.
Fifth printing 1981.
First published, Cornell Paperbacks, 1990.

International Standard Book Number 0-8014-0338-3 (cloth)
International Standard Book Number 0-8014-9735-3 (paper)
Library of Congress Catalog Card Number: 67-20519
PRINTED IN THE UNITED STATES OF AMERICA

♾ The paper used in the text of this publication meets the minimum requirements of American National Standard for Information Sciences—Permanence
of Paper for Printed Library Materials, ANSI Z39.48-1984.

To Kathleen

Contents

Preface to the 1990 Paperback Edition

God and Other Minds was published twenty-three years ago. Upon rereading it, I am gratified to discover the considerable extent of agreement between my present and former selves (although perhaps what that really shows is how little progress I've made in the last twenty-three years). Of course I have come to see things somewhat differently on a number of points of detail. Thus I think the formulation of the free will defense in terms of possible worlds and individual essences (as in *The Nature of Necessity*) is preferable to its formulation in *God and Other Minds* in terms of the sets of properties I called 'possible persons'. And perhaps it would have been wiser to consider the extended version of the First Mover argument Aquinas offers in the *Summa Contra Gentiles*, rather than the Third Way of the *Summa Theologiae*. In evaluating the theistic arguments, furthermore, I employed a traditional but improperly stringent standard; there may be plenty of good arguments for theism even if there aren't any that start from propositions that compel assent from every honest and intelligent person and proceed majestically to their conclusion by way of forms of argument that can be rejected only on pain of irrationality. After all, no philosophical arguments of any consequence meet *that* standard, and the fact that theistic arguments do not is not as significant as I thought. Still further, if I were to rewrite the book, I would perhaps devote less attention to Wittgensteinian claims and views about other minds, and more attention to the currently popular idea that the existence of other minds is, for each of us, a sort of scientific hypothesis.

There are more major points on which what I said also needs correction. First, after writing *God and Other Minds*, I came to see (as I think) that there is a form of the ontological argument that is perfectly sound, whatever its powers of compelling assent.[1] Second, when I considered and examined the ontological argument in *God and Other Minds*, I took it for granted that there are or could be merely possible beings, beings that do not exist but could have. This now seems to me a thoughtless mistake. I regret to say that I was taken in by such arguments as *Pegasus does not exist; therefore there is at least one thing that does not exist*. This argument, as I failed to realize, is no better than *the average woman has 2.36 children; therefore there is a woman who has 2.36 children*. The problem was insufficient attention to the semantics of quantifiers in English, or perhaps failure to distinguish objectual from substitutional quantification (in English) or, as it might have been put in the sixties, failure to distinguish the real logical form of a sentence from its apparent logical form. In any event it was an error. I therefore could not now cavalierly write, as I did then, that one can compare nonexistent objects such as Hamlet with existent objects such as Lyndon Johnson in point of the number of books written about each. True enough, the sentence 'More books have been written about Hamlet than about Lyndon Johnson' expresses a

[1]See *The Nature of Necessity* (Oxford University Press, 1974), chapter 10.

truth; but the truth it expresses does not pick out a pair of objects, one existent and the other nonexistent, predicating of them the relation of being such that more books have been written about the former than about the latter.

So on these points and some others I erred. But I remain unrepentant about the main epistemological conclusions of the book. The chief topic of *God and Other Minds* is the question of the rationality, or reasonability, or intellectual propriety of belief in God. My contention was that the strongest argument for the existence of God and the strongest argument for other minds are similar, and fail in similar ways; hence my "tentative conclusion": "if my belief in other minds is rational, so is my belief in God. But obviously the former is rational; so, therefore, is the latter." As I now see (with the acuity of hindsight), my chief aim was to make a suitable reply to the *evidentialist objection to theistic belief*: the objection that theistic belief is irrational or unreasonable or intellectually second- or third-rate because there is insufficient evidence for it. More exactly (and relying even more heavily on hindsight) my aim was to reply to that objection taken in the context or from the perspective of classical (Cartesian and Lockean) foundationalism.[2] The main argument of the book is really an argument against that objection, so taken.

From the perspective of classical foundationalism, the sort of rationality relevant to the evidentialist objection is really *justification*: being within one's epistemic rights, violating no epistemic duty or obligation. Among our chief intellectual obligations is that of believing a proposition that is not certain (i.e., either self-evident or incorrigible) only on the evidential basis of propositions that *are* certain. What I argued, in essence, is that from this point of view belief in other minds and belief in God are on an epistemological

[2]See my "Reason and Belief in God," in *Faith and Rationality*, ed. A. Plantinga and N. Wolterstorff (Notre Dame: University of Notre Dame Press, 1983).

par. In neither case are there cogent arguments of the sort required; hence if the absence of such arguments in the theistic case demonstrates irrationality, the same goes for belief in other minds. If you flout epistemic duty in accepting the one, then you flout it just as surely in accepting the other; hence if the former is irrational, so is the latter. But clearly the latter isn't irrational; this version of the evidentialist objection to theistic belief, therefore, is a failure. I also claimed, implicitly and in effect, that classical foundationalism can't be true, for a person flouts no epistemic duty in believing that there are other minds, whether or not there is good argumentative support for that belief. On these points I think I was correct.

Due to youth and inexperience and the influence of classical foundationalism, however, I failed to distinguish rationality in the sense of *justification*—being within one's intellectual rights, flouting no intellectual duties or obligations—from rationality in the sense of *warrant*—that property or, better, quantity, enough of which distinguishes knowledge from mere true belief.[3] (It is one of the achievements of contemporary epistemology to rediscover a clear distinction between justification and warrant—a distinction known to some of the medievals but lost in the *Anschluss* of classical foundationalism.) If we take rationality as *justification*, my conclusion was quite correct (although I would now argue for it slightly differently); belief in other minds and belief in God are in the same boat when it comes to justification, and a person can be entirely justified in accepting either or both, whether or not there are cogent arguments for either from other propositions she believes. If we take rationality as *warrant*, on the other hand, an entirely different galaxy of considerations becomes relevant. Indeed, so taken, this epistemological question is not ontologically or theologically neutral; pursued far enough, it transforms itself into an ontological or theo-

[3]See my "Justification in the Twentieth Century," forthcoming in *Philosophy and Phenomenological Research*, and chapter 1 of what I hope is my forthcoming book, *Warrant*.

Preface to the 1990 Paperback Edition

logical question. I explored these matters in Gifford Lectures given at the University of Aberdeen in 1987; I hope to explore them further in a book to be titled *Our Knowledge of God*.

ALVIN PLANTINGA

South Bend, Indiana
January 1990

Preface

IN this study I set out to investigate the rational justification of belief in the existence of God as He is conceived in the Hebrew-Christian tradition. Part I examines natural theology, an important traditional approach to this matter, by considering in turn the cosmological, ontological, and teleological arguments for the existence of God. These arguments are, I believe, worthy of serious and detailed study; and the last one is not, perhaps, completely without promise. Nevertheless it is open to a serious objection (developed in Chapter Four); along with natural theology generally it must finally be judged unsuccessful.

Part II considers natural atheology, the attempt, roughly, to show that, given what we know, it is impossible or unlikely that God exists. Here I consider the problem of evil, verificationism, the paradox of omnipotence, and an ontological disproof of God's existence. None of these survives close scrutiny;

the verdict must be that natural atheology is no more successful than natural theology.

Since neither natural theology nor natural atheology offers a
satisfying solution to the problem at hand, I try in Part III
another approach to it by exploring its analogies and connections with a similar question—the "problem of other minds."
In Chapters Eight and Nine, I defend the analogical argument
for other minds against current criticism and argue that it is
as good an answer as we have to the question of other minds.
But in Chapter Ten it turns out that the analogical argument
finally succumbs to a malady exactly resembling the one afflict-
ing the teleological argument. I conclude that belief in other
minds and belief in God are in the same epistemological boat;
hence if either is rational, so is the other. But obviously the
former *is* rational; so, therefore, is the latter.

My thanks are due to Professor Max Black for helpful edi-
torial suggestions, and to George G. Harper, who read the en-
tire manuscript and saved me from much stylistic gaucherie.
My thanks also to the *Journal of Philosophy* for permission to
incorporate a few paragraphs of "Kant's Objection to the Ontological Argument" (LXIII [1966]) in Chapter Two; to the
Philosophical Review for permission to reprint "A Valid Ontological Argument?" (LXX [1961]) as part of Chapter Two;
to the *Review of Metaphysics* for permission to reprint brief
portions of "Things and Persons" (XIV [1961]) in Chapters
Eight and Nine as well as sections of "Induction and Other
Minds" (XX [1966]), which here appear as parts of Chapters
Eight and Ten; and to Cornell University Press and George
Allen & Unwin Ltd for permission to include in Chapter Six a
revised version of "The Free Will Defence," which originally
appeared in *Philosophy in America*, Max Black, editor (Ithaca
and London, 1965).

Preface

I take this opportunity to record my abiding gratitude to several of my teachers, including Cornelius A. Plantinga, William K. Frankena, and Henry Stob. I must make special mention of William Harry Jellema, whose magnificent teaching and thinking kindled my enthusiasm for philosophy and have served as models ever since.

In writing this book I have had the benefit of stimulating discussion and penetrating criticism from a large number of friends, colleagues, and students—especially William P. Alston, Charles Landesman, Jr., Ian Mueller, and Nicholas Wolterstorff. I am particularly eager to acknowledge my indebtedness to the members and former members of the Wayne philosophy department—especially Richard L. Cartwright, Hector Castañeda, George Nakhnikian, and (perhaps most of all) Edmund L. Gettier, III, and Robert C. Sleigh, Jr. It would be hard to overestimate their contribution to this book; I have learned more from them than I can say.

ALVIN PLANTINGA

Calvin College
Grand Rapids, Michigan
January 1967

Part I

NATURAL THEOLOGY

One

The Cosmological Argument

IN this study I shall investigate the rational justifiability of a particular religious belief—the belief in the existence of God as He is conceived in the Judeo-Christian tradition. But the question arises: how can one approach this topic? How could one show that it is or is not rational to believe in God's existence? One important traditional approach is to be found in "natural theology," in which one gives *proofs* of some of the central beliefs of theism. But what would constitute a proof of God's existence? What would such a proof be like? Certainly not just any deductively valid argument with true premises will serve. For consider the following argument: If the Taj Mahal exists, God exists; the Taj Mahal exists; so God exists. Taking the first premise as a material conditional, any theist will hold that it is true; so what we have here, he must concede, is a deductively valid argument with true premises. And yet it is by no stretch of the imagination a proof of the existence of God.

God and Other Minds

What the natural theologian sets out to do is to show that some of the central beliefs of theism follow deductively or inductively from propositions that are obviously true and accepted by nearly every sane man (e.g., *Some things are in motion*) together with propositions that are self-evident or necessarily true. In this way he tries to show that certain pivotal religious beliefs—particularly the existence of God and the immortality of the soul—are rationally justifiable. And I think it is evident that if he succeeds in showing that these beliefs do indeed follow from those propositions, he succeeds in showing that these beliefs are rational. Since I am restricting my concern to the rationality of belief in the existence of God—a belief which is the foundation and center of any theistic religion—what I shall do in this and the three succeeding chapters is to consider carefully and in some detail three famous and traditional pieces of natural theology: what Kant called the cosmological, the ontological, and the teleological arguments for the existence of God. Although these arguments are famous and traditional, contemporary philosophers have had little or nothing to say about the first and third; and while they have said much about the second, much remains to be said.

The *locus classicus* for the cosmological argument is the "third way" of St. Thomas Aquinas:

The third way is taken from possibility and necessity and runs thus. We find in nature things that are possible to be and not to be, since they are found to be generated, and to be corrupted, and, consequently, it is possible for them to be and not to be. But it is impossible for these always to exist, for that which can not-be at some time is not. Therefore, if everything can not-be then at one time there was nothing in existence. Now if this were true, even now there would be nothing in existence, because that which does not exist begins to exist only through something already existing.

The Cosmological Argument

Therefore if at one time nothing was in existence, it would have been impossible for anything to have begun to exist; and thus even now nothing would be in existence—which is absurd. Therefore, not all beings are merely possible, but there must exist something the existence of which is necessary. But every necessary thing either has its necessity caused by another, or not. Now it is impossible to go on to infinity in necessary things which have their necessity caused by another, as has already been proved in regard to efficient causes. Therefore, we cannot but admit the existence of some being having of itself its own necessity, and not receiving it from another, but rather causing in others their necessity. This all men speak of as God.[1]

In order to consider this argument we need some kind of schematization of it. The following will perhaps serve our purpose initially:

(a) There are at present contingent beings ("things that are possible to be and not to be").

(b) Whatever can fail to exist, at some time does not exist.

(c) Therefore if all beings are contingent, then at one time nothing existed—from (b).

(d) Whatever begins to exist is caused to begin to exist by something else already existing.

(e) Therefore, if at any time nothing existed, then at every subsequent time nothing would exist—(d).

(f) Hence if at one time nothing existed, then nothing exists now—(e).

(g) Hence if all beings are contingent, then nothing exists now—(c), (f).

(h) Therefore, not all beings are contingent—(a), (g).

(i) Hence there is at least one necessary being—(h).

(j) Every necessary being either has its necessity caused by another being or has its necessity in itself.

---

[1] *Summa Theologica*, Q. 3, art. 3.

(k) It is impossible that there be an infinite series of necessary beings each of which has its necessity caused by another.

(l) Therefore there is a necessary being having of itself its own necessity, and this all men speak of as God— (i), (j), (k).

As it stands, this argument is singularly unconvincing. It has often been pointed out, for example, that (b) is not obviously true; and in any event (c) does not follow from it. For even if every being did fail to exist at some time or other, it surely would not follow that there is some time at which every being fails to exist—the inference looks like a simple quantifier mistake. And even if there is a time at which every being fails to exist, it scarcely follows that this time would have been in the *past*; perhaps that unhappy time is still to be looked for. Here Aquinas' commentators make a suggestion designed both to support (b) and to shore up the inference of (c) from it; but before we examine this suggestion we must ask a preliminary question: how, exactly, are we to understand the *modal* terms—*possible, contingent, necessary*—that the argument contains?

Aquinas says little about this, and his commentators say less. In Question II, Article 2, he points out that some propositions self-evident in themselves are not self-evident to us. A proposition is self-evident in itself, Aquinas says, if its subject contains its predicate; this characterization indicates pretty clearly that he takes these propositions to be necessarily true. Since, therefore, he maintains that the proposition *God exists* is self-evident in itself (but not to us), it is fairly clear that he takes that proposition to be logically necessary; and hence it is initially plausible to suppose that in the third way he sets out to demonstrate the existence of a logically necessary being. And indeed, Aquinas is very often understood in just this way.[2] On the other hand, P. T. Geach and Patterson Brown emphatically reject this interpretation, replacing the notion of logical necessity with the relatively obscure ideas of "imperishable existence that has no liability to cease"[3] and "inability to undergo any essential change in any of the ways permitted by the Aristotelian theories of matter and form, potentiality and actuality, and simplicity and complexity."[4] I shall consider both kinds of interpretation.

What does it mean, then, to say that a being is logically necessary? We might try the following explanation:

(m) *x* is a necessary being = def. the proposition *x exists* is logically necessary.

But (m) has the unfortunate consequence that a being A could be necessary while a being B identical with A would be merely contingent. Even if the proposition *God exists* is logically necessary, the proposition *The being worshipped by St. Francis exists* is not; and this despite the identity of God with the being worshipped by St. Francis. This awkwardness can be relieved as follows:

(n) *x* is a necessary being = def. (1) The proposition *x exists* is logically necessary, or (2) *x* is identical with some necessary being.

Many contemporary philosophers apparently believe that

[2] See, for example, C. B. Martin, *Religious Belief* (Ithaca, 1959), pp. 151–152; and J. J. C. Smart, "The Existence of God," in *New Essays in Philosophical Theology*, ed. A. Flew and A. MacIntyre (London, 1955), pp. 35–39, and many others.

[3] P. T. Geach and G. E. M. Anscombe, *Three Philosophers* (Oxford, 1961), p. 115.

[4] Brown, "St. Thomas' Doctrine of Necessary Being," *Philosophical Review*, LXXIII (1964), 76–90; quotation from p. 82.

7

necessary beings (in this sense of the term) are impossible; for it is a necessary truth, they think, that no existential statements are necessary. I shall discuss this claim in Chapter Two. For the moment let me say only that if "existential" is not given an extraordinary sense, the claim appears to be an unsupported dogma to which such propositions as *There is a prime number between 16 and 18* are counterexamples.

A point in favor of the Geach-Brown reading of St. Thomas is that under the present interpretation it is difficult indeed to grasp the distinction between beings "necessary in themselves" (necessary *a se*) and beings that have their necessity "caused by another" (necessary *ab aliter*). What are we to make of the suggestion that a necessary being has its necessity caused by another? No necessary being, of course, could be caused to come into existence, since it is impossible that a necessary being begin to exist. Nor can we suggest, presumably, that a necessary being has its necessity caused by another in case that other acts upon it in some specifiable way; the fact that a given being is a necessary being is itself a necessary fact, and hence there is no possible way of acting upon a necessary being such that if it were not acted upon in that way, it would not be necessary. How then are we to take this suggestion? We might try the following:

(0) *x* is a necessary being *ab aliter* if (1) *x* is a necessary being and there exists a necessary being *y* (distinct from *x*) such that the proposition *y exists* entails (or is entailed by?) the proposition *x exists*, or (2) *x* is identical with a being that is necessary *ab aliter*,

adding that *x* is necessary *a se* in case it is necessary but not necessary *ab aliter*. Now we must ask ourselves first how the term "entails" is being used here. If we identify entailment with strict implication (i.e., take it that *p* entails *q* if and only if the conjunction of *p* with the denial of *q* is necessarily false), then of course a necessary proposition is entailed by just any proposition. Further, any necessary being will be identical with some being *x* such that the proposition *x exists* is necessarily true. Suppose that there are two necessary beings *x* and *y*. Then *x* will be identical with some being *w* such that *w exists* is necessary; *y* will be identical with some being *z* such that *z exists* is necessary; *z exists* will entail and be entailed by *w exists*; hence *z* and *w* are both (by (o)) necessary beings *ab aliter*; hence (by (o)) so are *x* and *y*. What follows then is that if there are two or more necessary beings, all of them are necessary *ab aliter* (and hence none necessary *a se*).

We might try to avoid this difficulty by defining "entails" more narrowly so as to preclude the result that a necessary proposition is entailed by just any proposition. But none of the attempts to do this seem very satisfactory; some of them sacrifice such essential properties of entailment as transitivity, while others reject argument forms (e.g., the disjunctive syllogism) that are about as clearly cases of entailment as any we have.[5] And even if we did restrict entailment so as to preclude the so-called paradoxes of strict implication we should by no means have avoided the difficulty. For let *x* and *y* be any necessary beings. Again there will be a *z* identical with *x* and a *w* identical with *y* such that *z exists* and *w exists* are necessary. Now let R be some relation (there must be one) that *x* (and only *x*) bears to *w*. Then *the thing that bears R to w* is a necessary being, and the proposition *The thing that bears R to w exists* presumably entails *w exists* even in our restricted sense of entailment, whatever that is. But then it follows (by (o)) that *y* is necessary *ab aliter*, and by the same argument we can show

---

[5] See below, pp. 55–58.

that x is necessary *ab aliter*. Once more, then, we get the result that if there is more than one necessary being, there are no beings necessary *a se*.

There is a substantial difficulty, therefore, in glossing "necessary" as "logically necessary" in St. Thomas' third way; we then find no easy way to understand the distinction between necessity *a se* and necessity *ab aliter*. I do not know how to overcome this difficulty, and shall limit my concern with the proof to the part through step (i). To the objection that (i), though true, is of little interest to theism in that the number seven, for example, is a necessary being in the explained sense, we may reply that Thomas is speaking of beings capable (unlike the number seven) of bringing into existence or creating other beings;[6] and the conclusion that there is a necessary being of *that* sort is of considerable interest to theism. (It is, of course, a long step from (i) to *God exists*; but St. Thomas attempts to supply some of the necessary argument in the passages following Question II.) Furthermore, it is certainly plausible to suppose that there is at most *one* necessary being of this sort, in which case the category of beings necessary *ab aliter* will be empty. Of course it must be conceded that this does not remove the difficulty in understanding necessity *ab aliter*. We still have the peculiar result that on any plausible reading of "necessity *ab aliter*," if there are any beings necessary *ab aliter*, then there are no beings necessary *a se*; whereas what St. Thomas argues is that if there are any beings necessary *ab aliter*, then there is at least one being necessary *a se*. (It ought to be noted that these are not inconsistent; what their conjunction entails is only that there are no beings necessary *ab aliter*.)

Limiting our concern, then, to the argument up through step (i), let us return to the inference of

---

[6] And hence a clause to this effect should be added to definition (n).

The Cosmological Argument

(c) If all beings are contingent, then at one time nothing existed

from

(b) Whatever can fail to exist, at some time does not exist.

As I noted above, the inference is on the face of it flagrantly fallacious. Recognizing the need for repair, some of St. Thomas' commentators—for example, Gilson and Copleston—suggest that what we have here is a truncated version of the argument.[7] In Question 46, Article 2, Aquinas argues that for all we can prove philosophically, the world may have existed for an infinite stretch of time—that is to say, there is no sound argument against the supposition that for every time interval during which there were contingent beings, there was an earlier time interval during which contingent beings also existed. What Aquinas really means to show, so the suggestion goes, is that even if contingent beings have existed for an infinite stretch of time (in the sense just mentioned), there must still be a necessary being. And the premise to be added is that in any infinite stretch of time, every possibility is realized; a possibility that does not get itself realized in an infinite stretch of time is not worthy of the name, as Gilson puts it. The real structure of the proof, then, is more complicated and may be set out as follows:

(1) Either contingent beings have existed for an infinitely long time or they have not.

(2) Suppose contingent beings have not existed for an infinite stretch of time.

    (2a) Then there was at least one contingent being C

---

[7] E. Gilson, *The Philosophy of St. Thomas Aquinas*, tr. E. Bullough (Cambridge, 1929), p. 85; and F. C. Copleston, *Thomas Aquinas* (London, 1955), pp. 119–120.

that began to exist and was not brought into existence by a pre-existing contingent being—(2).

(d) Whatever begins to exist is caused to exist by something else already existent.

(2b) Hence C was caused to exist by some being B distinct from and pre-existing C—(2a), (d).

(2c) B is not contingent; hence B is a necessary being —(2a), (2b).

(i) There is at least one necessary being—(2c).

(3) So if contingent beings have not existed for an infinite stretch of time, then there is at least one necessary being—(2)–(i).

(4) Suppose contingent beings have existed for an infinite stretch of time—suppose, that is, that for every time interval during which contingent beings existed, there was an earlier time interval during which contingent beings existed.

(a) There are contingent beings now.

(a') In any infinite stretch of time, every possibility is realized.

(c) Therefore, if all beings are contingent, then at one time nothing existed—(a'), (4).

(d) Whatever begins to exist is caused to begin to exist by something already in existence.

(e) Therefore if at any time nothing existed, then nothing would exist at any subsequent time—(d).

(f) Hence if at one time nothing existed, then nothing exists now.

(g) Hence if all beings are contingent, then nothing exists now—(c), (f).

(h) Therefore not all beings are contingent—(g), (a).

(i) Hence there is at least one necessary being—(h).

(5) So if contingent beings have existed for an infinite

stretch of time, there is at least one necessary being—
(4)–(i).
(6) Hence there is at least one necessary being—(1), (3),
(5).

Now the inference of (6) from (1), (3), and (5) is certainly unexceptionable. Proposition (1) is necessarily true; (2) and (4) are hypotheses of conditional proofs, and hence beyond reproach. The question, then, concerns the arguments for (3) and (5). The argument culminating in (3) is valid; (d) is its only premise. Is (d) acceptable? Aquinas apparently thinks it self-evidently true. And, indeed, (d) is plausible; something like it has governed and directed a great deal of scientific inquiry. Nevertheless there are reasons for doubting that (d) is self-evident or necessarily true. Is it not logically possible that an elementary particle (or for that matter a full-grown horse) should just pop into existence, uncaused by anything at all? It is certainly hard to detect any inconsistency in that notion. Of course Aquinas needs only the *truth* of (d) for his argument; and while I am prepared to deny its necessity or self-evidence, I am certainly not prepared to deny its truth. Hence I propose to concede premise (d) (at least for the sake of discussion) and accept the argument for (3).

If we accept (d), then steps (d) through (i) in the argument for (5) appear to be impeccable. Our question, therefore, concerns the inference of (c) from (4) and (a'). Now (c) is a conditional proposition; hence if (4) and (a') entail (c), then the conjunction of (4), (a'), and the antecedent of (c) (call it (ac)) entails the consequent (cc) of (c). Our question, therefore, is whether the following argument is valid:

(4) For every time interval during which a contingent being existed, there was a preceding time interval during which a contingent being existed.

God and Other Minds

(a′) In any infinite stretch of time every possibility is realized.

(ac) Every being can fail to exist.

(cc) Hence at one time nothing existed.

This argument does not appear valid; to construct an explicitly valid argument with (4) and (a′) as premises and (cc) as conclusion, we should have to replace (ac) by

(p) It is possible that nothing exists.

(4), (a′), and (p) do entail (cc); and presumably Thomas thought that (ac) entails (p)—that is, presumably Thomas believed that (q) is necessarily true:

(q) If, for every being x, it is possible that x does not exist, then it is possible that nothing exists (that everything fails to exist).

Now the general principle of which (q) is an instantiation may be stated as follows:

(r) If, for every being x, it is possible that x has P, then it is possible that everything has P.

But (r) is not a valid principle. Perhaps we can see this most easily if we restrict the range of r to contingent propositions and let P be the property of being true. Then clearly enough for any contingent proposition p, it is possible that p is true; but (in view of the contingency of the denial of a contingent proposition) it is not possible that all contingent propositions are true. Therefore, (q) is not an instantiation of a valid principle of (modal) logic; (ac) does not *formally* entail p. Still St. Thomas might well argue that (q), though not a truth of logic, is nonetheless necessarily true. And it certainly is not clear that it is not. Could it be logically necessary that there is at least one being (capable of causing other beings to begin to

14

exist), although every being is logically contingent? It is plausible to suppose not. Hence I propose to accept St. Thomas' claim with respect to (q). The completed argument from (4) and (a') to (c) then goes at follows:

(4) For every time interval during which contingent beings have existed, there was a preceding time interval during which contingent beings existed.

(a') In any infinite stretch of time, every possibility is realized.

(ac) Every being can fail to exist—hypothesis.

(q) If every being can fail to exist, then it is possible that nothing exists—necessary truth.

(p) Hence it is possible that nothing exists—(ac), (q).

(cc) There was a time at which nothing existed—(4), (a'), (p).

This argument is valid; hence (4), (a') and (ac) entail (cc); hence (4) and (a') entail that if (ac) is true, so is (cc)—that is, (4) and (a') entail (c). Our problem, then, is to evaluate (a')—the claim that in an infinite stretch of time, every possibility is realized. Suppose we take a closer look at it. It is immediately clear that if it is to be of use in the argument, (a') must be so construed that its consequent is not necessarily false, or even known by us to be false. (Otherwise St. Thomas could use it to show, contrary to his own explicit disclaimer, that the world has not existed for an infinite stretch of time.) But just here the difficulty arises; it is by no means easy to interpret (a') in such a way that its consequent is possibly true. In evaluating the argument from (4) and (a') to (c), to be sure, we relied upon a rough and intuitive understanding of it; that a closer look is necessary becomes apparent when we notice that (understood in that same rough and ready way) (a') appears to contradict (4). For suppose that (4) and (a') are true. (4)

entails that past time is infinite. Furthermore, (4) is certainly not necessarily true (nor did St. Thomas think it was). Its denial is therefore possible, and hence, by (4) and (a′), *true*. But then the conjunction of (4) with (a′) entails (4) and also its denial; hence (a′) is inconsistent with (4). How, therefore, is (a′) to be construed?

What at first leaps rashly to mind is the suggestion that (a′) be taken as the claim that if past time is infinite, then every contingent proposition has been true at some time or other. But of course then it would have been true both that, for example, Napoleon was at Waterloo at 9:00 A.M. on January 5, 1862, and that he was not at Waterloo then. Nor can this formulation be succored by restricting it to propositions containing no specific time reference; for then we get the consequence that if past time is infinite, then Napoleon both was at Waterloo at some time or other and was never there. As a more serious attempt, let us try the following: Let S be a set of properties such that every property is either a member of S or logically equivalent to a conjunction or disjunction of members of S. And let us say that a proposition Q is a *world description* if (1) Q is a conjunctive proposition whose conjuncts are of the forms P *is instantiated,* and P *is not instantiated* (where "P" ranges over members of S), (2) Q asserts of every member of S either that it is instantiated or that it is not instantiated, and (3) Q is consistent. Thus, we might say, any world description specifies some possible world and any possible world is specified by some world description. Now perhaps we can restate (a′) as

(β) If past time is infinite, then for any world description WD there was a time t such that WD *at t* is true.

Now obviously there is at least *one* world description (WD1) entailing that there are no contingent beings. WD1 might, for example, contain as a conjunct the proposition that the property of *being a contingent being* is not instantiated. Hence if (β) is true, then if (4) is true and past time is infinite, there was a time at which no contingent beings existed. But if there were no necessary being, then by (d) there would have been no contingent beings subsequent to that time and hence none now.

But (β) is not without its difficulties. For let R be the property a contingent being has just in case it is a member of a set S of contingent beings such that, for any time t, at least one member of S exists at t. (St. Thomas clearly thinks it possible that there *be* such a set.) Then if past time is infinite, there was a time at which R *is instantiated* is true. But of course if WD1 was ever instantiated, R was never instantiated; hence (β) entails that if past time is infinite, then R was instantiated at some time and also was never instantiated—that is, (β) entails that past time is not infinite. Clearly, then, (β) is unsatisfactory as an explanation of (a').

There is one more formulation of (a') I wish to consider. Let us say that a property P is *nontemporal* in case it is possible that there be a pair of times t and t' such that something has P at t and nothing has P at t'. Redness would be nontemporal, while *eternality* or *everlastingness* would be temporal properties. (Furthermore, existence is to be construed as a property for the purposes of this discussion, and of course it will be a nontemporal property.) Given this definition, we can state (γ):

(γ) *If* a proposition P is such that:
   a) it is of one of the following four forms: *everything has Q, nothing has Q, something has Q,* and *something lacks Q* (where "Q" ranges over nontemporal properties), and
   b) P is possibly true,

then in an infinite stretch of time there is a time
t such that *P at t* is true.[8]

Notice that (γ) differs from (β) primarily in that it lays upon
the properties involved the restriction that they must be nontemporal in the above sense. (Of course the properties used to
show that (β) is unacceptable were *temporal* properties.)

We have already conceded St. Thomas the claim that if
there is no necessary being, it is possible that nothing exists.
So if there is no necessary being, the proposition *Nothing exists*
meets the conditions laid down in the antecedent of (γ); hence,
by (γ) if past time is infinite there was a time *t* such that
Nothing exists at t is true—that is, there was a time at which
nothing existed.

If (γ) evades the difficulties besetting (β), it nonetheless
has its own troubles. For consider the following artificial (but
relevant) properties: let us say that a physical object is *gred*
if and only if it is red and every physical object is green at some
time or other; and let us say that an object is *dred* if and only
if it is red and it is false that every physical object is green at
some time or other. Gredness and dredness are nontemporal
properties by our definition, for it is true that something is gred
(dred) at a given time only if at that time something is red.
Hence it may be true at one time but false at another that
something is gred (or dred). It then follows by (γ) that if past
time is infinite, then there was a time *t* at which something
was dred and a time *t'* at which something was gred. But if
so, then every physical object is green at some time or other
while some physical objects are never green; (γ) too entails
that past time is not infinite. Hence St. Thomas could accept
(γ) no more than (β) or (a′); for if he could, he could show

[8] This formulation of (a′) was suggested to me by Professor Robert Col-
lins Sleigh, Jr.

(contrary to his own explicit disclaimer) that the world has not existed for an infinitely long stretch of time.

The difficulty, then, is not that there are good reasons for thinking (a') false or no reasons for thinking it true; the difficulty is in so formulating the principle that it will function satisfactorily in the argument. Those commentators who recommend it do not so much as notice these difficulties. Of course my failure to find a reading of (a') that will satisfy the argument by no means shows that there is no such reading. But in the absence of an adequate version of (a') this statement of the third way is of at most dubious worth.

But perhaps a weaker premise than (a') could be employed in the proof. After all, St. Thomas needs, not the assertion that *every* logical possibility is realized in an infinite stretch of time, but only that every possibility of a certain restricted sort is. We might consider, therefore, adding to the argument:

(s) In any infinite stretch of time, any object which *can* fail to exist *does* fail to exist.

Now (s) alone is insufficient, for it does not guarantee that if past time is infinite, there was a time at which all contingent objects *simultaneously* failed to exist. Here perhaps we could employ a suggestion of Geach's; he surmises that St. Thomas means to treat the universe itself as one "great big object." [9] It is by no means clear, of course, that the universe *is* an object. It is by no means clear that if *a* and *b* are just any objects, then there is an object *c* composed of *a* and *b*. But even if the universe is an object, it is one of a peculiar kind indeed. We may see this by asking under what conditions the universe would not have existed. Suppose *S* is the set of contingent objects (not including the universe itself) existing at a given past time *t*. Now clearly enough it is not sufficient, for the nonexistence of

[9] *Op. cit.*, p. 115.

the universe at t, that some of the members of S fail to exist at t. And even the nonexistence of *all* the members of S at t is not sufficient; the universe's existing at t requires only that some (contingent) being or other exists at t; this is the only version of "the universe exists at t" that will serve in the argument. Hence the proposition that the universe exists at t is logically equivalent to the proposition that some contingent being exists at t. So if, in (s), we take the universe as itself an object, then (s) entails

    (s') if it is possible that no contingent being exists, then in any infinite stretch of time there will be a time at which no contingent being exists.

We have already conceded Thomas the premise that if there is no necessary being, then it is possible that no contingent being exists. Proposition (s') (and hence (s)) conjoined with that premise entails that if there is no necessary being, then if past time is infinite, there was a time at which no contingent being existed. Proposition (s) will therefore serve to bridge the gap between (b) and (c), given the supposition that past time is infinite. Nonetheless, (s) is not acceptable for Aquinas. It implies that if contingent beings have existed throughout an infinitely long stretch of time, then there was a time during that infinite stretch of time at which no contingent beings existed—that is, it entails that the world has not existed throughout an infinite stretch of time. For clearly it *is* possible that there be no contingent beings, nor would St. Thomas think otherwise. God was under no logical (or any other) compulsion to create the world. But then it follows by (s) that if past time is infinite, there was a time at which no contingent beings existed. And hence (s), like (a'), (β), and (γ), is too strong.

One final attempt: perhaps we can make progress by replacing (s) with

(t) If there is no necessary being, then in an infinite stretch of time any object which can fail to exist, does fail to exist.

Again, (t) will be strong enough only if we take the universe to be one of the objects under consideration. Given that, however, (t) entails

(u) If there is no necessary being, then if it is possible that no contingent beings exist, then in any infinite stretch of time there is a time at which no contingent beings exist.

And given the necessary truth of the proposition that it is possible that no contingent beings exist, (t) is equivalent to

(v) If there is no necessary being, then in any infinite stretch of time there is a time at which no contingent beings exist; that is,

(w) Contingent beings have existed for an infinite stretch of time only if there is a necessary being.

We began our examination of the third way by noting that St. Thomas appears to make an invalid inference: from

(b) Whatever can fail to exist at some times does not exist,

he infers

(c) If all beings are contingent, then at one time nothing existed.

We then moved to the suggestion that the real structure of the proof, contrary to appearances, is as follows: (1) Either contingent beings have existed for an infinite stretch of time or they have not. (3) If they have not, then (in view of (d)) there must be a necessary being. (5) On the other hand, if they have existed for an infinite stretch of time, then too there must be a necessary being. Why so? What reason is there for supposing (5) to be true? The current suggestion is that (t) is the premise from which this is to follow. And indeed it does follow from (t), for (t), as we have seen, is equivalent to (w)—the proposition that contingent beings have existed for an infinite stretch of time only if there is a necessary being. But (v) (and hence (t)) is of course no reason at all for (5); it just *is* (5) thinly disguised. Or, if that is putting the matter too strongly (in view of the fact that what has been demonstrated is only the equivalence of (5) and (t)), it is surely true that anyone who had any doubts about (5) will have, and have justifiably, the very same doubts about (t); it is not as if (t) wère widely accepted or independently plausible. These expedients, then, are of little help; the third way construed as an attempt to prove the existence of a logically necessary being is at best inconclusive.

P. T. Geach and T. P. Brown consider it a mistake to construe the argument in this way—that is, as an attempt to prove the existence of a logically necessary being. Geach's reasons for rejecting this interpretation appears to be that "the 'necessity' that is asserted of God is identified Aristotelian style with eternity—with imperishable existence that has no liability to cease." [10] But of course this is not much help: a being with "imperishable existence with no liability to cease" is a being that cannot cease existing, a being whose nonexistence is impossible. But our problem is precisely the force of "cannot" and "impossible." If the impossibility in question is not logical impossibility, of what sort is it? Causal or natural impossibility? A causally necessary being would be one (presumably) whose

---

[10] *Op. cit.*, p. 115.

existence was entailed by causal laws, or the laws of nature (but not by just any statement). What this suggestion might come to in the case of God is far from clear, since on St. Thomas' view God is responsible for the character of the causal laws themselves. God instituted these laws when he created the world; but God did not in instituting these laws bring himself or his necessity into existence. Thus it is not easy to see the alternative to construing Aquinas' "necessary being" as "logically necessary being." Furthermore, there is the fact (see above, p. 6) that on Aquinas' view God *is* a logically necessary being, which suggests that in proving the existence of a necessary being "that all men speak of as God" he may be trying to prove the existence of a logically necessary being.

Nevertheless there are two important considerations favoring the Geach-Brown interpretation. Brown points out that Aquinas seems to concede the existence of many *created* necessary beings;[11] and it is certainly not easy to see how a logically necessary being could have been created. And second, there is the difficulty I pointed out (above, p. 8) in making sense of the idea of a logically necessary being that is necessary *ab aliter*. Here the Geach-Brown interpretation—according to which a necessary being is one which possesses "imperishable existence with no liability to cease" (Geach) or which "could not begin or cease existing by any 'natural' process allowed by the Aristotelian physics" (Brown)—enjoys a clear superiority. For (as Brown points out) under this interpretation a being necessary *ab aliter* would be simply a *created* necessary being, a necessary being *a se* being uncreated. Accordingly this reading of the third way warrants examination.

The crucial difficulty here as in the previous case is in bridging the gap between

---

[11] *Op. cit.*, pp. 79–82.

(b) Whatever can fail to exist at some time does not exist
and

(c) If all beings are contingent then at one time nothing
   existed.

A contingent being is one with "a genuine liability to perish"
(Geach) or with "a built-in *process* of corruption" (Brown).
And (supposing as in the previous case, that the proof is designed to cover the possibility that the world has always existed) it is perhaps plausible to think that no being with such
a "built-in process of corruption" would survive an infinite
stretch of time. But what justifies the supposition that if all
beings were contingent and past time is infinite, then there
would have been a time at which all beings *simultaneously*
failed to exist? Proposition (a′) and its *epigoni* will be of no
more use here than they were previously. But perhaps Geach's
suggestion will be helpful: should we take the universe itself
to be one of the beings in the range of the quantifier of (c)'s
antecedent? If all things were contingent, then the universe
too would display a "built-in process of corruption" that would
have come to an inevitable fruition if past time is infinite. But
the universe, as previously remarked (above, p. 19) is a peculiar kind of object. For if the universe's failing to exist at a given
time entails that at that time no logically contingent being
exists (as must be the case if Geach's suggestion is to be relevant) then the proposition *The universe exists at t* is equivalent
to *Some (logically contingent) being or other exists at t.* And
if the universe is one of the objects in the range of the quantifier of (c)'s antecedent, it must also fall in the range of the
quantifier of

(i) There is at least one necessary being.

And so in proving (i) what we prove is that at least one element of a set of beings containing the universe as a member is a necessary being—that is, possibly the universe itself is the necessary being whose existence we have proved. Forced upon us by the exigencies of the proof, this introduces further complication. To say that the universe exists is only to say that something or other exists; what is it to say that the universe is a necessary being? Presumably this means that the universe has no built-in tendency to perish. But this, in turn, is not to say that some object (in the ordinary sense of "object") is a necessary being; it is to say only that there is no tendency for everything to fail to exist at the same time. In proving (i), then, what we prove is that either some object is a necessary being or else there is no tendency for everything to go out of existence simultaneously.

Similarly with

(1) There is a being necessary *a se.*

If we accept Geach's suggestion, then here too it is perhaps the universe itself that is the being necessary *a se.* Now a being is necessary *a se* in case it is necessary but uncreated, existent from eternity. To say that the universe is the being necessary *a se,* again, is not to say that some ordinary object with no tendency to corruption has existed from eternity; it is to say only that there have always been objects and there is no tendency for everything to go out of existence simultaneously—a conclusion in which the skeptic may cheerfully acquiesce. If we try to bridge the gap between (b) and (c) in this way, therefore, the conclusion of the third way will be vastly weakened and, indeed, of little interest to theism. Since the third way seems no more successful under this interpretation than under the previous one, we must conclude that this piece of natural theology is ineffective.

Two

The Ontological Argument (I)

THE ontological argument for the existence of God has fascinated philosophers ever since it was formulated by St. Anselm of Canterbury (1033–1109). It is doubtful, I think, that any person was ever brought to a belief in God by this argument, and unlikely that it has played the sort of role in strengthening and confirming religious belief that, for example, the teleological argument has played. To the unsophisticated, Anselm's argument is (at first sight at least) remarkably unconvincing, if not downright irritating; it smacks too much of word magic. And yet almost every major philosopher from the time of Anselm to the present has had his say about it; the last few years have seen a remarkable flurry of interest in it.

What accounts for this fascination? Not, I think, the religious significance of the argument, although no doubt that can be underrated. The cause is perhaps twofold. First, the ontological argument offers an enormous return on a pretty slim investment—a definition, and a perplexing but not altogether implausible premise connecting existence and "greatness," yield the theistic conclusion. Second, although the argument certainly looks at first sight as if it ought to be unsound, it is profoundly difficult to say what exactly is wrong with it. Indeed, it is doubtful that any philosopher has given a really convincing and thorough refutation of the ontological argument. Too often philosophers merely remark that Kant refuted the argument by showing that existence is not a predicate and that "one cannot build bridges from the conceptual realm to the real world." But it is very doubtful that Kant specified a sense of "is a predicate" such that, in that sense, it is clear both that existence is not a predicate and that Anselm's argument requires that it be one. Nor are the mere claims that no existential propositions are necessary or the above comment about bridge building impressive as refutations of Anselm—after all, he claims to have an *argument* for the necessity of at least one existential proposition. So one must either show just where his argument goes wrong, or else produce a solid argument for the claim that no existential (in the appropriate sense) propositions can be necessary—and this, I think, no one has succeeded in doing.

In this chapter I shall state Anselm's argument and examine some objections to it. First and most important is Kant's objection—an effort to find a *general* refutation that applies to every version of the argument. Kant, of course, thought that the argument fails because it presupposes that existence is a predicate. I believe that there is no such general refutation, and in the remainder of the chapter I shall look carefully at some contemporary restatements of Kant's objection.

I

Anselm states his argument as follows:

And so, Lord, do thou, who dost give understanding to faith, give me, so far as thou knowest it to be profitable, to understand that thou art as we believe; and that thou art that which we believe. And, indeed, we believe that thou art a being than which nothing greater can be conceived. Or is there no such nature, since the fool hath said in his heart, there is no God? . . . But, at any rate, this very fool, when he hears of this being of which I speak—a being than which nothing greater can be conceived—understands what he hears, and what he understands is in his understanding; although he does not understand it to exist.

For, it is one thing for an object to be in the understanding, and another to understand that the object exists. When a painter first conceives of what he will afterwards perform, he has it in his understanding, but he does not yet understand it to be, because he has not yet performed it. But after he has made the painting, he both has it in his understanding, and he understands that it exists, because he has made it.

Hence, even the fool is convinced that something exists in the understanding, at least, than which nothing greater can be conceived. For, when he hears of this, he understands it. And whatever is understood, exists in the understanding. And assuredly that, than which nothing greater can be conceived, cannot exist in the understanding alone. For, suppose it exists in the understanding alone; then it can be conceived to exist in reality; which is greater.

Therefore, if that, than which nothing greater can be conceived, exists in the understanding alone, the very being, than which nothing greater can be conceived, is one, than which a greater can be conceived. But obviously this is impossible. Hence, there is no doubt that there exists a being, than which nothing greater can be conceived, and it exists both in the understanding and in reality.[1]

This argument, it seems to me, is best construed as a *reductio ad absurdum*. Let us use the term "God" as an abbreviation for "the being than which none greater can be conceived." The argument then proceeds (in Anselm's own terms as much as possible) as follows:

---

[1] *Proslogion*, ch. ii.

The Ontological Argument (I)

(1) God exists in the understanding but not in reality—assumption for *reductio*.

(2) Existence in reality is greater than existence in the understanding alone—premise.

(3) A being having all of God's properties plus existence in reality can be conceived—premise.

(4) A being having all of God's properties plus existence in reality is greater than God—from (1) and (2).

(5) A being greater than God can be conceived—(3), (4).

(6) It is false that a being greater than God can be conceived—by definition of "God".

(7) Hence it is false that God exists in the understanding but not in reality—(1)-(6), *reductio ad absurdum*.

And so if God exists in the understanding, he also exists in reality; but clearly enough he does exist in the understanding (as even the fool will testify); accordingly he exists in reality as well.

A couple of preliminary comments: to say that a state of affairs is *conceivable* is to say that there is no logical impossibility in the supposition that it obtains. And to say specifically that a being having all of God's properties plus existence in reality is conceivable, is simply to say that it is possible that there is a being having all of God's properties plus existence in reality—that is, it is possible that God exists. To say that a being greater than God can be conceived, on the other hand, is to say that it is possible that there exist a being greater than the being than which it is not possible that there exist a greater.

The most famous attack upon the ontological argument is contained in a few pages of the *Critique of Pure Reason*—an attack which many think conclusive. Kant begins with the following general considerations:

If, in an identical proposition, I reject the predicate while retaining the subject, contradiction results; and I therefore say that the former belongs necessarily to the latter. But if we reject subject and predicate alike, there is no contradiction; for nothing is then left that can be contradicted. To posit a triangle, and yet to reject its three angles, is self-contradictory; but there is no contradiction in rejecting the triangle together with its three angles. The same holds true of the concept of an absolutely necessary being. If its existence is rejected, we reject the thing itself with all its predicates; and no question of contradiction can then arise. There is nothing outside it that would then be contradicted, since the necessity of the thing is not supposed to be derived from anything external; nor is there anything internal that would be contradicted, since in rejecting the thing itself we have at the same time rejected all its internal properties. "God is omnipotent" is a necessary judgment. The omnipotence cannot be rejected if we posit a Deity, that is, an infinite being; for the two concepts are identical. But if we say "There is no God," neither the omnipotence nor any other of its predicates is given; they are one and all rejected together with the subject, and there is therefore not the least contradiction in such a judgment. . . .

For I cannot form the least concept of a thing which, should it be rejected with all its predicates, leaves behind a contradiction.[2]

Here Kant seems to be arguing that no existential propositions are necessarily true—or is he, perhaps, arguing merely that no existential propositions are *analytic* in his more narrow sense? If the latter is his meaning, then what he says will be irrelevant to Anselm's proof. Perhaps that proof requires that *God exists* be necessarily true; it certainly does not require that *God exists* be analytic in Kant's sense. The second step of Anselm's argument as outlined above—that existence is greater than nonexistence—is presumably, according to Anselm, neces-

---

[2] *Critique of Pure Reason*, tr. N. K. Smith (London, 1929), pp. 502–503.

sarily true, but not necessarily analytic. If what Kant says is to be relevant, therefore, we must take it as a reason for supposing that no existential propositions are necessary.

But when we inspect this argument closely, it looks like a lot of fancy persiflage; what appear to be its premises seem to have no bearing at all on its conclusion. How are we to construe the argument? The conclusion, apparently, is that in rejecting the existence of a thing we cannot be contradicting ourselves. To be relevant in the present context this must be equivalent to the claim that no proposition which merely denies the existence of a thing or things of a specified sort is contradictory or necessarily false. Why not? Well, if we deny, for example, that God exists, "there is nothing outside it (i.e., God) that would then be contradicted, since the necessity of the thing is not supposed to be derived from anything external; nor is there anything internal that would be contradicted, since in rejecting the thing itself we have at the same time rejected all its properties." But how, exactly, is this relevant? The "necessity of the thing" in this instance would be the alleged fact that the proposition *God exists* is necessary. But what could Kant possibly mean when he says that there is nothing "outside of" God that could be contradicted by the denial of His existence? Presumably it is *propositions* that could contradict it; and there are plenty of them that do so, whether or not God exists. Does he perhaps mean to say that no *true* proposition would contradict the denial of God's existence? But this would be to hold that God does not exist, which is certainly nothing Kant is prepared to affirm. Does he mean that no *necessarily true* proposition would contradict it? But surely this would beg the whole question; for the claim that the proposition *God does not exist* is not inconsistent with any necessary proposition, is logically equivalent to the claim that *God exists* is not necessarily true. We do not seem to have much of an *argument* here at all. This paragraph, as it seems to me, is really no more than an elaborate and confused way of *asserting* that no existential propositions are necessary.

That Kant should have been unable to "form the least concept of a thing, which, should it be rejected with all its predicates, leaves behind a contradiction" is something of a surprise, given his views about mathematics. For he seems to believe that the true propositions of arithmetic and geometry are necessarily true, even if not analytic in his more narrow sense. But of course many of the truths of arithmetic are existential propositions. *There is a prime number between seventeen and twenty*, for example, or *The successor of six is greater than five* certainly appear to be necessarily true, as Kant himself urged. But surely they are also (*prima facie* at any rate) existential propositions. However that may be, the burden of Kant's objection to the ontological argument is contained in the following passage:

"*Being*" is obviously not a real predicate; that is, it is not a concept of something which could be added to the concept of a thing. It is merely the positing of a thing, or of certain determinations, as existing in themselves. Logically, it is merely the copula of a judgment. The proposition "God is omnipotent" contains two concepts, each of which has its object—God and omnipotence. The small word "is" adds no new predicate, but only serves to posit the predicate *in its relation* to the subject. If, now, we take the subject (God) with all its predicates (among which is omnipotence), and say "God is," or "There is a God," we attach no new predicate to the concept of God, but only posit the subject in itself with all its predicates, and indeed, posit it as an *object* that stands in relation to my *concept*. The content of both must be one and the same; nothing can have been added to the concept, which expresses merely what is possible, by my thinking its object (through the expression "it is") as given absolutely. Otherwise stated, the real contains no more than the merely possible. A hundred real thalers do not contain the least coin more than a hundred possible thalers. For as the latter signify the concept and the former the object and the positing of the concept, should the former contain more than the latter, my concept would not, in that case, express the whole object, and would not therefore be an adequate concept of it. My financial position, however, is affected very differently by a hundred real thalers than it is by the mere concept of them (that is, of their possibility). For the object, as it actually exists, is not analytically contained in my concept, but is added to my concept (which is a determination of my state) synthetically; and yet the conceived hundred thalers are not themselves in the least increased through thus acquiring existence outside my concept.

By whatever and by however many predicates we may think a thing—even if we completely determine it—we do not make the least addition to the thing when we further declare that this thing *is*. Otherwise it would not be exactly the same thing that exists, but something more than we had thought in the concept: and we could not, therefore, say that the exact object of my concept exists. If we think in a thing every feature of reality except one, the missing reality is not added by my saying that this defective thing exists.[3]

How, exactly, is what Kant says here relevant to Anselm's ontological argument? And how are we to understand what he says? The point of the passage seems to be that being or existence is not a real predicate; Kant apparently thinks this follows from (or is equivalent to) what he puts variously as "the real *contains* no more than the merely possible," "the *content* of both (i.e., concept and object) must be one and the same," "being is not the concept of something that could be *added to* the concept of a thing," and so on. An adequate concept, Kant believes, must contain as much content as the thing of which it is the concept; the content of the concept of

---

[3] *Ibid.*, pp. 504–505.

a thing remains the same whether the thing exists or not; and the existence of the object of a concept is not part of the content of that concept. But what *is* the content of a concept, or of an object? In what way do objects and concepts have content? Kant gives us very little help, in the passage under consideration, in understanding what it is to *add something* to a concept, what it means to say that a concept *contains* as much as an object, or what it is for a concept and its object both to have *content*—the *same* content.

Perhaps what he means is something like this: the content of a concept is the set of properties a thing must have to fall under or be an instance of that concept. The content of the concept *crevasse*, for example, includes, among others, the properties of *occurring on or in glaciers*, and *being more than one foot deep*. The content of the concept *the tallest man in Boston* will include, among others, the properties of *being a man*, *being in Boston*, and *being taller than any other man in Boston*. The content of an *object*, on the other hand, is the set of properties that object has; and a thing *a has* (at least) *as much content as* or *contains as much as* a thing *b* if every member of *b*'s content is a member of *a*'s content. But here we immediately encounter difficulty. For of course it will not be true that the concept of an object contains as much content as the object itself. Consider, for example, the concept *horse*. Any real horse will have many properties not contained in that concept; any real horse will be either more than sixteen hands high or else sixteen hands or less. But neither of these properties is in the content of the concept *horse* (although of course the property of being either more than sixteen hands high or else sixteen hands or less will be). Similarly for the tallest man in Boston: he will have the property of being married or else the property of being unmarried; but neither of these properties is part of the content of the concept *the tallest man in Boston*. This suggestion therefore requires amendment.

"By whatever and by however many predicates we may think a thing—even if we completely determine it—we do not make the least addition to the thing when we further declare that this thing *is*." This sentence provides a clue. We might note that to every existing object there corresponds its *whole concept:* the concept whose content includes all (and only) the properties the object in question has. (The content of the whole concept of an object will obviously contain many properties.) Now suppose we say that *the whole concept of an object O diminished with respect to P* is the concept whose content contains just those properties that (1) are members of the content of the whole concept and neither entail[4] nor are entailed by P, or (2) are entailed by properties meeting condition (1).[5] (Very roughly and inaccurately, a whole concept diminished with respect to P is what remains of a whole concept when P is deleted from its content.) Suppose, furthermore, that the Taj Mahal is pink and let C_1 and C_2 be, respectively, the whole concept of the Taj Mahal and the whole concept of the Taj Mahal diminished with respect to pinkness. Evidently there are possible circumstances in which C_2 but not C_1 would be exemplified by some actually existing object: perhaps these circumstances would obtain if the Taj Mahal were green, for example. (Of course C_1 could be exemplified only if C_2 were too.) Now perhaps Kant means to point out that existence differs from pinkness in the following respect. If C_3 is the whole concept of the Taj Mahal diminished with respect to *existence*, there are no possible circumstances in which C_3 but not C_1 has application; it is a

---

[4] Where a property P entails a property Q if and only if it is necessarily true that whatever has P has Q.

[5] Here I am indebted for a correction to Paul Mellema.

necessary truth that if C_3 is exemplified, so is C_1. Since the converse is also true, C_1 and C_3 are, we might say, equivalent concepts; in annexing *existence* to C_3 we don't really get a different concept. And if we add that a predicate (or property) P is a real predicate (or property) only if it is not the case that any whole concept diminished with respect to P is equivalent to the corresponding whole concept, we may conclude that existence, unlike pinkness, is not a real predicate; it "is not a concept of something which could be added to the concept of a thing." [6]

Giving a clear explanation of the claim that existence is not a real predicate, this interpretation also shows an interesting respect in which existence differs from other predicates or properties. Unfortunately, it seems to have no particular bearing on Anselm's argument. For Anselm can certainly agree, so far as his argument is concerned, that existence is not a real predicate in the explained sense. Anselm maintains that the concept *the being than which none greater can be conceived* is necessarily exemplified; that this is so is in no way inconsistent with the suggestion that the whole concept of a thing diminished with respect to existence is equivalent to the undiminished whole concept of that thing. Anselm argues that the proposition *God exists* is necessarily true; but neither this claim nor his argument for it entails or presupposes that existence is a predicate in the sense just explained.

What *does* Kant's argument show then? How could anyone be led to suppose that Kant's claim did dispose of the ontological argument? This last question is not altogether easy to answer. What Kant's argument does show, however, is that

---

[6] For a fuller and more detailed consideration of this objection, see my "Kant's Objection to the Ontological Argument," *Journal of Philosophy*, LXIII (1966), 537–546.

one cannot "define things into existence"; it shows that one cannot, by adding existence to a concept that has application contingently if at all, get a concept that is necessarily exemplified. For let C′ be any whole concept and C be that whole concept diminished with respect to existence. If the proposition *There is an object to which C applies* is contingent, so is *There is an object to which C′ applies*. Kant's argument shows that the proposition *There is an object to which C applies* is logically equivalent to *There is an object to which C′ applies*; hence if either is contingent, so is the other. And this result can be generalized. For *any* concept C, singular or general, if it is a contingent truth that C is exemplified, it is also a contingent truth that the concept derived from C by annexing existence to it is exemplified. From a concept which has application contingently—for example, *crow*, we cannot, by annexing existence to it, get a concept that necessarily applies; for if it is a contingent truth that there are crows, it is also a contingent truth that there are existent crows.

But of course Anselm need not have thought otherwise. Schopenhauer describes the ontological argument as follows: "On some occasion or other someone excogitates a conception, composed out of all sorts of predicates, among which, however he takes care to include the predicate actuality or existence, either openly or wrapped up for decency's sake in some other predicate, such as perfection, immensity, or something of the kind." [7] If this *were* Anselm's procedure—if he started with some concept that has instances contingently if at all and then annexed *existence* to it—then indeed his argument would be subject to Kant's criticism. But he didn't, and it isn't. And Kant's objection shows neither that there are no necessary

[7] *The Ontological Argument*, ed. A. Plantinga (New York, 1965), pp. 66–67.

existential propositions nor that the proposition *God exists* is not necessary—any more than it shows that *There is a prime between fifty and fifty-five* is a contingent proposition.

II

Kant's disapproval of the ontological argument centers on his claim that existence is not a predicate or quality. Many contemporary philosophers have followed Kant's lead here: Ayer, Wisdom, and Broad substantially agree that—in Broad's words—"The Ontological Argument presupposes that existence is a quality or power," and that

the assumption that existential propositions are of *logically* the same form as characterizing propositions . . . makes the Ontological Argument seem plausible. But it is certainly false. . . . Let us begin with the two negative propositions *Cats do not bark* and *Dragons do not exist*. It is obvious that the first is about cats. But, if the second be true, it is certain that it cannot be about dragons, for their will be no such things as dragons for it to be about. The first might be expressed, on the conditional interpretation, by the sentence "If there were any cats, none of them would bark." On the instantial interpretation it might be expressed by the sentence "There are cats, and none of them bark." Suppose you try to express the negative existential proposition the same way. On the first alternative it would be expressed by the sentence "If there were any dragons, none of them would exist." On the second alternative it would be expressed by the sentence "There are dragons, and none of them exist." Both these sentences are self-contradictory and meaningless. So if you try to analyse negative existential propositions in the same way as negative characterizing propositions, you will find that they are all self-contradictory. But it is plain that *Dragons do not exist* is *not* self-contradictory. It is not only logically possible but is almost certainly true.

Now consider the two affirmative propositions *Cats scratch* and *Cats exist*. On the conditional interpretation the former would be

The Ontological Argument (I)

expressed by the sentence "If there were any cats none of them would fail to scratch." On the instantial interpretation it would be expressed by the sentence "There are cats, and none of them fail to scratch." Suppose you try to express the affirmative existential proposition in the same way. On the first alternative it would be expressed by the sentence "If there were any cats, none of them would fail to exist." On the second alternative it would be expressed by the sentence "There are cats, and none of them fail to exist." Now both these sentences are mere platitudes. So if you try to analyse affirmative existential propositions in the same way as affirmative characterizing propositions, you will find that they are all platitudes. But it is plain that *Cats exist* is not a mere platitude. . . . So it is certain that existential propositions need a different kind of analysis.[8]

Broad is arguing for the conclusion that existence is not a quality. He takes it for granted, apparently, that if (and perhaps only if) existence *were* a quality, then existential propositions (both affirmative and negative) would be *about* their subjects. But negative existentials, he says, are not, if true, about their subjects, for there would then be nothing for them to be about. By the same token the contradictories of true negative existentials are not about their subjects either. So neither true negative existentials nor the corresponding affirmative existential propositions are about their subjects. The premise Broad appeals to, however, has a still more general consequence: if *Dragons do not exist* is true, then no subject-predicate propositions of any sort are about dragons.[9] And this is plainly outrageous. For even if *Dragons do not exist*

---

[8] C. D. Broad, *Religion, Philosophy and Psychical Research* (London, 1953), pp. 182–183. Cf. A. J. Ayer, *Language, Truth and Logic* (London, 1947), p. 43; and John Wisdom, *Interpretation and Analysis* (London, 1931), p. 62.

[9] Cf. R. Cartwright, "Negative Existentials," *Journal of Philosophy*, LVII (1960), 633.

were not about dragons (but surely it is) the same could not be said for *Dragons do not have fur* or *Dragons are beasts of fable.* One can hope for what does not exist, and search for it, as Ponce de Leon demonstrated. One can even draw pictures of it. Why, then, cannot one talk about or refer to what does not exist? The fact, of course, is that one can; it is not at all difficult, for example, to tell stories about ghosts—indeed, I have seen it done. And when one tells a story about ghosts, then what one says is presumably about ghosts. Any objection to the ontological argument requiring the premise that no propositions are about ghosts or dragons is more than dubious.

But Broad has another and more important argument for the conclusion that existential statements are not about their subjects. He implicitly argues that if they were, they would yield to the same kind of analysis as do what he calls *characterizing propositions.* Now a negative characterizing proposition —for example, *Cats do not bark*—is equivalent to a proposition of the same form as either

(a) There are some cats and none of them bark

or

(b) If there were any cats, none of them would bark.

But obviously the negative existential *Dragons do not exist* is not equivalent to either of the corresponding propositions of the indicated forms; for it is certainly contingent and probably true, while they are both, Broad says, "contradictory and meaningless." Similarly for affirmative existentials: an affirmative characterizing proposition—for example, *Cats scratch*—is equivalent to a proposition of the form of

(c) There are some cats and all of them scratch

or

The Ontological Argument (I)

(d) If there were any cats, all of them would scratch.

Affirmative existentials do not yield to this analysis, for surely *Cats exist* is equivalent neither to *There are some cats and all of them exist* nor to *If there were some cats, all of them would exist*. *Cats exist* is a synthetic proposition, while the above two, Broad says, are "mere platitudes," that is (as the context makes clear) tautologies.[10]

Is Broad right? We might note first that not nearly all "characterizing propositions" (propositions about their subjects) are of the forms (a)–(d). *Buffalo once abounded on the Great Plains*, for example, does not say either that there are some buffalo and all of them once abounded on the Great Plains, or that if there were some buffalo all of them would once have abounded on the Great Plains. The same holds for *Cats are more intelligent than dogs, Snakes come in many colors*, and *Lions display varying degrees of friendliness*. More important (since the conclusion of the ontological argument is a singular existential) Broad neglects singular characterizing propositions altogether. No doubt he means to hold that propositions of the form *A has P* (where "A" does duty for singular referring expressions and "P" for expressions denoting properties) are really of one of the following forms:

(e) A exists and A has P.
(f) If A existed, A would have P.

But not every singular proposition about its subject is of one of these forms either: consider

(g) Cerberus is my favorite beast of fable.

This is true (let us suppose) and about Cerberus; but surely

---

[10] Of course Broad is mistaken about *There are some cats and all of them exist*; since it entails the contingent *There are some cats*, it is not a tautology.

it is false that Cerberus exists and has the property of being my favorite beast of fable. It is also false that if Cerberus existed, he would have the property of being my favorite beast of fable—if Cerberus existed I would be much less favorably inclined toward him. If this is a *material* conditional, of course, it is true; but in that case it is equivalent to *Either Cerberus does not exist or Cerberus is my favorite beast of fable*, which, since its first disjunct does not entail (g), is not equivalent to the latter. Hence (g) is not equivalent to the corresponding propositions of the forms (e) and (f).

So not all singular characterizing propositions are of the indicated forms. Why, then, must existential propositions be so, to be about their subjects? But suppose we grant for the moment Broad's thesis about existential propositions. How, exactly, is this thesis supposed to bear on Anselm's argument? As follows, presumably. Essential to Anselm's argument is some premise entailing the legitimacy of comparing an existent with a nonexistent being. As I formulated the argument (above, p. 29), that proposition is

(2) Existence in reality is greater than existence in the understanding alone

which presumably entails that an existent being is greater than a nonexistent one. Now Broad claims that

(1) no comparison can be made between a nonexistent term and anything else except on the hypothesis that it exists and (2) on this hypothesis it is meaningless to compare it with anything in respect of the presence or absence of existence.[11]

This follows, he believes from the supposed fact that existence

---

[11] *Op. cit.*, p. 181.

is not a quality. Now it is not at all clear to me that this claim does follow from it. But in any event the claim is surely false. One certainly *can* compare, for example, Hamlet with President Johnson in point of the number of books written about each; and when a man says *More books have been written about Hamlet than about Lyndon Johnson,* he certainly need not commit himself to *If Hamlet had existed more books would have been written about him than about Lyndon Johnson.* And while it is true that Superman is a comic-book figure much stronger than any actual man, it is no doubt false that if Superman existed he would be a comic-book figure much stronger than any actual man. Finally, one certainly *can* compare a nonexistent thing to an existent thing with respect to existence; to do this is simply to say that the one exists and the other does not. One of the principal differences between Cerberus and Louis XIV, for example, is that the latter (for better or worse) really did exist.

Broad has not established, then, that existence is not a predicate, or that existential propositions are not about their subjects. It is perhaps possible to *specify* some sense of "about" such that in that sense, existential propositions are not about their subjects. But how may we be assured that Anselm's argument requires existential propositions to be about their subjects in that sense of "about"—or, for that matter, in the ordinary sense? Anselm needs some such premise as *If A exists and B does not, then A is greater than B.* Why must he go on to add that *A exists* is *about A?* It certainly *appears* to be about A; but Anselm need not commit himself on that issue at all. Broad has not shown that existence is not a quality; and what he deduced from this—that no categorical comparison between existents and nonexistents can be made—is false. Hence he has not succeeded in refuting the ontological argument.

III

In "Existence, Predication and the Ontological Argument," Jerome Shaffer tries, like Kant and Broad, to furnish general grounds for rejecting any argument relevantly like Anselm's.[12] Shaffer begins by pointing out that existential sentences can be tautological. If, for example, we take "God" as an abbreviation for "an almighty being who exists and is eternal," then "God exists" is tautological in that it is equivalent to "an almighty being who exists and is eternal, exists." And here he is surely correct. But he goes on to argue that even "if we are given a tautological existential assertion like 'particulars exist' (where 'particular' is defined as 'existent object') or 'God exists' this leaves open the question whether there is a God." How so? ". . . If someone uses the sentence 'God exists' tautologically, he tells us only that being an existent is a logical requirement for being God. . . . In the case of the Ontological Argument the only valid conclusion is an intensional statement about the meaning of the concept of God." [13]

The version of the ontological argument Shaffer considers in his paper goes as follows:

Let the expression "God" mean "an almighty being who exists and is eternal." Therefore "God is an almighty being who exists and is eternal," is true by definition and that entails "God exists." [14]

Shaffer's comment is apposite with respect to *this* argument, for

---

[12] *Mind*, LXXI (1962), 307.

[13] *Ibid.*, p. 323. It does not seem to me that Shaffer has shown that there are tautological existential *assertions*, if an existential assertion is one that asserts the existence of some object or other (or asserts that some concept has instances, as he puts it). What he has shown is that sentences of the form *x exists* or *There are x's* can be used (given suitable definitions) to make tautological assertions; but in none of the examples he gives are these assertions existential in the sense just mentioned.

[14] *Ibid.*, pp. 307–308.

its conclusion is the proposition that an almighty being who exists and is eternal, exists—that is, anything that is an almighty being who exists and is eternal, exists. And, indeed, as Shaffer says, this does not entail that there are any almighty beings who exist and are eternal. But this argument is not Anselm's; the latter simply deduces a contradiction from the proposition *The being than which it is not possible that there be a greater exists in the understanding but not in reality,* together with the assertion that existents are greater than non-existents. And if this procedure covertly involves annexing existence to some concept such as *almighty and eternal being,* that must be *shown* to be so.

But Shaffer maintains further that *no* extensional assertions (i.e., assertions entailing that some concept applies to some actually existing object) can be necessarily true,[15] for "they do not merely tell us what the requirements are for being an A, but, starting with these requirements, tell us whether anything meets these requirements." [16] This is no doubt so; but one wonders why it is taken to imply that no such propositions are necessarily true. If it is a reason for supposing that no affirmative extensional propositions are necessarily true, it is also a reason for supposing that no negative existential propositions are either; for the latter certainly tell us with respect to a given set of "requirements" whether anything meets them. But surely it is necessarily true that nothing meets the requirements of being a married bachelor or an octogenarian under the age of sixty; that there are no such things is necessarily true if anything is. Further: it certainly *appears* to be necessarily true that the concept *prime number between fifty and fifty-five* has ex-

---

[15] His word here is "tautological"; but if he takes this term to be narrower than "necessarily true," his claim will have no bearing on Anselm's argument.

[16] Shaffer, *op. cit.,* p. 323.

tension; it is *true* that the number fifty-three exemplifies it; and how could that truth be merely contingent? Shaffer recognizes this difficulty and deals with it as follows:

What makes this case puzzling is that we have no idea what would count as establishing that the concept of a number has extension or that it does not have extension. We can investigate whether the concept of a number is a legitimate one, clear and self-consistent; we can note its logical connection with other mathematical concepts; and we can frame propositions which state these connections, even propositions like "there exists a number which is even and prime." But what would count as showing that the concept over and above its intensional content, has extension as well? Where would one look for traces, signs, evidences, intimations or testimonies of the nature of numbers? Nothing would count as showing that the concept of numbers had extension over and above its intensional content, and this is to say that the notion of extension does not apply here. The most that can be said is that numbers *are* intensional objects.[17]

But can this really be true? One thing that ordinarily counts as showing that a given concept has extension, is showing that there is at least one thing to which the concept applies. Now surely the least prime is a number; but there is a least prime; hence there is at least one number; hence the concept *number* has extension. And if we find special difficulties in the claim that there are numbers, we may take instead the concept *prime number between fifty and fifty-five.* Have we really no idea of what would count as establishing whether this concept has extension? Surely we do; we establish this by determining whether it applies to something—that is, by determining whether there is a prime between fifty and fifty-five. Here we certainly have an idea of the appropriate procedure—it is not even *difficult,* let alone impossible. "Nothing would count as

---

[17] *Ibid.,* pp. 324–325.

showing that the concept of number had extension *over and above its intensional content,* and this is to say that the notion of extension does not apply here" (my italics). If this means that while we can easily enough show, with respect to the concept *prime between fifty and fifty-five* that it has intensional content, we nevertheless cannot show that it has extension, it is clearly false. But perhaps it means that the intension of the concept itself determines whether it has extension. This seems to be so for the concept in question. But does it follow that the notion of extension does not apply here? Only if, presumably, we embrace a special sense of "extension" such that concepts that necessarily have extension in the usual sense are said to have none in the new sense. It will then indeed follow that if Anselm is right, the concept *God,* since it necessarily has extension in the usual sense, has none in the new sense. But this will leave Anselm utterly unruffled.

IV

The last contemporary refutation of the ontological argument I shall consider is William P. Alston's impressive "The Ontological Argument Revisited." [18] After rejecting traditional explanations and arguments for the dictum that existence is not a predicate, Alston suggests a more adequate reading of it which, he thinks, really does refute Anselm's argument. In this section I shall consider in detail both Alston's objection to Anselm's argument and the relevant portions of the more general doctrine of predication his article contains.

Alston begins by distinguishing several "modes of existence" including existence in the understanding, existence in reality, and legendary or fictional existence. The "standard objections"

---

[18] *Philosophical Review,* LXIX (1960), 452–474. Reprinted in *The Ontological Argument,* ed. A. Plantinga (New York, 1965), pp. 86–110. Page references are to this volume.

(to be found in Ayer, Wisdom, and Broad—see above, p. 38) are vitiated, he says, by a failure to make this distinction. For,

granted different modes of existence, we can restate the argument in a form which is not open to the standard objections. We can get our subject of predication by presupposing the existence of a perfect being in some nonreal mode, where the existence is obvious. Then we can argue that an analysis of this being shows that it possesses the characteristic of real existence.

It is interesting that St. Anselm's version of the Ontological Argument (in his *Proslogium*) is explicitly in this form. . . . Instead of saying, with Descartes, that existence is contained in the idea of a perfect being, Anselm speaks of a being than which nothing greater can be conceived, which he initially supposes to have a certain kind of existence—existence in the understanding. . . . He can then raise the question of what can (or must) be attributed to this being; the argument is, of course, that real existence, on pain of contradiction, must be attributed to it. . . . In this form the argument has recognized the principle that all predication presupposes the existence of a subject, and so is not subject to any attack based on this principle.[19]

Alston next suggests some general points about predication:

An existential statement has the function of setting up a subject for predication. Now that we have recognized different modes of existence, we can add a further stipulation: the kind of existence which is being stated will place limits on the sorts of predication that can be made with respect to that subject, that is, on the logical status of statements which can be made about it.[20]

Some examples follow. If a man says "old man Karamazov had three sons," what he says presupposes fictional existence for old man Karamazov and his sons. This being so the proposition *Either all of old man Karamazov's sons have died or else*

---

[19] *Ibid.*, pp. 94–95.
[20] *Ibid.*, p. 99.

at least one is still living does not follow from what he says, as it would if what his statement presupposed was the *real* existence of Karamazov and his sons. In general,

we can say that the kind of considerations which are relevantly adduced in defending or attacking a subject predicate statement, and the sorts of implications which can be drawn from it, are a function (in part) of the kind of existence presupposed. . . .

An existential statement determines a logical framework within which predications can be made of what has been said to exist. It can be construed as a license to make certain sorts of subject predicate statements, and not others. . . .

An existential statement has the same sorts of implications as the subject predicate statements it licenses and to that extent falls within the logical framework it determines.[21]

Now how, exactly, does this bear on the ontological argument?

Anselm escapes the standard criticism by presupposing existence in the understanding so as to get a subject of which he can show real existence to be necessarily predicated. But . . . the statement which he is claiming to be necessarily true is a statement about a being in the understanding, and as such exhibits the logical features of statements based on a presupposition of mental existence. . . . Existence in the understanding shares with other nonreal modes of existence the following features. For each existent in some nonreal mode, we can specify two sorts of real existence. First, there is some real existent of a given sort . . . the existence of which is entailed by the nonreal existence of the thing in question. . . . Whenever something exists in my understanding, there are real thoughts, ideas, images and so forth, in my mind which would ordinarily be said to be about this thing. . . . Let us call such a real existent the *real correlate* of a nonreal existent. . . .

Now it seems to be a defining feature of all nonreal modes of

---

[21] *Ibid.*, pp. 100–101.

existence that any statement about something which exists in such a mode will have no implications with respect to real things, except for its real correlate and any implications that might have. . . . Any statement which attaches a predicate to something which exists in my understanding can have no implications for the real world except for the fact that I have, or have had, certain thoughts.

This means that if "The being than which nothing greater can be conceived exists in reality" is to be interpreted as the attribution of a predicate to a being in the understanding, it can have no implications with respect to the real world other than the fact that Anselm, or whoever else forms this concept, had a certain idea in his mind. . . .

"The perfect being exists in reality" can only be claimed to be necessarily true, at least on the grounds adduced by Anselm, provided we construe "exists in reality" as a predicate of the perfect being, the existence of which in the understanding has been presupposed. But this gives us a statement the logical status of which sharply distinguishes it from an ordinary statement of real existence and prevents it from having the sort of religious significance for the sake of which the conclusion was sought.[22]

Alston's criticism of Anselm's argument can be encapsulated as follows:

(a) Anselm's argument is successful only if its conclusion predicates real existence of a being assumed to have existence in the understanding

and

(b) No statement about a being presupposed to have existence in the understanding entails that it really exists.

Suppose we begin with (b). Presumably it is to follow from

(b1) If real existence were predicated of a being assumed to

---

[22] *Ibid.*, pp. 102–105.

have mental existence, the resulting proposition would lack the entailments that make the proposition *God exists* religiously interesting.

But (b1) is not entirely clear. The idea, presumably, is that there is no difficulty in attributing real existence to a being B assumed to exist in the understanding. The result of doing this, however, is not equivalent to the proposition B *exists in reality*; the former lacks the latter's entailments "for the real world." And so we can predicate either mythical or real existence of a being existing in the understanding. The Chimera, for example, exists in the understanding, and presumably mythical existence ought to be predicated of it. But here a question arises: exactly how does one predicate real existence of a being—for example, God—presupposed to have existence in the understanding? What is the resulting proposition—that is, the proposition that God, presupposed to exist in the understanding, exists in reality? Alston seems to suggest that there *is* such a statement. What statement is it? Is there a clue in the fact that "the various modes of existence . . . are carried over bodily into fiction and dreams and exist there with all their interconnections intact"? [23] Within the realm of fiction there are beings presented as having real existence, and also beings presented as having dream existence (such as the Grand Inquisitor, who is a figure in a dream of Ivan's in *The Brothers Karamazov*). The Red Queen was a character in Alice's dream; Alice herself has real existence in the story. Similarly someone might write a novel in which the main character writes novels about what is presented in the novel as a fictional character named Dead-eye Dick.

Can we find an analogous situation in the case of existence in the understanding? Can we see what it would be, for example,

---

[23] *Ibid.*, p. 109.

to predicate dream existence of something presupposed to exist in the mind? Suppose I imagine a certain egregious animal that is a cross between a kangaroo and a dragon fly. Suppose I name it Ferdinand. Then Ferdinand has existence in the mind. Suppose further I report a dream I had about Ferdinand. Is this a case where I am (in the relevant way) predicating dream existence of a being presupposed to exist in the understanding? No. For the statement that I dreamt about that being Ferdinand I imagined yesterday has the implications that *any* similar dream statement has—it entails that I really did have a dream. But to be parallel to the fiction case, it can have no such implications. So how *can* I predicate dream existence of a being presupposed to exist in the mind?

The crucial case, however, is that of predicating real existence of a being *B* presupposed to exist in the understanding. Now the result of the predication is not, according to Alston, to entail that *B* really exists. Must we say that *B*, which exists in the understanding, is *thought of* as existing in reality?

On this interpretation Anselm's conclusion would be equivalent to the proposition that

(c) God exists in the understanding and is thought of as existing in reality.

Now Alston concedes that the conclusion of Anselm's argument, if he is predicating real existence of a being existing in the understanding, is necessarily true. And of course (c) is not necessarily true; it entails that someone believes that God exists in reality, which is certainly contingent. So apparently the statement Anselm makes when he predicates real existence of a being that exists in the understanding—the statement "the logical status of which sharply distinguishes it from an ordinary statement of real existence and prevents it from having the sort of religious significance for the sake of which the conclusion was sought"—is not (c). But what statement is it? What statement is it that results when Anselm predicates real existence of a being he presupposes to exist in the understanding?

Perhaps, then, we should understand Alston as holding that one *cannot* predicate real existence of a being presupposed to exist in the understanding. At any rate he certainly means to hold that one cannot *assert a proposition entailing that such a being really exists* by predicating real existence of it. Why not?

"It seems to be a defining feature of all nonreal modes of existence that any statement about something which exists in such a mode will have no implications with respect to real things, except for its real correlate and any implications that might have." How are we to take "implication" here? In explaining the notion of "real correlates," Alston points out that any statement about some being that exists in a nonreal mode *entails* the real existence of the real correlate of that thing. So presumably we may read "implications" in the quoted statement above as "entailments." So taken, the principle needs more careful statement. For I am no part of the real correlate of the Chimera; but the proposition *The Chimera is my favorite beast of fable* is about the Chimera and entails that I exist. Similarly for such a statement as *More books have been written about Hamlet than about Lyndon Johnson*; this is about Hamlet and entails something about Lyndon Johnson. Further, a man may mistakenly *believe* that Cerberus really exists; in that case, no doubt, he might assert that Boston was once really visited by Cerberus. Boston is certainly not the real correlate of Cerberus.

We might note with respect to the first difficulty that the counterexamples are about me and Lyndon Johnson as well as the Chimera and Hamlet; they are not *merely* about beings existing in some nonreal mode. And the second difficulty can be met as follows: what is important here is not whether the being in question *exists* in some nonreal mode, but whether the statement in question (or the maker of that statement) *presupposes* that it does. Hence (c) can be restated:

> (c1) If p is any statement merely about some being presupposed to have existence in some nonreal mode, then any statement about real things entailed by p will be about the real correlate of p's subject.

There is another perplexing matter here, however. Why cannot a statement presuppose both existence in reality *and* existence in the understanding for its subject? It is clear, I think, that many beings exist both in the understanding (as Alston understands that phrase) and in reality. For Alston apparently means to use that phrase in pretty much the way Anselm does; but in the latter's use, from the fact that someone hears and understands the name "the Taj Mahal," it follows that the Taj Mahal exists in the understanding. But of course it also exists in reality; so many things exist both in reality and in the understanding. Anselm's proof is designed to show that God has just this status. But if beings often exist both in the understanding and in reality, there seems to be no reason why a statement might not presuppose such dual existence for its subject: a statement like *The Taj Mahal is generally but mistakenly believed to be pink* is a good candidate for this status. Such a statement, of course, is about a being presupposed to have existence in the understanding; nevertheless it entails that the Taj Mahal really is not pink. But no doubt (c1) can easily be restated so as to accommodate this matter:

> (c2) If p is a statement merely about some being presupposed to have some nonreal mode of existence, but not presupposed to have existence in reality, then any statement about real things entailed by p will be about the real correlate of p's subject.

Is (c2) true? There is a question about entailment that must be resolved before we can tell—a question interesting enough, perhaps, to warrant a digression. If we take it that p entails q just in case the conjunction of p with the denial of q is necessarily false, then any necessary statement is entailed by any statement whatever. Alston does not believe that what he says constitutes an argument against the existence of necessary existential statements. But if we construe entailment as above, then (c2) entails that there are no necessary existential statements, that is, necessary statements attributing real existence to something. For any necessary existential statement (e.g., there is a least prime number) would then be entailed by any statement at all and hence by any statement merely about a being for which some nonreal mode of existence was presupposed. Now (c2) entails that any statement about the real world entailed by such a statement would be about the real correlate of the statement's subject; the least prime is not, presumably, the real correlate of any such statement; hence *There is a least prime*—which is certainly a necessary existential if there are any at all—could not be both necessary and existential.

But perhaps the inadequacy of this characterization of entailment is revealed by the very fact that it implies that every proposition entails every necessary statement. There is no denying the oddity of supposing, for example, that *All bachelors are unmarried* entails every truth of arithmetic, including either Goldbach's conjecture or its denial. C. I. Lewis, however, once restated a very simple argument that was known to the medievals and has never, I think, been satisfactorily answered. Lewis argues that a contradiction entails just any proposition as follows: An explicit contradiction consists in the conjunction of a proposition p with its denial not-p. This conjunction, clearly enough, entails p. But p entails the disjunction of itself with any proposition q. The contradiction also entails the denial of *p*; hence it entails the conjunction of *p or q* with the denial of *p*. But this clearly entails *q*. Schematically, we can put the argument thus:

> Suppose (1) *p* and not-*p*,
> then (2) *p* (from 1)
> and (3) *p* or *q* (from 2)
> and (4) not-*p* (from 1);
> hence (5) (*p* or *q*) and not-*p* (from (3) and (4));
> and hence (6) *q*.

At what points is this argument vulnerable? It might be said that a proposition *p* does not entail its disjunction with just any proposition—after all *Johnson will be elected* does not entail *Either Johnson will be elected or else we will have a communist president*. But "or" in line (3) must be construed "truth functionally"; line (3) asserts only that at least one of its disjuncts is true. And certainly from the truth of a given proposition it follows that at least one disjunct of any disjunction of which it is a disjunct, is true. So step (3) is certainly entailed by step (2) and hence (by the transitivity of entailment) by step (1). Again, the argument form by which (2) and (4) follow from (1) certainly yields entailments; but (2) and (4) certainly entail their conjunction (line (5)) which again by the transitivity of entailment is entailed by line (1).[24] So line (1) entails line (5). Alan Anderson and Nuel Belknap deny that (5) entails (6).[25] But surely it does. If I am given a pair (any pair) of propositions *p* and *q* and am told that at least one of them is true and *p* is false, I can certainly infer that *q* is true. If this is not an entailment step, it is hard to see what

[24] Or if this is objected to, we may note that (1) entails (5) (given that it entails (3) and (4)) by the principle that if *p* entails *q* and also entails *r* then *p* entails the conjunction of *q* with *r*.

[25] "Tautological Entailments," *Philosophical Studies*, XIII (1962), 9, 17–20.

would be one. But then since (1) entails (5), and (5) entails (6), (1) entails (6).

Various attempts have been made to avoid Lewis' conclusion by denying that one or another of his inferences is an entailment step. But these denials have consequences quite as paradoxical as the conclusion they are designed to avoid. The proposal of Anderson and Belknap has the paradoxical conclusion that the disjunctive syllogism is not in every case a valid entailment step; other proposals entail that entailment is not transitive;[26] still others reject the general validity of the step from the conjunction of p with q to p and to q. But all of these are quite as paradoxical as the admission that a contradiction really does entail just any proposition. Indeed, the denial of *any* of the principles involved in Lewis' argument—that p *and* q entails p and entails q, that p entails that at least one of the pair of propositions $\{p\ q\}$ is true, that the argument forms conjunction and disjunctive syllogism are entailment steps, and that entailment is transitive—will be at least as paradoxical as Lewis' conclusion. No doubt we are not inclined initially to think that a contradiction entails just any proposition you pick; but why can we not discover (through discovering an argument like Lewis') that our initial inclinations were mistaken?

It is therefore hard to avoid the conclusion that a contradiction entails every proposition. But then by contraposition it follows that the denial of a contradiction is entailed by just any proposition. Let us say that a proposition is *formally true* if it is the denial of any proposition that formally (i.e., by means of the usual rules of logic) entails an explicit contradiction; then every formally true proposition is entailed by every proposition. This result does not, of course, entail that just any *necessary* proposition is entailed by every proposition. For a proposition

---

[26] See, for example, Timothy Smiley, "Entailment and Deducibility," *Proceedings of the Aristotelian Society,* LIX (1959), 233–254.

like *There is no least prime* does not formally entail a contradiction—to deduce a contradiction from it we must employ as additional premises certain truths of arithmetic which no doubt are necessarily true but need not be taken as truths of logic. Nonetheless if we admit that any formally true proposition is entailed by every proposition, our objection to the suggestion that every necessary proposition enjoys the same status pretty much evaporates: and with it goes the objection to the above characterization of entailment.

To return then to Alston's principle (c); if we characterize entailment as I have been suggesting, (c2) has the consequence that there are no necessary propositions asserting real existence. But perhaps we can take advantage of the difference between entailment and formal entailment to restate (c2) as (c3):

(c3) If *p* is any statement merely about a being presupposed to have existence in some nonreal mode (but not presupposed to have existence in reality as well), then any statement about real things *formally* entailed by *p* will be about the real correlate of *p*'s subject.

This version of (c) no longer entails that there are no necessary existential propositions. This is small consolation, however, for Anselm can accept (c3) with utter equanimity. He maintains, not that *God exists in reality* formally follows from *God exists in the understanding* alone, but from the latter together with the principle that existence in reality is greater than existence in the understanding alone. And the latter principle, while no doubt necessarily true, according to Anselm, need not be supposed to be a truth of logic. Accordingly Anselm is not refuted by the observation that *God exists in reality* is not formally entailed by *God exists in the understanding*. And of course it is obvious that we cannot strengthen (c3) by replacing its consequent with "then any statement about real things formally entailed by the conjunction of p with any necessary statement will be about the real correlate of p's subject." For then once more the principle will entail that there are no necessary existential statements; so revised the principle is equivalent to (c1). But perhaps we might make one last attempt:

(c4) If p is any statement merely about a being presupposed to exist in some nonreal mode (but not presupposed to exist in reality as well) then any statement about real things that is formally entailed by the conjunction of p with a necessary statement, and is not about the real correlate of p's subject, will be formally entailed by the necessary statement in question alone.

If (c4) is true, Anselm's argument is unsuccessful: he sets out to deduce a contradiction from the supposition that God exists in the understanding alone, together with what he takes to be the necessary truth that existence in reality is greater than existence in the understanding alone. This deduction is possible only if the conjunction of *God exists in the understanding* with the necessary principle formally entails that God exists in reality. But the latter is certainly not formally entailed by the necessary principle alone, and is also not about the real correlate of God. Hence if (c4) is true, Anselm's argument must be invalid.

Sadly enough, however, (c4) appears to be too strong. For consider again the least prime. It certainly exists in the understanding. Now the proposition *It is false that the least prime exists in the understanding but not in reality* is necessarily true (since it is necessary that there is a least prime). Conjoined with *The least prime exists in the understanding,* it formally entails *The least prime exists in reality,* which by itself it does not formally entail. So here we have a counter instance to (c4): we have a proposition p (*The least prime exists in the understanding*) merely about some being presupposed to have existence in some nonreal mode (but not presupposed to exist in reality) such that there is a statement that (1) is formally entailed by p's conjunction with a necessary proposition, but not by that necessary proposition alone, and (2) is not about the real correlate of the subject of p. Indeed, (c4), though more subtle than (c2), is like the latter in entailing that there are no necessary existential statements.

The project of finding a satisfactory statement of (c)—that is, one that will defeat Anselm's argument but not entail that there are no necessary existential statements—is beginning to look implausible. But suppose we did have an adequate statement of it. Why should we accept it? What are the reasons in its favor? Alston does not explicitly argue for c; his procedure is to give some examples that illustrate it.[27] Presumably he hopes that in reflecting upon these examples we will be led to see that the principle holds quite generally. And, indeed, the examples do illustrate the principle; restricted to cases of the sort the examples typify, the principle would be sound. But as a perfectly general principle, it seems to be without support and without a great deal of initial plausibility; it is hard to see that Anselm, for example, ought to feel even the smallest obligation to accept it.

We recall that (c) was the support for Alston's claim that real existence cannot be predicated of a being presupposed to exist in some nonreal mode—that existence is not a predicate. Since we have been able to find neither a satisfactory statement of (c) nor any reason for accepting it, we cannot use it to object to Anselm's argument. Now Alston maintains that existential statements in general are not predicative. But are there not alternative accounts that seem just as plausible? If subject-predicate propositions have presuppositions, presumably it is either the proposition itself or the person asserting it that does the presupposing. Now why not suppose that on any occasion when a man makes a subject-predicate statement he (or the statement he makes) presupposes the existence in the understanding (or the "existence in the conceptual realm") of the statement's subject? Consider the first alternative. If a man says *The Taj Mahal is green but the Taj Mahal has no existence in the understanding*, what he says is peculiar in the same way as *The Taj Mahal is green but I do not believe it*. And if we take the second alternative—that it is the propositions themselves (rather than persons) that presuppose existence for their subjects—then presumably the "conceptual existence" of a thing follows from the fact that it is the subject of some subject-predicate proposition. Hence *The Taj Mahal is green but the Taj Mahal does not have conceptual existence* would be necessarily false. But whether it be persons or propositions that presuppose, on this account all attributions of real existence would be subject-predicate propositions predicating real existence of a being presupposed to exist in the understanding (or the conceptual realm). It is only propositions ascribing existence in the understanding (or conceptual existence) that could be construed as impredicative. I mention this alternative account, not because I believe that it is true, but because it seems quite as plausible as the account Alston gives; and unlike the latter, it does not stigmatize Anselm's argument if we construe the latter as essentially involving the predication of real existence of a being presupposed to exist in the understanding.

Alston's objection to Anselm's argument could be encapsulated, I said, in the following two premises:

(1) Anselm's argument is successful only if it treats existence as a predicate by predicating real existence of a being assumed to have existence in the understanding, and

(2) No statement about a being having existence in the understanding entails that the being in question really exists.

We have found reason to mistrust (2); (1), it seems to me, is also dubious. For Anselm proposes to show that the proposition *God exists in reality* is true by showing that *God exists in the understanding but God does not exist in reality* is necessarily false. But how, exactly, does his procedure involve treating existence as a predicate? Not, surely, just in arguing that a proposition of the form *x exists in the understanding but not in reality* is necessarily false. But then how? Presumably the answer is that Anselm is treating existence as a predicate in ascribing real existence to a being presupposed to exist in the understanding. Here we should note that Anselm's argument can easily be restated so that the notion of existence in the understanding plays no part in it, in which case it cannot be thought to involve predicating real existence of a being presupposed to exist in the understanding:

(1) Suppose that the being than which it is not possible that there be a greater does not exist—assumption for *reductio*.
(2) Any existent being is greater than any nonexistent being.
(3) The Taj Mahal exists.
(4) Hence the Taj Mahal is greater than the being than which it is not possible that there be a greater—(1), (2), (3).

(4) is necessarily false; hence the conjunction of (1), (2), and (3) is necessarily false; (2) is necessarily true; hence the conjunction of (1) and (3) is necessarily false; hence *The Taj Mahal exists* entails *The being than which none greater can be conceived exists*. But the former proposition is obviously true; hence the latter is too.

The Ontological Argument (I)

We have no reason to believe, therefore, either that existence in reality cannot be predicated of a being presupposed to exist in the understanding, or that Anselm's argument necessarily involves predicating real existence of such a being. I think the conclusion to be drawn is that we do not yet have a general refutation of Anselm's ontological argument.[28]

---

[28] For a brief comment on Frege's objection (in the *Foundations of Arithmetic*) to the ontological argument, see my "Kant's Objection to the Ontological Argument," *op. cit.*

Three

The Ontological Argument (II)

I ARGUED in Chapter Two that none of the attempts to give a general or wholesale refutation of the ontological argument and its variants has succeeded. No one has produced, it seems to me, a sense for the term "predicate" such that in that sense it is clear both that existence is not a predicate and that Anselm's argument requires it to be one. Nor has anyone shown, it seems to me, that existential statements (or an appropriate subclass of them) are not necessary. Every general argument of this sort with which I am acquainted involves some unsupported premise that does not seem self-evident and that Anselm would scarcely be obliged to accept. Why should Anselm not reply in these cases that his argument shows the premise to be mistaken? There is no substitute, I think, for tackling Anselm's argument directly and in detail. In this chapter I shall not argue that no version of the ontological argument can possibly succeed, but only that none of the more obvious ways of stating it do in fact succeed.

64

The Ontological Argument (II)

The essential portion of Anselm's argument (as I stated it above, p. 29) goes as follows:

Let "God" be an abbreviation for "the being than which none greater can be conceived."

Then

(1) Suppose God exists in the understanding but not in reality.
(2) Existence in reality is greater than existence in the understanding alone.
(3) A being having all of God's properties plus existence in reality can be conceived.

Therefore,

(4) A being having all of God's properties plus existence in reality is greater than God—(2), (1).

So

(5) A being greater than God can be conceived—(3), (4).

(5), however, appears to be self-contradictory; since it was deduced from (1) with the help of the allegedly necessarily true premises (2) and (3) and the definition of "God," it follows that (1) is necessarily false. But God does exist in the understanding; hence he exists in reality as well.

Now when Anselm defines "God" as "the being than which none greater can be conceived," I think we can represent his intent by replacing that phrase with "the being than which it is not (logically) possible that there be a greater," or "the greatest possible being." Some philosophers object that the notion of a being than which it is not possible that there be a greater is self-contradictory or nonsensical and that the ontological argument is therefore wrecked before it leaves port.[1] But this is far from obvious. As they correctly point out, it seems impossible to state a set of principles enabling us to compare just any two beings with respect to greatness. If this is true it is not easy to see its relevance; for even if it is false that every possible being can be compared with every other possible being with respect to greatness, it scarcely follows that there is *no* possible being that can be thus compared with every other possible being. And how could a being be greater than the God of Christianity: how could an eternal, omnipotent, omniscient, morally perfect being whose essence is love be improved upon?

Given, then, that "being than which none greater can be conceived" is to be read as "being than which it is not possible that there be a greater," step (3) of the argument becomes

(3') It is possible that there be a being having all of the properties of the greatest possible being plus existence in reality.

That is, step (3) simply asserts that it is possible that God (the greatest possible being) exists. And (5) then becomes

(5') It is possible that there be a being greater than the being than which it is not possible that there be a greater

which certainly does not have the ring of truth. Indeed, on the plausible doctrine that if a given proposition p is logically necessary, then the proposition that p is logically necessary is itself logically necessary, (5') seems necessarily false. Our problem, then, in determining whether the argument is sound, is to determine whether (2) is true and whether (4) follows from (1) and (2).

---

[1] See, for example, C. D. Broad, *Religion, Philosophy and Psychical Research* (London, 1953), pp. 177–180.

The Ontological Argument (II)

But first of all we must determine what (2) *says*. What is it to say that existence in reality is greater than existence in the understanding alone? Given step (3), the minimum premise that can be used to deduce (4) will be something like

(2a) If A has every property (except for *nonexistence* and any property entailing it) that B has and A exists but B does not, then A is greater than B,

which is a relatively weak premise. It does not, of course, entail that every existent being is greater than every nonexistent being. The idea behind it is as follows: if a being A shares with a being B all of the latter's properties that make for greatness and in addition A exists while B does not, then A is greater than B. So, for example, if there were an actual being that shared with, say, Superman, all the latter's properties that make for greatness, that being would be greater than Superman.

Now according to (3) there is a possible being (call it R) that has all of God's properties plus existence; the idea is to go on from there to show that this being R would be greater than God. To carry through the argument formally, we must *instantiate* (2a) onto R and God by replacing "A" and "B" in (2a) with "R" and "God":

(2b) If R has every property (except for *nonexistence* and any property entailing it) that God has and R exists but God does not, then R is greater than God.

But now consider the antecedent of (2b); it asserts that R has every property (with the noted exception) that God has. One property God has is that of being the being than which it is not possible that there be a greater; hence R has this property too. But then R is the being than which it is not possible that there be a greater; since, furthermore, R exists, the being than which it is not possible that there be a greater exists; hence the antecedent of (2b) is self-contradictory.

The following consideration may mollify anyone who finds the procedure of the last paragraph too highhanded: there is, presumably, some set S of properties so connected with the description *the being than which it is not possible that there exist a greater* that a being meets or exemplifies that description just in case it has every property in S. But then by hypothesis R has every property in S, in which case R is identical with the being than which it is not possible that there exist a greater; in which case the latter exists. The antecedent of (2b) is thus self-contradictory.

But how does this affect the proof? Since we have already conceded (above, pp. 55–58) that a self-contradictory proposition entails just any proposition, we must admit that the antecedent of (2b) entails just any proposition, in which case it entails the consequent of (2b); (2b), therefore, is true and indeed necessarily true, as is (2a) as well. Accordingly we cannot very gracefully object to it.

In trying to restate the proof more formally, then, we have the following:

(1)   God exists in the understanding but not in reality.

(2)   If A has every property (except for nonexistence and any property entailing it) that B has, and A exists and B does not, then A is greater than B.

(3)   It is possible that there be a being having of the properties of God plus existence in reality.

Now step (4) (A *being having all of God's properties plus existence in reality is greater than God*) was to follow from steps (1) and (2). I think we can see that it does if we restate it:

(4a)   If there is a being that has all the properties of God plus existence in reality, then there is a being that is greater than God.

It is a principle of logic that if a pair of propositions p and q jointly entail r, then p entails that q implies r.[2] Now step (1) asserts that God does not exist. The antecedent of (4a) (*There is a being having all of God's properties* (with the noted exception) *plus existence in reality*), however, entails that God does exist. Hence the antecedent of (4a) conjoined with (1) is self-contradictory and entails every proposition including, of course, the consequent of (4a). But then by the above principle it follows that (1) entails that if the antecedent of (4a) is true, so is its consequent—that is, (1) entails (4a). Hence we can scarcely object to (4) either.

To follow the proof further we must deduce

(5)   It is possible that there is a being greater than God

from the preceding steps. And if we can deduce (5), then the proof will apparently be successful. But *can* we? Consider this tempting expedient: first we insert

(4b) If p is possible and p entails q, then q is possible.

Then from (4b) together with (3) and (4a) we deduce (5) as follows:

(3)   It is possible that there is a being having all of God's properties plus existence in reality.

(4a) If there is a being having all of God's properties plus existence in reality, then there is a being greater than God.

(4b) If p is possible and p entails q, then q is possible.

Hence

(5)   It is possible that there be a being greater than God,

which entails (since it is identical with) the proposition that it

---

[2] I.e., $[(p.q) \to r] \to [p \to (q \supset r)]$.

is possible that there be a being greater than the being than which it is not possible that there be a greater. What has gone wrong? The error, of course, is in supposing that (4a) is an *entailment*; we can deduce (4a) from (1), but to perform the deduction we must construe (4a) as a *material* conditional. The *necessity* of (4a) does not follow from (1); but it is the latter that is needed if we are to deduce (5) from (3), (4a) and (4b). The fact is that nothing of interest follows from (1)–(4); the suggestion is good for nothing but bedeviling graduate students.

The difficulty with this version of the proof obviously centers on step (2). Indeed, it is bound to, since (1) is the hypothesis of a *reductio* and thus quite beyond reproach, and (3) is quite apparently true, saying only, as it does, that it is possible that God exists. And the difficulty with (2) is that it has a self-contradictory antecedent; this guarantees its *truth*, but precludes its functioning in some of the important ways conditionals typically function—(2b) cannot function, for example, as the major premise of a sound *modus ponens* argument. More to the present point, it cannot function as the conditional premise in a sound argument of the sort in which one demonstrates the possibility of a proposition *q* by deducing it from *p entails q* and *it is possible that p*. Suppose, therefore, we try replacing (2b) by

(2c) If A has every property B has except for (1) nonexistence, (2) any property that entails nonexistence, and (3) any property that entails that A is identical with B, and A exists and B does not, then A is greater than B.

This suggestion does not fall victim to the ills besetting the previous version; for when we instantiate (2c) onto the greatest possible being and R as we did before, its antecedent will not oblige us to attribute to R the property of being the being than which it is not possible that there be a greater. But if (2c) does not share every defect of (2b), it still shares the crucial one; its antecedent is also self-contradictory. For consider the antecedent of the appropriate instantiation of (2c). It attributes to R every property of God that entails neither that R does not exist nor the R is identical with God. Now the property *is identical with God or is worshiped by Voltaire* does not entail either nonexistence or identity with God; hence by (2c's) antecedent R has that property. The same holds for the property *is identical with God or is not worshiped by Voltaire*; hence R has this property too. Further, of course, God has either the property of being worshiped by Voltaire or the property of not being worshiped by him; and by the antecedent of (2c) R shares that property with him. But then obviously R has a pair of properties that entail its identity with God; hence the antecedent of (2c) entails both that R is identical with God and that R exists; hence it entails that God exists, but also, of course, that God does not exist. So (2c) is no better than (2b).

The fate of (2c) naturally drives us on to

(2d) If A is distinct from B and has every property B has except for nonexistence and any property A alone has, and A exists but B does not, then A is greater than B.

A little reflection, however, reveals that (2d) is no better than (2c); for God, presumably, is not alone in having the property of either being God or being prime; nor is he alone in not being prime. Hence R would have each of these properties and so, once more, would be identical with God, rendering the antecedent of (2d) self-contradictory.[3] Hence (2d) will not do either.

---

[3] If this example is too bizarre, consider instead the property of being divine or human.

So far then we have not succeeded in finding an appropriate version of (2). Let us consider next the following three possibilities:

(2e) If A exists and B does not, then A is greater than B.

(2f) If A does not exist, then it is possible that there exist a being greater than A (since A itself would be greater if it existed).

To state the third possibility, let us suppose that we have composed a list of properties that make for greatness, and let us call the properties on this list "l-properties." Then

(2g) If A has every l-property that B has and A exists and B does not, then A is greater than B.[4]

I shall consider only (2e), although what I say about it will also apply, for the most part, to (2f) and (2g).

Now (2e) is peculiar, but not wholly implausible or obviously false. If we are at all willing to compare nonexistents with existents with respect to greatness (and the reasons for not doing so are tenuous), then (2e) has something to recommend it. After all, nonexistent objects really do not amount to much when it comes to greatness. Is not the merest earthworm really a good deal more impressive than the most exalted but merely fictitious being? Perhaps so (and then again perhaps not); in any event (2e) is not obviously false. And given (2e), our argument can be restated as follows: suppose

(1) God does not exist in reality.

(2e) If A exists and B does not, then A is greater than B.

---

[4] (2f) was suggested to me by Keith Lehrer and (2g) by Peter De Vos. Gaunilo also attributes something like (2e), (2f), or (2g) to Anselm: see "On Behalf of the Fool" in *The Ontological Argument*, ed. A. Plantinga (New York, 1965), p. 11.

The Ontological Argument (II)

(3) The Taj Mahal exists.[5]
(4) The Taj Mahal exists and God does not—(1), (3).
(5) If the Taj Mahal exists and God does not, then the Taj Mahal is greater than God.
(6) The Taj Mahal is greater than God—(4), (5).
(7) It is false that the Taj Mahal is greater than God.

Propositions (6) and (7), of course, are inconsistent. Proposition (7) is presumably to be thought of as necessarily true, being equivalent to

(7′) It is false that the Taj Mahal is greater than the being than which it is not possible that there be a greater.

Proposition (5) appears to follow quite properly from (2e); (3) is indisputable and (4) certainly follows from (1) and (3). Hence the conjunction of (1), (2e), and (3) is inconsistent. Since (2e) is allegedly necessary, (1) and (3) are inconsistent; but (3) is obviously true; hence (1) is false.

The monk Gaunilo objected that if Anselm's argument is acceptable, then so is this one: "You can no longer doubt that this island which is more excellent than all lands exists somewhere, since you have no doubt that it is in your understanding. And since it is more excellent not to be in the understanding alone, but to exist both in the understanding and in reality, for this reason it must exist. For if it does not exist, any land which really exists will be more excellent than it; and so the island already understood by you to be more excellent will not be more excellent." [6] This objection may or may not apply to the previous versions of Anselm's argument; it does apply to this one. Perhaps we can restate it more formally. By employing (2e)

---

[5] If we take as our premise here *The number seven exists*, then we get the conclusion that (1) is necessarily false.

[6] *Loc. cit.*

73

as a premise we can produce an argument of the very same form as Anselm's, with a preposterous conclusion: suppose

(1) The greatest possible horse[7] does not exist.

(2e) If A exists and B does not, then A is greater than B.

(3) The least impressive horse in Kentucky exists.

(4) The least impressive horse in Kentucky exists and the greatest possible horse does not—(1), (3).

(5) If the least impressive horse in Kentucky exists and the greatest possible horse does not, then the least impressive horse in Kentucky is greater than the greatest possible horse—(2).

(6) The least impressive horse in Kentucky is greater than the greatest possible horse—(4), (5).

(7) It is false that the least impressive horse in Kentucky is greater than the greatest possible horse.

And obviously in this way we can go on to prove the existence of the greatest possible thing of any kind you please. Even more unsettling, perhaps, is the fact that, given the premise that *greater than* is transitive, we can show that there is no greatest actual being. For suppose there were a greatest actual being *a*. Then it would follow that:

(1) The being greater than *a* does not exist.

(2e) If A exists and B does not, then A is greater than B.

(3) The Taj Mahal exists.

·

·

·

(6) The Taj Mahal is greater than the being greater than *a*—(2e), (3).

---

[7] "Greatest possible horse" is to be read as "the horse than which it is not possible that there be a greater."

(7) The being greater than *a* is greater than *a*.[8]

(8) The Taj Mahal is greater than *a*—(6), (7).

But of course (8) tells us that the Taj Mahal is greater than the greatest actual being and hence is false; so (1) is false. It follows, therefore, that if there were a greatest actual being *a*, then the being greater than *a* would exist; hence there is no greatest actual being. But if there is no greatest *actual* being, then there is no such thing as the being than which it is not *possible* that there be a greater either—for the latter, if it existed, would of course be the greatest actual being. Hence by using this form of argument we can show that God both does and does not exist. Obviously, then, this form is not altogether impeccable.

Now it might be objected here that we ought to lay certain restrictions on the range and substituend sets of the variables "A" and "B" in our statement of (2e). After all, we got our paradoxical results by substituting for "B" such expressions as "the being greater than the greatest possible being," "the being greater than the greatest actual being," "the being greater than the being than which it is not possible that there be a greater," and the like. And these descriptions, it may be argued, are one and all logically incapable of exemplification in the sense that any proposition entailing that one of them is exemplified is necessarily false. Perhaps, then, we can improve matters by restricting the substituend sets of the variables "A" and "B" in such a way that they contain no descriptions that are logically incapable of exemplification. (We can accomplish the same result by prefacing (2e) with "where A and B are possible beings.")

----

[8] One may properly view this premise with suspicion; but as we shall see the reasons for rejecting it are equally reasons for rejecting step (7) in our statement of Anselm's argument.

This expedient does not accomplish much. In the first place it seems dreadfully *ad hoc*. The basic idea of (2e) was that existent objects are all greater than nonexistent ones; *necessarily* nonexistent objects, one would think, would then be pretty insignificant indeed—scarcely worth talking about, if not altogether beneath notice. Any reason for thinking that every existing object is greater than any *contingently* nonexisting object would (one would think) be as good a reason for supposing that every existing object is greater than any object that necessarily fails to exist. But the latter principle is just what is being deleted from (2a) by the proposed restriction.

Even if we waive this objection, however, (2e) so amended will be unsuccessful. For even if we respect the restriction we can still use the argument form to produce outrageous results. One thing we can show, for example, is that if there are any Guatemalans at all, there are an infinite number of them. For suppose there is at least one, and call him Hector. Now there is a Guatemalan greater than Hector. For suppose there is none: then the Guatemalan greater than Hector does not exist. But then by (2e) Hector is greater than the Guatemalan greater than Hector. Hence it is false that there is no Guatemalan greater than Hector. Our proof, however, depended upon no special facts about Hector; hence we can generalize our conclusion to the result that for any Guatemalan there is a greater. Given that the relation *greater than* is transitive, irreflexive, and asymmetrical, it follows that the set of Guatemalans is infinite. Hence if there are any Guatemalans at all, there is an infinite set of them.

By employing (2e) in an argument of the same form as Anselm's we can deduce a preposterous conclusion; something is amiss with this version of Anselm's argument. But what? What are the possibilities? Step (1) (God does not exist) is the hypothesis of the *reductio;* steps (3) (The Taj Mahal exists) and (4) (The Taj Mahal exists and God does not) are certainly beyond reproach. Apparently there are just three possibilities. Either (5) (If the Taj Mahal exists and God does not, then the Taj Mahal is greater than God) does not follow from (2e), or (2e) is false, or (7) (It is necessarily false that the Taj Mahal is greater than God) is false.

With respect to the first of these possibilities, it might be pointed out that not every grammatically proper replacement for variables like "A" and "B" in a statement like (2e) will yield a true sentence, even if the statement in question is true. It is true that if A can run the mile in three and a half minutes and B cannot, then A is faster than B; but it scarcely follows that if nobody can run a mile in three and a half minutes and George cannot, then nobody is faster than George. Even if it is true that if A exists and B does not, A is greater than B, it surely does not follow that if Nick exists and nobody does not, Nick is greater than nobody. But if not just any grammatically admissible substitutes for "A" and "B" may appear in their substituend sets, which must be ruled out? To hold that instantiating a proposition containing variables onto names of nonexistents is *always* unsound practice is just to reject (2e) and is going too far: *If Pegasus is mythological then Pegasus does not really exist* certainly follows quite properly from the corresponding quantified statement containing a variable in place of "Pegasus."

It is no doubt true that any term which replaces "A" or "B" in (2e) must be a "referring term"—but only in a sense of that phrase in which "Pegasus" is (though "nobody" is not) a referring term. It is also reasonable to insist, perhaps, that any substituend for "A" and "B", though it need not name a being having "existence in reality," must name one having some kind of status or other—fictional or legendary or "existence in the understanding." ⁹ But obviously this will not disqualify the move from (2e) to (5). Indeed, it might serve to defend the argument against the Gaunilonian sort of objection: for while it is not easy to characterize this condition on the substituend set of "A" and "B," it seems fairly clear that "God" meets it while "the greatest possible horse," "the being greater than the being than which it is not possible that there be a greater," "the Guatemalan greater than Hector," and so on, do not. To restrict the range of the variables involved in (2e), incidentally, is equivalent to qualifying it by replacing its implicit, fully universal quantifier with some such restricted quantifier. And hence the first possibility really reduces to the second; for if (2c) is true as it stands, that is, with the understood strictly universal quantifier *for any objects A and B*, then (5) certainly does follow from it.

It is therefore hard to see any reason for rejecting the inference of (5) from (2e). Should we instead reject (2e)? It is certainly hard to see that it is false or nonsensical, though also hard to find much reason for supposing it true. Still it would be disturbing if our only objection to the ontological argument were that this premise, though not obviously false, is not obviously true either.

Accordingly, let us consider

> (7) It is necessarily false that the Taj Mahal is greater than the being than which it is not possible that there be a greater.

Now if (6) (the proposition resulting from (7) by deleting "it is necessarily false that") is, or is equivalent to

---

⁹ Cf. R. Cartwright, "Negative Existentials," *Journal of Philosophy*, LVII (1960), 638.

(6′) The Taj Mahal really exists and the being than which
it is not possible that there be a greater really exists and
the former is greater than the latter,

then (6) is self-contradictory and (7) is clearly true. But then
if the proof is to succeed, (6) so taken (i.e., as (6′)) must follow from (4) and (5), in which case (5) must be equivalent to

(5′) If the Taj Mahal exists and God does not, then there
really is such a thing as the Taj Mahal and there really
is such a thing as God and the former is greater than
the latter.

And (5′) certainly does not appear to follow from (2e); a proposition of this form would follow from (2e), it seems, only if
the range of the latter's variables were restricted to existent
beings, in which case (2e) could not be instantiated upon "the
Taj Mahal" and "God" without a prior proof that God exists.
If (2e) is understood in some *outré* fashion according to which
it does entail (5′), then in that same way of understanding it,
(2e) will entail the following: If the Taj Mahal exists and the
Chimera does not, then there really is such a thing as the Taj
Mahal and there really is such a thing as the Chimera and the
former is greater than the latter. This is clearly false. Hence if
(2e) entails it, (2e) is false. Hence either (2e) does not entail
(5′) or else (2e) is false. And hence if we understand (6) in
such a way that (7) is clearly true, the rest of the proof falls
to pieces.

Is (6) necessarily false even if it is not to be construed as
(6′)? It is a principle of logic that if a proposition is necessarily
false then so is its conjunction with any other proposition.
Hence if (6) is necessarily false, so is

(6″) The greatest possible being does not exist and the great-

79

est possible being is (for that very reason) a lesser being than the Taj Mahal.

But (6″) does not at any rate *appear* to be necessarily false. We can easily imagine someone who accepted (2e) as accepting (6″), and indeed accepting its second conjunct on the grounds that its first conjunct is true. Here I am inclined to think that when we speak of the being than which it is not possible that there be a greater, we mean to be talking about a being such that *if it exists* there cannot be a greater being; it does not follow that even if it fails to exist there cannot be a greater.[10] If existent and nonexistent beings can be categorically compared, then perhaps the truth of the matter is this: if the being than which it is not possible that there be a greater really does exist, then indeed nothing can be greater than it; but if it does not (e.g., if it is merely fictional) then many things may be its superior.

There are other propositions that resemble (6) in form and are not necessarily false. Suppose the meanest man in North Dakota is Dirk Miedema, a resident of Ypsilanti renowned throughout the area for his meanness. Suppose also that Frederick Manfred writes a story about a fictional Bismarck resident named Larz, further characterized as (among other things) the meanest man in North Dakota. Now suppose (as Anselm does) that it is possible to compare categorically an existent being with a nonexistent (with respect to meanness). If it is possible, then what are we to say about Larz and Dirk? Of each we can correctly predicate, it seems, *being the meanest man in North Dakota.* Is Larz meaner than Dirk? or *vice versa*? If the categorical comparison *is* possible, then either

---

[10] Unless comparisons involving nonexistent terms are necessarily hypothetical (see above, p. 42) in which case (2e) will be of no use to the argument anyway.

The Ontological Argument (II)

(a) The meanest man in North Dakota is not meaner than (or identical with) Dirk Miedema, who lives in North Dakota,

or

(b) The meanest man in North Dakota is not meaner than (or identical with) Larz, a North Dakota resident

will be true and hence consistent.

Suppose there were a story about the (merely fictional) greatest man in the state of Washington. If we agree, again, that existent and nonexistent beings may be compared with respect to greatness, would we be obliged to claim that the greatest man in Washington is really greater than, say, Jim Whittaker, one of America's leading mountain climbers? Surely not. Similarly for the greatest possible being: if it does not exist then if one can compare existents with nonexistents (with respect to greatness) at all, there may be many things superior to it.

The difficulty with this version of the ontological argument, then, is that if the relevant propositions of the form *a is greater than b* are so construed that they do not entail the existence of *a* and *b*, then (6) is not necessarily false and (7) is not true.[11] Now what we need for a really thorough examination of this issue is a complete and accurate account of the predication of properties of nonexistent beings. Unfortunately I am not able to give such an account. Nonetheless this last form of the ontological argument is as specious as the preceding one. No doubt there are other reasonable interpretations of this Anselmian argument; I can scarcely claim to have refuted the argument

---

[11] And this suggestion also disposes of the versions of the ontological argument that replace (2e) by (2f) and (2g) (above, p. 72).

überhaupt. But until other interpretations are suggested, the verdict must be that the ontological argument is unsuccessful.

II

Charles Hartshorne and Norman Malcolm maintain that Anselm stated two quite different ontological arguments.[12] Like Kant, they reject one of these arguments (roughly on the grounds that it necessarily involves what they take to be the false proposition that existence is a predicate). They believe, however, that the other one is a perfectly sound argument for the existence of God. In this section I shall consider this second ontological argument as Malcolm states it.

I shall not be concerned with the question whether Malcolm has interpreted Anselm correctly; instead I shall stick to Malcolm's exposition of this version of the ontological argument, hoping to show that the argument is invalid. In essence, the proof is an attempt to deduce God's necessary existence from our conception of Him as a being than which none greater can be conceived by showing "that the notion of contingent existence or of contingent nonexistence cannot have any application to God." [13] Malcolm's account of the proof falls into two parts: an exposition and expansion of Anselm's argument and a summary of it. In order to get the argument in its entirety before us, I shall begin by examining the summary.

Let me summarize the proof. If God, a being a greater than which cannot be conceived, does not exist then He cannot *come* into existence. For if He did He would either have been *caused* to come

---

[12] See, for example, Hartshorne, *Man's Vision of God* (New York, 1941), and *Anselm's Discovery* (La Salle, 1965), which are entirely devoted to this argument, and Malcolm, "Anselm's Ontological Arguments," *Philosophical Review*, LXIX (1960), 41–62 (reprinted in *The Ontological Argument*, ed. Plantinga (New York, 1965), pp. 136–59).

[13] Malcolm, *op. cit.*, p. 49.

into existence or have *happened* to come into existence, and in either case He would be a limited being, which by our conception of Him He is not. Since He cannot come into existence, *if He does not exist His existence is impossible* [my italics—A. P.]. If He does exist He cannot have come into existence (for the reasons given), nor can He cease to exist, for nothing could cause Him to cease to exist nor could it just happen that he ceased to exist. So *if God exists His existence is necessary* [my italics—A. P.]. Thus God's existence is either impossible or necessary. It can be the former only if the concept of such a being is self-contradictory or in some way logically absurd. Assuming that this is not so, it follows that He necessarily exists.[14]

The structure of the main argument here seems to be the following:

(1) If God does not exist, His existence is logically impossible.

(2) If God does exist, His existence is logically necessary.

(3) Hence either God's existence is logically impossible or it is logically necessary.

(4) If God's existence is logically impossible, the concept of God is contradictory.

(5) The concept of God is not contradictory.

(6) Therefore God's existence is logically necessary.

I take it that (3) is equivalent to the assertion that "the notion of contingent existence or of contingent nonexistence cannot have any application to God"[15]; and in fact (3) follows from (1) and (2). Before examining the argument for (1) and (2), however, I wish to consider the intended meaning of the phrase "logically necessary" as it occurs in the proof. It seems reasonable to understand the assertion *God's existence is log-*

---

[14] *Ibid.*, pp. 49–50.
[15] *Ibid.*, p. 49.

ically necessary as equivalent to the assertion *The proposition "God exists" is logically necessary.* I think this is Malcolm's intention:

> It may be helpful to express ourselves in the following way: to say, not that *omnipotence* is a property of God, but rather that *necessary omnipotence* is; and to say, not that *omniscience* is a property of God, but rather that *necessary omniscience* is. We have criteria for determining that a man knows this and that and can do this and that, and for determining that one man has greater knowledge and abilities in a certain subject than another. . . . That God is omniscient and omnipotent has not been determined by the application of criteria: rather these are requirements of our conception of Him. They are internal properties of the concept, although they are also rightly said to be properties of God. *Necessary existence* is a property of God in the *same sense* that *necessary omnipotence* and *necessary omniscience* are His properties.[16]

It is a requirement of our conception of God that He is omnipotent; it is merely putting this point a different way, I believe, to say that the proposition *God is omnipotent* is logically necessary. The sense in which necessary omnipotence is a property of God is that the proposition *God is omnipotent* is necessary. And necessary existence, says Malcolm, is a property of God in the same sense in which necessary omnipotence and necessary omniscience are. To say "God necessarily exists," then, is to say the same as "*God exists* is a necessary proposition." This interpretation receives confirmation from the following sentence: "The a priori proposition 'God necessarily exists' entails the proposition 'God exists,' if and only if the latter also is understood as an a priori proposition: in which case the two propositions are equivalent." [17] Taking "logically necessary" and "a priori" as synonyms here, this passage seems

---

[16] *Ibid.,* p. 50.
[17] *Ibid.*

to mean that *God necessarily exists* is equivalent to "*God exists*" *is necessary*. I am assuming further that for Malcolm a proposition is logically necessary if and only if its contradictory is self-contradictory. If Malcolm's reconstruction of Anselm's argument is correct, therefore, the proposition *God does not exist* is self-contradictory.

I turn now to premises (1) and (2) of the argument as outlined above. The first step in the argument given in the summary for (1) is to show that from the conception of God as the greatest conceivable being it follows that it is logically impossible for God to come (or to have come) into existence. For if He had either been caused to come into existence, or merely happened to come into existence, He would be a limited being. This inference seems quite correct; it follows from our conception of God that:

(a) N [18] (God never has and never will come into existence).

In the summary Malcolm apparently deduces (1) from (a). But this seems to be a mistake; for (a) does not entail (1) although it entails a proposition similar in some respects to the latter. Taking (a) and the antecedent of (1) as premises and the consequent of (1) as the conclusion, the deduction of (1) from (a) is equivalent to the following argument:

(a) N (God never has and never will come into existence).

(1a) God does not exist—antecedent of (1).

Therefore

(1c) N (God does not exist)—consequent of (1).

But (1c) does not follow from (a) and (1a). What does follow is (1c'): God never will exist. That is, the proposition *It*

---

[18] "N (. . .)" is to be read as "It is necessarily true that . . ."

is logically necessary that God never comes into existence entails:

(1') N (If there is a time at which God does not exist, then there is no subsequent time at which He does exist).

But (1'), of course, cannot play the role assigned to (1) in Malcolm's argument, for (1') cannot help to show that the notion of contingent existence does not apply to God. The argument for (1) in the summary seems invalid, then.

In the exposition of the proof there seem to be *two* different though related arguments whose conclusions entail (1). I believe that Malcolm's reply to the above criticism would be to appeal to one of these arguments. The one I am referring to runs along the following lines: if God did not exist, and if the fact that He did not were merely contingent, then either He is prevented from existing or He merely happens not to exist. But it is contrary to the concept of God to suppose that anything could prevent Him from existing; and if the supposition that He merely happens not to exist is consistent, then if He did exist He would have "mere duration rather than eternity." But it is a requirement of our concept of God that He is an eternal Being; hence it cannot be true both that God does not exist and that the proposition *God does not exist* is logically contingent. I shall consider this argument after examining the argument in the summary for premise (2) of the proof.

Proposition (2) is deduced from (a) (see above) together with

(b)   N (God never has ceased and never will cease to exist).

Proposition (b), like (a), is deduced from the proposition that God is a being than which no greater can be conceived. Taking (a) and (b) together with the antecedent of (2) as premises and the consequent of (2) as conclusion we get the following inference:

The Ontological Argument (II)

(a) N (God never has begun and never will begin to exist).

(b) N (God never has and never will cease to exist).

(2a) God exists—antecedent of (2).

Therefore

(2c) N (God exists)—consequent of (2).

Once again it is apparent that (2c) does not follow from (a), (b), and (2a). What does follow is:

(2c′) God always has existed and always will exist.

To put it differently, (a) and (b) together entail the following necessary conditional:

(2′) N (If at *any* time God exists, then at *every* time God exists).

If God cannot (logically) come into or go out of existence, it is a necessary truth that if He ever exists, He always exists. But it does not follow that if He exists, the proposition *God exists* is necessary. The correct definition of "God" might contain or entail that He never comes into or goes out of existence, in which case it would be a necessary truth that He never has and never will either begin or cease to exist. But nothing has been said to show that the fact, if it is a fact, that there is a being so defined is a necessary fact. The argument given in the summary for (2), then, is also invalid.

Allow me to venture a guess as to the origin of the confusion here. One way of advertising the necessary truth of a conditional, in English, is to inject some modal term into the consequent. We might say, for example, "If Jones is a bachelor, he cannot be married"; and in so saying, of course, we do not mean to assert that if Jones is a bachelor, the proposition *Jones is unmarried* is necessary. What we do mean is that *If Jones is a bachelor, he is unmarried* is necessary. Similarly here:

it is a necessary truth that if God exists, He always has and always will. A proper (though misleading) way of putting this is to say: if God exists, He cannot fail to exist eternally. But this assertion, which is equivalent to my (2′) above, and which does follow from (a) and (b), should not be confused with (2), which does not so follow.

Now the argument given in the summary for (1) and (2) contains an omission. Malcolm argues that God cannot merely happen to begin to exist nor merely happen to cease to exist, and also that He cannot have been caused either to begin to exist or to cease to exist. But he does not consider the possibility that it just happens that God always has and always will exist (and so happens neither to begin nor cease existing, nor is caused either to begin or cease existing), nor does he consider the possibility that it just happens that God never has existed and never will exist. Malcolm's reply, as I have intimated, is that if either of these were the case, then if God exists, He has mere duration rather than eternity. After arguing that it is contrary to the concept of God to suppose that He depends upon anything for existence or that He could be prevented from existing, Malcolm considers the possibility that God just happens to exist:

Some may be inclined to object that although nothing could prevent God's existence, still it might just *happen* that He did not exist. And if He did exist that too would be by chance. I think, however, that from the supposition that it could happen that God did not exist it would follow that, if He existed, He would have mere duration and not eternity. It would make sense to ask, "How long has He existed?" "Will He still exist next week?" "He was in existence yesterday but how about today?" and so on. It seems absurd to make God the subject of such questions. According to our ordinary conception of Him, He is an eternal being. And eternity does not mean endless duration, as Spinoza noted. To ascribe eternity to something is to exclude as senseless all sentences that imply that it has duration.[19]

The principle of this argument seems to be the contention that if God merely happened to exist He would have duration rather than eternity. In order to see whether the argument holds up we must ask what it is to "happen to exist" and what it is to have mere duration rather than eternity. Now Malcolm appears to be using the locution "happens to exist" in such a way that the sentence *God just happens to exist* is equivalent to the conjunction of the following four sentences:

God just happens to exist = (a) God exists,
                                   (b) *God exists* is logically contingent,
                                   (c) God is not caused to exist, and
                                   (d) *God is not caused to exist* is logically necessary.

I am not sure about the inclusion of (d), but my argument will hold without it. The situation with respect to the terms "duration" and "eternity" is not quite so clear, unfortunately. But at any rate the last sentence of the above quotation makes it apparent that if something has eternity, it does not have duration. We must therefore inquire what it is to have duration. First of all it appears that if God had duration it would make sense to ask "How long has He existed?" "He was in existence yesterday, but how about today?" and so forth. Now Malcolm is quite correct, surely, in holding that such questions cannot sensibly be asked about God. But he seems mistaken in inferring the sensibility of these questions from the proposition that God just happens to exist. Let us agree that our normal

___
[19] *Op. cit.*, p. 48.

conception of God includes or entails that He is not caused to exist and that His existence has neither beginning nor end. It will then be true and necessarily true that

(7) If God exists, then there is a being whose existence is not caused and who has neither beginning nor end.

The whole conditional is necessary, but we have no reason so far for supposing that either its antecedent or its consequent is. It may be a logically contingent truth, if it is a truth, that there actually is a being so conceived. And if God, so defined, does exist, the four conditions I suggested as constituting the meaning of "God happens to exist" will all be fulfilled. But the question "How long has God existed?" will not "make sense." For in asking the question one implies that He does exist. And the assertion that God exists entails the assertion that He has always existed. Hence anyone who understands the question already knows the answer; to ask that question seriously is to betray misapprehension of the concept of God. Similarly the question "Will He still exist next week?" will be absurd. For it also implies that He does exist; but in the conception suggested above the conjunction *He does exist now, but next week He will no longer exist* is contradictory. Hence I conclude that *God merely happens to exist* does not entail that God has duration in any sense involving the logical propriety of questions of the sort Malcolm mentions.

Further on in the same passage, however, Malcolm seems to introduce a slightly different sense of "duration":

If a thing has duration then it would be merely a *contingent* fact, if it was a fact, that its duration was endless. The moon could have endless duration but not eternity. If something has endless duration it will *make sense* (although it will be false) to say that it will cease to exist, and it will make sense (although it will be false) to say that something will *cause* it to cease to exist. A being with endless duration is not, therefore, an absolutely unlimited being.[20]

Here it is suggested that the assertion *God has duration* has three components. That assertion entails (a) that any statement specifying the temporal limits of God's existence is contingent, (b) that *God will cease to exist* is sensible, and (c) that *God will be caused to cease to exist* is sensible. (c) appears to entail (b); perhaps it is also meant to entail (a), but I leave that question on one side. Now it seems clear that the proposition *God merely happens to exist*, understood as above, does not entail (b). If an adequate definition of "God" includes or entails that He never comes into or goes out of existence, it obviously will not "make sense" to suppose that God will cease to exist. For *God will cease to exist* entails *There is a time at which God exists and a later time at which He does not.* But under the definition in question that proposition is contradictory. Hence the supposition that God merely happens to exist does not entail (b). Nor does it entail (c), since (c) entails (b).

The situation with respect to (a) is a bit more complicated. Suppose we take the assertion

(8)   God has neither beginning nor end

as a specification of God's temporal limits in the somewhat Pickwickian sense that it denies any such limits to His existence. There are two possible interpretations of this proposition:

(8a) If God exists, then He always has existed and always will exist,

and

(8b) God does exist and He always has existed and always will exist.

On the interpretation I have been suggesting, (8a) is logically necessary; (8b) is contingent, though each of its conjuncts entails the remaining two. Accepting the second interpretation of (8), then, we might say that the proposition *God merely happens to exist* entails that God has duration. But this is a weak sense indeed of "duration"; in fact to say that God has duration in that sense is to say no more than that *God exists* is logically contingent—which, after all, was the essential component of the contention that God merely happens to exist. In particular this in no way implies that questions of the sort Malcolm mentions are legitimate; nor does having duration in this sense constitute a limitation. It is a mistake, therefore, to suppose that God's happening to exist is inconsistent with His being "that than which none greater can be conceived."

Malcolm supports the argument I have just criticized by an exegesis of a passage in Anselm's *Responsio I:*

> In *Responsio I* Anselm adds the following acute point: if you can conceive of a certain thing and this thing does not exist then if it *were* to exist its nonexistence would be *possible*. It follows, I believe, that if the thing were to exist it would depend on other things both for coming into and continuing in existence, and also that it would have duration and not eternity. Therefore it would not be, either in reality or in conception, an unlimited being.[21]

The first point here seems to be that the proposition *God can be conceived but does not exist* entails the proposition *If God existed, His nonexistence would be possible.* This seems correct. But Malcolm draws the further inference that if God were to exist, then He would "depend upon other things" and would have mere duration rather than eternity. This argument comes to the following:

---

[21] *Ibid.*

The Ontological Argument (II)

(9) If the existence of God were logically contingent, God would depend upon other beings both for coming into existence and for continuing in existence, and God would have duration rather than eternity.

I believe I have already shown that from the supposition that God's existence is logically contingent it does not follow that He has duration rather than eternity, except in the trivial sense in which predicating duration of God is saying no more than that the proposition *God exists* is logically contingent. But it seems equally clear that God's dependence upon other things does not follow from the supposition that His existence is logically contingent. Malcolm states his argument in such a way that any statement of contingent existence entails that the subject of the statement depends upon other things both for coming into and for continuing in existence. But this is surely a mistake. For suppose that certain elementary physical particles—for example, electrons—have always existed (in which case they surely do not depend upon anything for coming into existence) and that there is nothing upon which they depend for their continued existence: it would not follow that the statement "Electrons do not exist" is self-contradictory, or that the existence of electrons is logically necessary.

Perhaps Malcolm had the following in mind here: even if electrons depend upon nothing at all for coming into or continuing in existence the assertion that they do not so depend is contingent. But the assertion that God does not depend upon anything is necessary. And it is inconsistent to hold both that God's existence is contingent and that it is a necessary truth that He depends upon nothing at all either for coming into or for continuing in existence. I think this is the heart of Malcolm's argument. But I must confess inability to see the inconsistency. Malcolm is entirely correct in taking it that the

93

proposition *God does not depend upon anything for coming into or continuing in existence* is logically necessary. As he says, the necessity of this proposition follows from the fact that God is conceived, in the Hebraic-Christian tradition, as a being than which nothing greater can be conceived. And hence an adequate definition of the word "God" must include or entail that He is dependent upon nothing whatever. But the assertion that a being so defined exists, that the definition actually applies to something, may well be, for all that Malcolm and Anselm have said, a contingent assertion. It is a necessary truth that if God exists, then there is a being who neither comes into nor goes out of existence and who is in no way dependent upon anything else. But from this it does not follow, contrary to Malcolm's argument, that the proposition *There is a being who neither comes into nor goes out of existence and who depends upon nothing* is necessary; nor does it follow that *God exists* is necessary. Malcolm's reconstruction of the ontological argument therefore fails.

Four

The Teleological Argument

IF the ontological argument smacks of trumpery and word magic, the teleological proof is as honest and straightforward as a Norman Rockwell painting. No doubt it is on this account that it has enjoyed a wide popular appeal. Kant, who had little but contempt for the ontological and cosmological arguments, believed that the teleological proof

always deserves to be mentioned with respect. It is the oldest, the clearest, and the most accordant with the common reason of mankind. It enlivens the study of nature, just as it itself derives its existence and gains ever new vigor from that source. . . . Reason, constantly upheld by this ever-increasing evidence which, though empirical, is yet so powerful, cannot be so depressed through doubts suggested by subtle and abstruse speculation, that it is not at once aroused from the indecision of all melancholy reflection, as from a dream, by one glance at the wonders of nature and the majesty of the universe—ascending from height to height up to the all-highest.[1]

---

[1] *Critique of Pure Reason*, tr. N. K. Smith (London, 1953), p. 520.

In many ways the teleological argument is more difficult to discuss and assess than are the two theistic proofs already examined. This difficulty arises mainly, perhaps, from the circumstance that it is an inductive or analogical argument; and the logic of such argumentation is not nearly as well understood as the logic of deductive argument. Furthermore, questions involving degrees of difference between widely disparate classes of things (does the universe resemble a machine more than it does an animal? or is it more like a vegetable?) become essentially relevant; and it is hard indeed to see how to answer them.

A classic statement of the argument is to be found in David Hume's *Dialogues Concerning Natural Religion:*

Look round the world: contemplate the whole and every part of it: you will find it to be nothing but one great machine, subdivided into an infinite number of lesser machines, which again admit of subdivisions, to a degree beyond what human faculties can trace and explain. All these various machines, and even their most minute parts, are adjusted to each other with an accuracy, which ravishes into admiration all men, who have ever contemplated them. The curious adapting of means to ends, throughout all nature, resembles exactly, though it much exceeds, the productions of human contrivance; of human design, thought, wisdom and intelligence. Since therefore the effects resemble one another, we are led to infer, by all the rules of analogy, that the causes also resemble; and that the author of nature is somewhat similar to the mind of man; though possessed of much larger faculties, proportioned to the grandeur of the work, which he has executed.[2]

Hume's treatment of the argument in the *Dialogues* is widely hailed as a masterpiece of philosophical criticism. "Hume's destructive criticism of the argument," says Norman

---

[2] Ed. with an introduction by Norman Kemp Smith (New York, 1947), p. 143.

The Teleological Argument

Kemp Smith, "was final and complete." [3] And there is much to be said for this estimate—Hume's discussion is matchless for clarity, imagination, and grace. Since contemporary discussion of the argument is sparse we can probably do no better than to consider carefully what Hume has to say about it. He presents essentially two objections to the argument from design; I shall argue that one of these is finally inconclusive while the other is sound.

I

I begin with a connected system of objections whose unity is easier to see than to characterize. The design argument as stated is an argument by analogy and may be put schematically as follows:

(1) The "productions of human contrivance" are the products of intelligent design.
(2) The universe resembles the productions of human contrivance.
(3) Therefore probably the universe is a product of intelligent design.
(4) Therefore probably the author of the universe is an intelligent being.

The objection is that the universe is not, after all, very much like the productions of human design and intelligence—not enough like them to support the argument. Why not?

But can you think, Cleanthes, that your usual phlegm and philosophy have been preserved in so wide a step as you have taken, when you compare to the universe houses, ships, furniture, machines; and from their similarity in some circumstances infer a similarity in their causes? . . . But can a conclusion, with any propriety, be transferred from parts to the whole? Does not the great dispropor-

[3] *Ibid.*, p. 3.

tion bar all comparison and inference? From observing the growth of a hair, can we learn anything concerning the generation of a man? [4]

Although this objection is not easy to evaluate, taken by itself it does not seem very strong. Philo, in that dialogue, apparently suggests that no whole can resemble its parts (or some set of its parts) sufficiently to support an analogical inference. But surely this is not so. I know that large parts of the North Cascades Wilderness Area contain more than seven Douglas firs to the acre (and have no contrary evidence); I can reasonably conclude that the North Cascades Wilderness Area itself probably contains seven or more Douglas firs to the acre. On just the information cited, my conclusion certainly seems to be more probable than not. The *general* conclusion that one cannot properly argue from parts to whole is false. Everything depends upon the specific whole and parts in question.

Philo follows this objection with one that does take into account the nature of the relevant whole:

When two species of objects have always been observed to be conjoined together, I can infer, by custom, the existence of one whenever I *see* the existence of the other. And this I call an argument from experience. But how this argument can have place, where the objects, as in the present case, are single, individual, without parallel, or specific resemblance, may be difficult to explain. And will any man tell me with a serious countenance, that an orderly universe must arise from some thought and art, like the human; because we have had experience of it? To ascertain this reasoning, it were requisite that we had experience of the origin of worlds; and it is not sufficient, surely, that we have seen ships and cities arise from human art and contrivance.[5]

---

[4] *Ibid.*, p. 147.
[5] *Ibid.*, p. 150.

The Teleological Argument

There are several suggestions contained here. One is that we could arrive at inductive conclusions about the origin of the universe only if we had had experience of the origin of various universes, which, of course, would be difficult to manage. But this suggestion is too strong; it implies that we could make no sound inductive inference concerning the origin, for example, of the largest crow in the Amazon jungle, since we obviously cannot have had experience of various largest crows in the Amazon. The passage also suggests that the universe is unique and singular, hence not sufficiently like the products of human contrivance (or anything else, presumably) to support an analogical argument whose conclusion ascribes some property to it. Again, if the suggestion is that nothing unique and singular can figure as the subject of a sound analogical argument, the suggestion is too strong; for surely we can reason in this way about the largest crow in the Amazon jungle.

And why can we not evade the objection altogether? Note, first, that there are certain connections between analogical and straightforward inductive arguments. An analogical argument may have the following form:

(a) (5) The members of class γ have A.
     (6) a resembles the members of γ.
     (7) Therefore probably a also has A.

Now if a resembles the members of γ, there will be some (possibly complex) property that it shares with them. This property will determine a class; wherever there is an argument of form (a), therefore, there will be one of the following form:

(b) (8) The members of γ are members of β and have A.
     (9) a is a member of β.
     (10) Probably a has A.

And the argument from design as stated by Cleanthes can

easily be recast so as to fit this form: γ would be the class of "objects of human contrivance"; β would be the class of things "exhibiting the curious adaptation of means to ends" or the "nice adjustment of means to ends"; A would be the property of being the product of intelligent design and a would be the universe.

Now if it happens that the members of γ are the only members of β of which we know whether or not they have the property A, we can restate the argument as follows:

(c) (11) Every member of β of which we know whether or not it has A, in fact has A.

(12) a is a member of β.

(13) Therefore probably a has A.[6]

The argument of form (c) is a good deal stronger than the corresponding arguments of forms (a) and (b). And the mentioned condition is satisfied in the case of the argument from design. Clearly we do not know of any member of the class of things exhibiting curious adaptation of means to ends that is not the product of conscious and intelligent design: even if we know that a thing was not designed *by man* we do not know that *God* did not design it, unless we already know that God did not design the universe (in which case it is pointless to consider the teleological argument). Hence the argument may be restated as follows:

(14) Everything that exhibits curious adaptation of means to ends and is such that we know whether or not it was the product of intelligent design, in fact was the product of intelligent design.[7]

---

[6] In an argument of this form, β will be the *reference class*, A the *sample property*, and those members of β of which we know whether they have a constitute the *sample class*.

[7] Why not cast (14) in the more familiar form: (11′) All examined

The Teleological Argument

(15) The universe exhibits curious adaptation of means to ends.

(16) Therefore the universe is probably the product of intelligent design.

This is perhaps the strongest version of the teleological argument. And it may appear that the objection we are now considering—that the universe is unique, does not much resemble machines, and so on—has no bearing at all upon it. That this is so, however, is not clear. How does the fact that the universe is single or unique affect the argument? It would seem to be relevant only if it implies that there are no classes of which the universe is a member (or perhaps no classes which contain it and other things), and hence no reference class for the argument. But, of course, there are any number of classes to which both the universe and many other things belong: the class of very large things, for example, or of things more than fifty years old. The mere fact that a thing is unique does not of course entail that it has no property in common with anything else.

The fact that the universe is single or unique, therefore, does not invalidate the argument. But perhaps we should construe Hume's objection as a query: *is* there an appropriate reference class for the argument? To investigate this question we might try taking as its reference class the union of the class of, say, Chevrolets with the unit class of the universe. Then our argument will proceed as follows:

(17) Every member of the class of Chevrolets plus the universe, of which we know whether or not it is the prod-

A's are B? Because this asserts more than the teleological arguer can claim to know. There are many members of the reference class—eyes, for example—that he has examined without discovering either that they are or that they are not products of intelligent design. The class of examined members of the reference class is not always identical with the sample class; in these cases an argument of the form (11') cannot be used.

uct of intelligent design, is indeed the product of intelligent design.

(18) The universe is a member of the class of Chevrolets plus the universe.

(19) Probably the universe is the product of intelligent design.

Here our argument is of the proper form and has true premises; it is none the less preposterous. Why? We might consider the following analogue: suppose I do not know whether Julius Caesar was snub-nosed. I can then construct a class K by annexing Julius Caesar to the class of snub-nosed persons and argue as follows:

(20) Every member of K such that I know whether or not he is snub-nosed, is.

(21) Julius Caesar is a member of K.

(22) So probably Julius Caesar is snub-nosed.

On the other hand, I can construct a class H by annexing Julius Caesar to the class of non-snub-nosed persons, and by an argument exactly paralleling (20)–(22) with H replacing K, conclude that Julius Caesar is not snub-nosed. But it is not easy to see just what is shown by the fact that it is possible to construct these two arguments. That the argument (20)–(22) can be paralleled by another inductive argument with a conclusion inconsistent with (22) does not show that (20)–(22) is not an acceptable argument. For the perfectly proper argument whose conclusion is that the largest crow in the Amazon is black (and whose major premise is that all observed crows have been black) may be paralleled in similar fashion by an argument whose reference class is the class I of white birds plus the largest crow in the Amazon jungle. In this latter case one of these arguments is stronger than the other in that its reference class—the class of crows—is somehow more appropriate or proper: but it is certainly not easy to say what this appropriateness consists in.

Hume, indeed, in the passage quoted above (p. 98) may be taken to suggest that in a good inductive argument the reference class is always a *species* or some other natural kind. No doubt this would rule out arguments (17)–(19) and (14)–(16), as well as the argument from design; but it is much too strong. There certainly are proper inductive arguments with reference classes such as the class of houses built between 1925 and 1935, the class of overweight adult human males, and the class of creosoted railroad ties and telephone poles.

Nevertheless, the class of crows is a better reference class than *I* is; an argument with *I* as its reference class is preposterous. Perhaps the reason is that for every argument of this sort (i.e., with a reference class like *I*) for the conclusion that the crow in question is not black, there is another just like it, and just as strong, for the opposite conclusion. The objection to (20)–(22) as a reason for supposing that (22) (Julius Caesar is snub-nosed) is more probable than not on our total evidence is just that the same total evidence yields an argument exactly analogous to it, and of the same strength, for the denial of (22).

Is this objection available in the case of the argument (17)–(19)? If so, there must be available a nonempty class of objects known not to be the products of intelligent design; from this we may then construct our reference class by taking its union with the unit class of the universe. But what class would this be? Mountains, plants, and the like will not serve, since we do not know that they are not the products of God's intelligent design. Taking such objects as numbers and propositions to exist necessarily (and hence not by design) we might conceivably try to construct an appropriate reference class by annexing the universe to—for example—the set of prime numbers.

This argument is utterly outrageous, but perhaps deserved by anyone who suggests an argument like (17)–(19). On the other hand, (17)–(19) could then be replaced by (23)–(25):

(23) Every *contingent* object such that we know whether or not it was the product of intelligent design, *was* the product of intelligent design.

(24) The universe is a contingent object.

(25) So probably the universe is designed.

To this argument certainly, and possibly to (17)–(19), the objection to (20)–(22) cannot be sustained. So we still do not have a clear objection to either. Nevertheless (17)–(19) (and possibly (23)–(25)) is preposterous, and its eccentricity certainly arises from the bizarre character of its reference class. Even if we are unable to specify an acceptable general rule that eliminates it, (17)–(19) must be rejected.

A very great deal of Hume's criticism of the argument is devoted to the claim that the universe does not really resemble the "objects of human contrivance" to which Cleanthes likens it. Philo suggests that the world resembles an animal more than a machine, and a vegetable more than either.[8] Will this suggestion rule out (17)–(19)? And how, exactly, is it relevant to the argument from design restated as an inductive argument with "things that exhibit curious adapting of means to ends" as its reference class? Perhaps as follows: if the reference class of an inductive argument can be partitioned into a pair of classes of objects widely disparate in character, the argument is to a certain degree weakened. If in addition all the members of its sample class are of a sort very different from some of the reference class minus the sample class, the argument is weaker still. In the extreme case, where the reference class is the set of Chevrolets plus the universe, or crickets plus Martians, and the

---

[8] *Op. cit.*, pp. 171, 172, 176.

sample class consists exclusively in each case of objects from just one of the two classes whose union forms the reference class, it may be maintained reasonably, perhaps, that the argument is altogether worthless. The members of the reference class must themselves resemble each other to some degree and in particular the members of the sample class must resemble, to some degree, the members of the reference class minus the sample class.[9] If I argue that all adult lions are over five feet long on the basis of my examination of some lions in Krueger Park, my argument is not very strong. If I argue that all adult animals are over five feet long on the same basis, my argument is weaker still, if not worthless.

No doubt all this is so. Still, it is not of much help. For naturally enough the members of any class resemble each other in some respect; the problem is to specify how much and in what respects the members of the sample class must resemble those of the reference class minus the sample class. If my sample class consists of crows observed in Washington's Whatcom County and my reference class is that of crows in the state generally, the fact that some members of my reference class but none of my sample class reside outside Whatcom County is of little consequence; not so if my sample class consists only of crows and my reference class is animals generally. But it is difficult if not altogether impossible to give rules for detecting the sorts of differences that disqualify an argument; and in criticizing the argument from design Hume does not do so.

Still, even if we cannot give rules for detecting relevant differences or for determining appropriate degrees of similarity, we are able to do this in practice; the fact is that we often recognize, as in the case of some of the arguments mentioned, that the sample class does not resemble the reference class minus the sample class in the relevant respects. No doubt. But

---

[9] *Ibid.*, p. 144.

what, exactly, is the trouble with the reference class of the teleological argument? True enough, the universe does not greatly resemble a spring loom or a golf club. It may even be, as Hume suggests, that it resembles an animal or a plant more than the products of human contrivance—or at any rate that there are some products of human contrivance to which it bears less similarity than it does to some plants or animals. This, however, is not to the point, since plants and animals themselves (as well as some of their parts) have the reference property: they too exhibit the curious adaptation of means to ends. Eyes, for example, are often cited as having this property.

The upshot of this objection about the reference class of the argument from design is best construed, I think, as the question whether its sample class resembles the reference class minus the sample class sufficiently to support an inference of any strength at all: Hume has given us no answer to this question. And how are we to decide whether the admitted differences do or do not disqualify the argument? Philo concedes that the universe certainly seems initially to resemble things we know to be designed; the impression that the universe has been designed is hard to avoid: "A purpose, an intention, or design strikes everywhere the most careless, the most stupid thinker; and no man can be so hardened in absurd systems, as at all times to reject it." [10] Kant thinks the analogy of the universe (or the parts we are acquainted with) to the products of design is sufficient to support some such argument and at any rate better than any thing else at hand: "But at any rate we must admit that, if we are to specify a cause at all, we cannot here proceed more securely than by analogy with those purposive productions of which alone the cause and mode of action are fully known to us." [11] And the fact is that the universe

---

[10] *Ibid.*, p. 214.
[11] Kant, *op. cit.*, p. 522.

The Teleological Argument

does seem to resemble in certain important respects, and with certain qualifications, things we know to be designed. Perhaps it also resembles such things as animals and trees; and surely there are the differences Hume points out between the universe and things we know to be designed. But there seems to be no reason to think that these differences ruin the argument.

The just conclusion is that the teleological argument is weaker, perhaps much weaker, than the inferences by which we establish that almost all crows are black; but there is no justification here for taking the further step of claiming that it has no force at all. This objection is therefore inconclusive.

II

Hume's second objection begins with the existence of evil in the world. Philo suggests at two points that the existence of evil (or at any rate of the amount and variety of evil we actually find) is *logically inconsistent* with the existence of God.[12] If true, this would of course be an utterly devastating objection to the argument from design: it would then follow that the evidence at our disposal precludes instead of supports its conclusion. Cleanthes, indeed, appears to agree with Philo that the existence of an all-powerful, omniscient, and perfectly good deity is inconsistent with the existence of evil;[13] he therefore proposes to discuss the existence of a deity not so exalted but nonetheless "finitely perfect." I think this claim is entirely mistaken, but since it is more naturally regarded as an independent argument against the existence of God, I shall defer what I have to say about it to Part II (see below, pp. 115–155). But this is not the extent of Hume's objection from evil:

Let us allow, that, if the goodness of the Deity (I mean a goodness like the human) could be established on any tolerable reasons

---

[12] Hume, *op. cit.*, pp. 199, 201.
[13] *Ibid.*, p. 203.

a priori, these phenomena, however untoward, would not be sufficient to subvert that principle; but might easily, in some unknown manner, be reconcilable to it. But let us still assert, that as this goodness is not antecedently established, but must be inferred from the phenomena, there can be no grounds for such an inference, while there are so many ills in the universe, and while these ills might so easily have been remedied, as far as human understanding can be allowed to judge on such a subject. I am skeptic enough to allow, that the bad appearances, notwithstanding all my reasonings, may be compatible with such attributes as you suppose: But surely they can never prove these attributes.[14]

Just how is this to be understood? There seem to me to be two possibilities. In the first place, Philo may be asserting that the existence of evil *disconfirms* the existence of God; that is, offers evidence for the proposition that there is no God. This alone would not refute the argument, however, for even if what we know about the world contains a set of propositions disconfirming the existence of God, it may contain another set confirming it. My total evidence may give me some reason for supposing that proposition false, but a stronger reason for supposing it true. Does Hume mean to add that the negative evidence from evil is so strong that the rest of our knowledge, no matter what it was, could not possibly furnish stronger evidence *for* God's existence? Although this seems a fairly natural reading of Hume, it is dubious indeed—or at any rate is much too strong a claim if the existence of God is logically compatible with the existence of evil.[15]

Hume's argument can be so stated as to avoid this extravagant claim. For we may understand him as contending, not that there *could not* be any evidence which, when conjoined

---

[14] *Ibid.*, p. 211.

[15] A proposition *p* confirms a proposition *q* so strongly that there is no proposition *r* (consistent with *p*) such that the conjunction of *p* with *r* confirms the denial of *q*, only if p *entails* q.

with the existence of evil, confirms the existence of God, but rather that the conjunction of evil with the evidence actually at our disposal does not support this conclusion. On the evidence to which the teleological argument draws our attention, says Hume, the existence of a powerful designer who is morally indifferent is as probable as the existence of God; but then on that evidence it is not more probable that God exists than that he does not. And this objection certainly has a great deal of force. It is an instance of a more general objection that seems to me correct.

In arguing that God exists, the theist typically means to argue for a proposition equivalent to a conjunction of which the following are conjuncts:

(a) The universe is designed.
(b) The universe is designed by exactly one person.
(c) The universe was created *ex nihilo*.
(d) The universe was created by the person who designed it.
(e) The creator of the universe is omniscient, omnipotent, and perfectly good.
(f) The creator of the universe is an eternal spirit, without body, and in no way dependent upon physical objects.

Now we can put the objection as follows: the teleological arguer may have some evidence (not very strong, perhaps, but not completely negligible) for (a); but with respect to (b)–(f) our evidence is altogether ambiguous. In the case of propositions (b)–(f) our total evidence affords in each case an argument *against* it as strong as any it yields *for* it.

Consider (b), for example. In many cases things exhibiting the degree of unity the universe exhibits (supposing we could ascertain this) have been designed by just one person; but in just as many, such things (e.g., Chevrolets) are the work of several persons. Perhaps, Philo suggests, the universe was designed by a *committee* of deities of some sort. (Or perhaps it is the first unsteady attempt of an infant deity, or the last feeble effort of a superannuated one.[16]) The point is that on our evidence a proposition inconsistent with (b) is just as probable as is (b) itself; but then it follows that (b) is not more probable than not on our evidence. The same comment holds for (c)–(f). Consider the conjunction of (d) with (f), says Philo: our evidence affords an argument *against* it in that every intelligent person we know about has had a body; so probably all intelligent persons have bodies, in which case the designer-creator of the universe does too. In the same way we may argue that he is dependent upon physical objects in various ways, and had parents.

Cleanthes, to be sure, tries to reply to this line of reasoning: "You start abstruse doubts, cavils and objections: You ask me, what is the cause of this cause? I know not; I care not; that concerns not me. I have found a deity; and here I stop my enquiry. Let those go farther, who are wiser or more enterprising." [17] But of course the point is that if (b)–(f) are no more probable on his evidence than their negations, Cleanthes has not really found a deity at all. His evidence supports the claim that the universe was designed, but nothing stronger.

Philo himself carries this objection too far; he tries to employ it against (a) as well: "The world plainly resembles more an animal or a vegetable than it does a watch or knitting loom. Its cause, therefore, it is more probable, resembles the cause of the former. The cause of the former is generation or vegetation. The cause, therefore, of the world, we may infer to be something similar or analogous to generation or vegetation." [18] As Demea points out, however, that the world has a vegetative or

---

[16] Hume, *op. cit.*, p. 167.

[17] *Ibid.*, p. 163.

[18] *Ibid.*, p. 177.

generative origin is not inconsistent with (a);[19] hence the fact that our evidence supports that proposition as strongly as it does (a), does nothing to show that it does not support (a). It is not as if we know that things with a vegetative or generative origin are *not* the product of intelligent design.

If Philo's first objection to the argument from design is inconclusive, his second is much stronger. And so that argument seems no more successful, as a piece of natural theology, than the cosmological and ontological arguments. Now of course these three are not the only arguments of their kind; there are also, for example, the various sorts of moral arguments for God's existence. But these are not initially very plausible and do not become more so under close scrutiny. And so it is hard to avoid the conclusion that natural theology does not provide a satisfactory answer to the question with which we began: Is it rational to believe in God?

---

[19] *Ibid.*, pp. 178–179.

Part II

NATURAL ATHEOLOGY

Five

The Problem of Evil

IF natural theology cannot answer our question, perhaps natural atheology—the attempt to prove the central beliefs of theism false—can. Like the natural theologian, the natural atheologian draws his premises from the class of propositions that are necessarily true or accepted by common sense; his conclusions, however, are quite different.

The most impressive argument of natural atheology has to do with the problem of evil. Many philosophers have held that the existence of evil constitutes, in one way or another, a problem for those who accept theistic belief.[1] Those contemporary philosophers who here find a difficulty for the theist claim, for the most part, to detect *logical inconsistency* in the beliefs he typically accepts. So H. J. McCloskey:

Evil is a problem for the theist in that a *contradiction* is involved

---

[1] David Hume and some of the French Encyclopedists, for example, as well as F. H. Bradley, J. McTaggart, and J. S. Mill.

in the fact of evil, on the one hand, and the belief in the omnipotence and perfection of God on the other.[2]

And J. L. Mackie:

I think, however, that a more telling criticism can be made by way of the traditional problem of evil. Here it can be shown, not that religious beliefs lack rational support, but that they are positively irrational, that the several parts of the essential theological doctrine are *inconsistent* with one another.[3]

Essentially the same charge is made by Henry Aiken in an article entitled "God and Evil." [4]

These philosophers, then, and many others besides, hold that traditional theistic belief is self-contradictory and that the problem of evil, for the theist, is that of deciding which of the relevant propositions he is to abandon. But just which propositions are involved? What, according to these authors, is the set of theistic beliefs whose conjunction yields a contradiction? The authors referred to above take the following five propositions to be essential to traditional theism: (a) that God exists, (b) that God is omnipotent, (c) that God is omniscient, (d) that God is wholly good, and (e) that evil exists. Here they are certainly right; each of these propositions is indeed an essential feature of orthodox theism. And it is just these five propositions whose conjunction is said by our atheologians to be self-contradictory.

The first point to note is that of course these five propositions do not by themselves *formally* entail a contradiction; to get a formally contradictory set the atheologian must add some proposition or other. But of course he cannot add just any proposition he pleases. What conditions must be met by

---

[2] "God and Evil," *Philosophical Quarterly*, X (1960), 97.

[3] "Evil and Omnipotence," *Mind*, LXIV (1955), 200.

[4] *Ethics*, XLVIII (1957–58), p. 79.

the proposition he adds (which I shall call (f)) if his accusation is to be made good? First, the conjunction of (f) with (a)–(e) must formally entail a contradiction. But what further condition must it meet? If (f) were *necessarily* true then (a)–(e) would formally entail the denial of (f); and perhaps we could say of any proposition which formally entails the denial of a necessarily true proposition that it is self-contradictory, at any rate in a broad sense of that term. On the other hand, if (f) were an essential part of theism, then, although it would not follow that there is a contradiction in (a)–(e), there would be one in some larger set of beliefs accepted by any theist. So to make good his claim the atheologian must provide some proposition which is either necessarily true, or essential to theism, or a logical consequence of such propositions. And none of the atheologians I quoted above seems to have realized the difficulty of that task. Certainly none of them has succeeded in producing such a proposition. McCloskey, for example, seems not to have noticed that an additional premise is required in order to deduce a contradiction, so (naturally enough) he makes no attempt to provide one. Mackie, however, recognizes that

the contradiction does not arise immediately; to show it we need some additional premises, or perhaps some quasi-logical rules connecting the terms "good," "evil," and "omnipotent." These additional premises are that good is opposed to evil, in such a way that a good thing always eliminates evil as far as it can, and that there are no limits to what an omnipotent thing can do.[5]

And Aiken, in the passage referred to above, tacitly adds two premises that come to the same as Mackie's.

Now Mackie's second additional premise, if a bit imprecise, is on the whole unexceptionable. It needs a small qualification

---

[5] *Op. cit.*, p. 200–201.

that Mackie himself no doubt intended; what we must say is that there are no *nonlogical* limits to what an omnipotent being can do. God is omnipotent only if God can perform any action that it is logically possible for him to perform. But the other additional premise suggested by Mackie—that a good thing always eliminates evil as far as it can—does not seem to be true at all, let alone necessarily true. For both the theist and his opponent presumably regard any case of *pain* as an evil; but if so, then the proposition in question is clearly *false*. A physician who can eliminate the pain in your knee only by removing your leg does not forfeit his claim to moral excellence by failing to do so. It will be objected, of course, that since God, unlike the physician, is omnipotent, the case stands very differently with him. And so it does. Still, the proposition suggested by Mackie does not meet the conditions mentioned above; it must be qualified or restricted in some way. How?

The physician escapes culpability because he cannot, or justifiably believes that he cannot, eliminate the evil in question without also eliminating a greater good.[6] So perhaps we can say that a person is not morally culpable in producing an evil *E*, if he justifiably believes that he can produce *G*, a good that outweighs *E*, only by producing *E*; nor culpable in failing to eliminate an evil if he justifiably believes that he can eliminate it only by eliminating a greater good. Perhaps we can restate Mackie's proposition in the following way:

(f_1) A person *P* is wholly good only if
    (1) *P* holds no belief such that his holding it is morally censurable, and there is no belief he fails to hold such that his failing to hold it is morally censurable, and
    (2) *P* tries to eliminate every state of affairs that he

---

[6] I.e., a good state of affairs that outweighs the evil state of affairs.

believes is evil, and that he believes he can eliminate without eliminating a greater good.

Now what Mackie needs is a necessary proposition that con-
nects (b), (c), and (d) on the one hand with (e) on the other
—that is, one connecting God's goodness, omniscience, and
omnipotence with the existence of evil. Proposition (f_1), however, says nothing about omniscience and omnipotence. As a
step toward repairing that defect we might note that an omniscient person automatically satisfies the first condition laid down
in (f_1); for it is hard to see how a person could be morally
censurable for holding a belief he knows to be true or for failing to hold a belief he knows to be false. And the second condition can be stated more simply, since a reference to belief is
no longer needed:

(f_2) An omniscient person P is wholly good only if he tries
to eliminate every evil state of affairs that he can eliminate without eliminating a greater good.

An omnipotent being in the sense mentioned above can perform (roughly) any logically consistent action; hence either it
is a logically necessary truth that evil exists or else God is able
to eliminate any case of evil whatever. No reputable theologian,
so far as I know, has held that the proposition *There is evil* is
logically necessary; accordingly, I shall assume henceforth that
God can eliminate every case of evil whatever. On the other
hand, we cannot blithely assume that every case of evil is one
which an omnipotent being can eliminate without eliminating
a greater good. It has been held, for example, that in some
cases a display of courage and fortitude in the face of suffering
outweighs the suffering in question; and not even God can
eliminate Jones's suffering without eliminating Jones's courage
and fortitude in his suffering. Under what conditions will an

omnipotent being be unable to eliminate one state of affairs without also eliminating another? Since such a being can perform (roughly) any logically consistent action, the atheologian might be inclined to hold that God is unable to eliminate a state of affairs S without eliminating a state of affairs S' only if S is a logically necessary condition of S'; that is, only if the proposition S' *obtains* entails the proposition S *obtains*.[7] Following this line of thought, he might be tempted to restate (f) for an omnipotent, omniscient being as follows:

(f_3) An omnipotent, omniscient person is all good only if he eliminates every evil state of affairs which is not a logically necessary condition of a good state of affairs that outweighs it.

This, however, is too liberal. Consider any evil state of affairs E such that there is a good state of affairs G which outweighs it. G-and-E (the state of affairs that obtains just in case both G and E obtain) is a good state of affairs, and it is also a logically sufficient condition of E. Hence, any evil E which is outweighed by at least one good G, is a logically necessary condition of a good state of affairs (G-and-E) which outweighs it. But this means that an omnipotent and omniscient being could permit as much evil as he pleased, without, under (f_3), forfeiting his claim to omnibenevolence, so long as for every evil state of affairs he permits, there is a greater good. That is to say, he could permit as much evil as he pleased, provided that there was a balance of good over evil in the universe as a whole; and this would be so even if it were within his power to create a better universe just be excising some or all of the evil states of

---

[7] And wherever a state of affairs S' is a logically necessary condition of a state of affairs S I shall say that S entails S'.

affairs which in fact obtain. Therefore (f_3) is not the proposition for which the atheologian is looking.

How can we repair (f_3)? Its inadequacy lies in its suggestion that an evil state of affairs E is not a good candidate for elimination if at least one good state of affairs G entails it; this is too weak, for there may be a state of affairs better than G that does not entail E, which state of affairs would then be preferable to G. To strengthen (f_3) we must add that an evil need not be eliminated only if some good G entails it, such that every state of affairs *better* than G *also* entails it; an all-good being will eliminate every evil E such that for every good entailing E, there is a greater good that does not entail it. Here one is inclined to object that perhaps some conjunctive state of affairs which included some of the goods which entail E, *as well as* those which do not, might be better than any good state of affairs composed solely of goods which do not entail E. To raise this objection, however, is to forget that by hypothesis for *every* good state of affairs which entails E, there is a better state of affairs which does not. So, in particular, for any good state of affairs containing conjunctively some good state of affairs entailing E, there is a better state of affairs which does *not* contain any good entailing E. It seems, therefore, that what follows is at least part of the proposition the atheologian is looking for:

(f_4) An omnipotent, omniscient person is wholly good only if he eliminates every evil which is such that for every good that entails it, there is a greater good that does not entail it.

The atheologian may be saddened to note, however, that the conjunction of (a)–(e) and (f_4) is not a formally contradictory set either. If it *were* formally contradictory, (a)–(d) and (f_4) would jointly entail the denial of (e)—that is, they would entail that there is no evil at all. But they do not entail that; what they entail is

(g) Every evil E is entailed by some good G such that every good greater than G also entails E.

And hence the atheologian must add still another proposition to the set (a)–(e) and (f_4) in order to get a formally contradictory set. The proposition he adds must, of course, meet the very same conditions that (f_4) had to meet; it must be necessarily true or an essential part of theism or a consequence of such propositions. Furthermore, this proposition must entail, in conjunction with (a)–(e) and (f_4), the denial of (g):

There is at least one evil state of affairs such that for every good that entails it, there is a greater good that does not.

Let us say that an evil state of affairs is *justified* just in case it is false that for every good that entails it there is a greater good that does not. To convict the theist of inconsistency, the atheologian must deduce the proposition that there is unjustified evil from (a)–(e) and (f_4) together with propositions which are necessarily true or essential to theism or consequences of such propositions. Now it looks very much as if the only proposition that is essential to theism and relevant to the deduction in question is (e) itself—the proposition that evil exists. Hence, it looks as if the atheologian must deduce the existence of unjustified evil from (e) together with necessary propositions. But if this is so, then he must hold that

(h) If there is any evil, there is unjustified evil

is entailed by some set of necessary propositions and is itself, therefore, necessarily true. Here some contemporary atheologians apparently mistake the logic of the situation. They seem to suppose that the *theist*, if he doesn't wish to accept the charge of inconsistency, must show that every evil state of affairs *is* justified. McCloskey, for example, says that a certain argument proposed by some theists,

if valid, justifies only some evil. A belief that it justifies all the evil in the world is mistaken, for a second argument, by way of supplement to it, is needed. This supplementary argument would take the form of a proof that all the evil that occurs is *in fact* valuable and necessary as a means to greater good. Such a supplementary proof is in principle impossible; so, at best this fifth argument can be taken to show only that some evil *may* be necessary for the production of good, and that the evil in the world may perhaps have a justification on this account.[8]

But if the argument in question does show that the evil in the world *may perhaps* have a justification, then surely it suffices to rebut the charge of *contradiction*. What McCloskey must show is that it is *logically impossible* that there is evil and that all of it is justified; if it is even possible that all evil is justified, then, surely, there is no contradiction in the joint assertion of (a)–(e).

No atheologian, so far as I know, has proved or even tried to prove that the proposition *If there is any evil in the world, then there is unjustified evil* is necessarily true. Indeed, it is hard to see what form such a proof could take. In an admirable reply to the article by Aiken mentioned above, Nelson Pike claims that no such proof could be given:

If the proposition "There is good reason for evil in the theistic universe" (i.e., "there are motives or other factual considerations which, *if known*, would render blaming God for evil inappropriate") *could* be true, then the logic of the phrase "perfectly good person" allows that the propositions "God is a perfectly good per-

---

[8] *Op. cit.*, p. 105.

son" and "God allows evil in the world although he could prevent it" could be true together. This point rests on the fact that a perfectly good person can allow evil, provided he has a good reason. Since the first of the three propositions just mentioned is clearly not contradictory and thus could be true, the conjunction of the latter propositions is also free of contradiction and the contention that a perfectly good person would *of necessity* prevent evil if he could is shown, beyond question, to be in error.[9]

Pike does not here explain what, in his view, might constitute good reasons for God's allowing evil to occur; but let us suppose for the moment that in his view the only good reason an omnipotent and omniscient being could have for allowing an evil state of affairs would be that the evil in question is not such that for every good which entails it there is a greater good that does not. So taken, Pike's position amounts to the claim that

(h) If there are any evil states of affairs, there are unjustified evils

is not a necessary proposition.

If this is Pike's meaning, then I think he is right; but perhaps this is not an altogether foregone conclusion. At any rate it may be worth while asking what sort of argument the atheologian *could* produce for the necessity of (h). He might try arguing first that if a state of affairs is evil then it cannot be a logically necessary condition of a good state of affairs. But this is not true at all, let alone necessarily true. Any pair consisting of a good G and an evil E where G outweighs E will provide a counterexample, for G-and-E will be a good of which E is a necessary condition.

---

[9] "God and Evil: A Reconsideration," *Ethics*, LXVIII (1957–1958), 119. Cf. also Pike's "Hume on Evil," *Philosophical Review*, LXXII (1963), 184–188

The Problem of Evil

Taking his cue from this objection to his first try, the atheologian might assert that (i) is necessarily true:

(i) Any good G which entails an evil E is or is equivalent[10] to a conjunctive state of affairs one conjunct of which is E and the other a good that (1) outweighs and is logically independent of E, and (2) is better than G.

Proposition (i) evidently entails

(j) Every evil state of affairs is such that for every good that entails it, there is a greater good that does not,

and (j), asserting as it does that every evil state of affairs is unjustified, surely entails (h).

But is (i) necessarily true? The answer seems to be that we have already noted one apparent counterexample to it: the case of the man whose magnificent bearing of pain outweighs the evil of the pain itself. It seems impossible to analyze this situation into a conjunctive state of affairs one conjunct of which is *Jones's being in pain* while the other is some good state of affairs which outweighs and is logically independent of Jones's being in pain, and is better than his magnificent bearing of the pain. On the other hand, however, the atheologian might protest that

(k) Someone's bearing pain is never a good state of affairs;

that at best the bearing of pain, no matter what noble qualities of character are exhibited, is a matter of making the best of a bad situation. And, indeed, (k) appears to be entailed by (i), since no good state of affairs consisting in someone's bearing pain (magnificently, or in some other laudable way) meets

---

[10] States of affairs S and S' are *equivalent* if and only if S entails and is entailed by S'; they are logically independent if neither S nor the complement of S (the state of affairs which obtains just in case S does not) either entails or is entailed by S'.

the condition laid down in (i). Hence if (k) is false, so is (i). Now (k), of course, is a moral or ethical judgment.

At this point it may be helpful to review the logic of the situation. The atheologian claims that the set of propositions (a)–(e), admittedly an essential part of theistic belief, is contradictory. It is evident at first sight that the set is not *formally* contradictory; some proposition must be added to the set if a contradiction is to be deduced from it formally. This proposition must, if the atheologian's claim is to be vindicated, be either necessarily true or an essential part of theism or a consequence of such propositions. Now (f_4) appeared to be the appropriate necessary proposition connecting omniscience, omnipotence, omnibenevolence, and the elimination of evil. However, (a)–(e) + (f_4), is not a formally contradictory set either; a further proposition must be added. This further proposition, whatever it is, must of course meet the very same condition (f_4) had to meet; it too must be necessary, or an essential part of theism, or a consequence of propositions falling into those two classes; and in conjunction with (a)–(e) + (f_4) it must entail

(g) There is some unjustified evil.

The only proposition essential to theism and relevant to the deduction of (g) from propositions which are either necessary or essential elements of theism, however, appears to be (e) itself. Since that is so the atheologian must find a necessary premise from which

(h) If there is any evil then there is unjustified evil

follows; and this necessary proposition is to be added to the set (a)–(e) + (f_4). The last suggestion was that it is (i) which is to be added; and (a)–(e) + (f_4) + (i) clearly is a contradictory set. (i), however, appears to entail (k), an ethical proposition which the theist may well dispute. The question before us, then, is this: Can the atheologian justifiably add *moral judgments* (or propositions that entail moral judgments) to the set (a)–(e) + (f₄) in attempting to deduce a contradiction from the theist's position? And if he may, what conditions must these moral judgments meet?

Some philosophers have thought that some moral judgments, at any rate, are, if true, necessarily true. Even if this view were correct, however, the atheologian could not properly add *just any* necessary moral judgment to (a)–(e) + (f₄) in attempting to show that the theist's position is necessarily false. For after all, the point of his whole endeavor is to show that the theist's beliefs are *irrational*; but moral judgments are notoriously the sort of propositions about which careful and rational people can and do disagree. Let us say that a moral judgment is *self-evident* if no reasonable person who understood and carefully considered it would believe its denial. Now any moral judgment the atheologian can justifiably add to (a)–(e) + (f₄) must be, I should think, either self-evident or an essential part of theism; nor may he add any proposition (whether a moral judgment or not) nontrivially entailing a moral judgment that meets neither of these conditions.[11] This criterion may not always be

---

[11] And this requires a revision in our statement of the conditions which must be met by any proposition the atheologian can justifiably add to the set (a)–(e) in order to show that the theist's position is contradictory. These conditions may be stated more accurately as follows:

The atheologian can justifiably add a set S of statements to (a)–(e) if and only if

(1) Each of S's members is either necessarily true or an essential element of theism or self-evident or a deductive consequence of such propositions, and

(2) The only moral judgments nontrivially entailed by the set S are self-evident or essential elements of theism

where a proposition *p* nontrivially entails a moral judgment *m* if and only if there is an argument such that its only premise is *p*, its conclusion is *m*, easy to apply; but at any rate it does rule out many moral judgments.

In particular, it rules out (k). Reasonable persons who understand and carefully consider it do sometimes deny (k). Hence the atheologian cannot justifiably add any proposition entailing (k) to (a)–(e) + (f₄) in order to deduce a contradiction from the theist's position; he cannot, therefore, add (i).

So far, then, we have not been able to find a proposition, necessarily true or an essential part of theism or a consequence of such propositions, which in conjunction with (a)–(e) + (f₄) entails a contradiction. Indeed, we have not so much as produced a plausible candidate. If this does not show that there is *no* such proposition, it suggests that finding one is much more difficult than most atheologians seem to suppose.

There is another matter of interest here. One may distinguish a priori atheological arguments, whose main counterpart in natural theology is the ontological argument, from a posteriori atheological arguments, which correspond to such arguments as the cosmological and teleological proofs. What we have been considering so far is an a priori atheological argument, one whose conclusion is that the theist's position is self-contradictory. But an a posteriori argument from evil may also be given. The atheologian might hold, for example, that we actually find certain kinds of evil that no good state of affairs, no matter how impressive, could possibly outweigh—severe, protracted, and involuntary human pain, for example. That there *is* severe, protracted, and involuntary human pain is an obvious fact of experience, on a par, roughly, with such venerable premises of natural theology as that there are objects standing in causal relations with one another. But if it is true

---

and each of its steps follows from preceding steps by an argument form whose corresponding conditional is self-evident.

The Problem of Evil

that no good state of affairs ever outweighs such a case of pain, then no good state of affairs ever entails an evil state of affairs consisting in such a case of pain; and hence no such evil state of affairs is ever justified. And from the fact that unjustified evil occurs, it follows that there is no omnipotent, omniscient, wholly good being. This argument is an a posteriori one, for one of its premises—that there is severe, protracted, involuntary human pain—is clearly not a priori (nor an essential part of theism).

The tricky premise, of course, is the claim that

(1) No case of severe, protracted, involuntary human pain is ever outweighed by any good state of affairs.

The theist will certainly deny that (1) is true; and it is very difficult indeed to see how one could *show* it to be true. The atheologian cannot, of course, advance his case by maintaining that (1) is *analytic* or *true by definition* in the sense in which a proposition is analytic just in case it can be reduced to a truth of logic by replacing some of its terms with their definitions. For suppose he succeeded in producing some reasonably plausible definition of, say, "good state of affairs" such that the result of substituting it for "good state of affairs" in (1) was a truth of logic; the theist would then retort that the suggested definition does not express what he means by "good state of affairs"; and if the atheologian were to convince him that the definition was correct with respect to the ordinary use of that phrase, the theist would simply admit that he had been misusing the phrase in question, retract his agreement to (f_4) (a wholly good, omnipotent, omniscient being would eliminate every evil state of affairs which is such that for every good state of affairs that entails it, there is a better state of affairs that does not) and replace (f_4) by something like (f₅) A wholly good, omnipotent, omniscient being would eliminate every state of affairs which is such that for every *valuable* state of affairs that entails it, there is a more valuable state of affairs that does not.

Further, he would add, although perhaps no *good* state of affairs can ever outweigh protracted and severe human pain, *valuable* states of affairs can perfectly well do so. And now, the argument is exactly where it was before the atheologian made his claim of analyticity.

The atheologian's only recourse at this point is to claim that (1), though not analytic, is nonetheless necessarily true. He might argue, for example, that it is utterly inconceivable that any good state of affairs outweigh protracted and severe human pain. The theist, of course, will demur; and here the disputants seem to reach an impasse. The most that can be said for the atheologian who accepts (1) is, I think, that the existence of protracted and severe human pain provides *him* with a decisive reason for believing that God does not exist; but he could hardly claim that the *theist* is involved in any difficulty here. For he cannot claim (without stooping to name-calling) that (1) is a proposition which no reasonable person who understood it would deny; one of the hallmarks of such moral judgments as (1) is just that reasonable persons can and sometimes do disagree about them.

Six

The Free Will Defense

CHAPTER FIVE suggests that the set of propositions (a)–
(e) (above, p. 116) is, contrary to the atheologian's claim,
consistent. And in Chapter Five we assumed, for purposes of
argument, that a morally perfect, omniscient, and omnipotent being would permit an evil state of affairs to exist only
if that evil state of affairs were a logically necessary condition
of a good which outweighed it. This assumption is by no
means self-evident, however, and apologists for traditional theism
have often denied it; they have suggested that perhaps there
are certain good states of affairs that an omnipotent God cannot bring about without permitting evil, despite the fact that
these goods are not a logically sufficient condition of any evil
at all. This suggestion on their parts is sometimes called *the
free will defense*; in this chapter I shall explain and examine
it.

First of all, a distinction must be made between *moral evil*
and *physical evil*. The former, roughly, is the evil which results

from human choice or volition; the latter is that which does not. Suffering due to an earthquake, for example, would be physical evil; suffering resulting from human cruelty would be moral evil. This distinction, of course, is not very clear and many questions could be raised about it; but perhaps it is not necessary to deal with these questions here. Given this distinction, the free will defense is usually stated in something like the following way. A world containing creatures who freely perform both good and evil actions—and do more good than evil—is more valuable than a world containing quasiautomata who always do what is right because they are unable to do otherwise. Now God can create free creatures, but He cannot causally or otherwise determine them to do only what is right; for if He does so then they do not do what is right *freely*. To create creatures capable of moral good, therefore, He must create creatures capable of moral evil; but He cannot create the possibility of moral evil and at the same time prohibit its actuality. And as it turned out, some of the free creatures God created exercised their freedom to do what is wrong: hence moral evil. The fact that free creatures sometimes err, however, in no way tells against God's omnipotence or against His goodness; for He could forestall the occurrence of moral evil only by removing the possibility of moral good.

In this way some traditional theists have tried to explain or justify part of the evil that occurs by ascribing it to the will of man rather than to the will of God. At least three kinds of objections to this idea are to be found in both traditional and current writings. I shall try to develop and clarify the free will defense by restating it in the face of these objections.

I

The first objection challenges the assumption, implicit in the above statement of the free will defense, that free will and causal determinism are logically incompatible. So Antony Flew:

> To say that a person could have helped doing something is not to say that what he did was in principle unpredictable nor that there were no causes anywhere which determined that he would as a matter of fact act in this way. It is to say that if he had chosen to do otherwise he would have been able to do so; that there were alternatives, within the capacities of one of his physical strength, of his I.Q., of his knowledge, open to a person in his situation. . . .
>
> There is no contradiction involved in saying that a particular action or choice was: *both* free, and could have been helped, and so on; *and* predictable, or even foreknown, and explicable in terms of caused causes. . . .
>
> If it is really logically possible for an action to be both freely chosen and yet fully determined by caused causes, then the keystone argument of the Free Will Defence, that there is contradiction in speaking of God so arranging the laws of nature that all men always as a matter of fact freely choose to do the right, cannot hold.[1]

Flew's objection, I think, can be dealt with in fairly summary fashion. He does not, in the paper in question, explain what he means by "causal determination" (and of course in that paper this omission is quite proper and justifiable). But presumably he means to use the locution in question in such a way that to say of Jones's action A that it is *causally determined* is to say that the action in question has causes and that given these causes, Jones could not have refrained from doing A. That is to say, Flew's use of "causally determined" is presumably such that one or both of the following sentences, or some sentences very much like them, express necessarily true propositions:

---

[1] "Divine Omnipotence and Human Freedom," in *New Essays in Philosophical Theology*, ed. A. Flew and A. MacIntyre (London, 1955), pp. 150, 151, 153.

(a) If Jones's action A is causally determined, then a set S of events has occurred prior to Jones's doing A such that, given S, it is causally impossible for Jones to refrain from doing A.

(b) If Jones's action A is causally determined, then there is a set S of propositions describing events occurring before A and a set L of propositions expressing natural laws such that

(1) The conjunction of S's members does not entail that Jones does A, and

(2) The conjunction of the members of S with the members of L does entail that Jones does A.

And Flew's thesis, then, is that there is no contradiction in saying of a man, both that all of his actions are causally determined (in the sense just explained) and that some of them are free.

It seems to me altogether paradoxical to say of anyone all of whose actions are causally determined that on some occasions he acts freely. When we say that Jones acts freely on a given occasion, what we say entails, I should think, that either his action on that occasion is not causally determined, or else he has previously performed an undetermined action which is a causal ancestor of the one in question. But this is a difficult and debatable issue; fortunately we need not settle it in order to assess the force of Flew's objection to the free will defense. The free will defender claims that the sentence "If there are free actions, not all of them are causally determined" expresses a necessary truth; Flew denies this claim. This strongly suggests that Flew and the free will defender are not using the words "free" and "freedom" in the same way. The free will defender apparently uses the words in question in such a way that the sentences "Some of Jones's actions are free" and "Jones did action A freely" express propositions inconsistent with the proposition that all of Jones's actions are causally determined. Flew, on the other hand, claims that with respect to the ordinary use of these words, there is no such inconsistency. It is my opinion that Flew is mistaken here; I think it is he who is using these words in a nonstandard, unordinary way. But we need not try to resolve that issue; for the free will defender can simply make Flew a present of the word "freedom" and state his case using other locutions. He might now hold, for example, not that God made men free and that a world in which men freely do both good and evil is more valuable than a world in which they unfreely do only what is good; but rather that God made men such that some of their actions are *unfettered* (both free in Flew's sense and also causally undetermined) and that a world in which men perform both good and evil unfettered actions is superior to one in which they perform only good, but fettered, actions. By substituting "unfettered" for "free" throughout his account, the free will defender can elude Flew's objection altogether.[2] So whether Flew is right or wrong about the ordinary sense of "freedom" is of no consequence; his objection is in an important sense merely verbal and thus altogether fails to damage the free will defense.

II

Flew's objection, in essence, is the claim that an omnipotent being could have created men who were free but nonetheless causally determined to perform only right actions. According to a closely allied objection, an omnipotent being could have made men who, though free, and free from any such causal

---

[2] Since this is so, in what follows I shall continue to use the words "free" and "freedom" in the way the free will defender uses them.

determination, would on every occasion freely refrain from performing any evil actions. Here the contemporary spokesman is Mackie:

If God has made men such that in their free choices they sometimes prefer what is good and sometimes what is evil, why could he not have made men such that they always freely choose the good? If there is no logical impossibility in a man's freely choosing the good on one, or on several occasions, there cannot be a logical impossibility in his freely choosing the good on every occasion. God was not, then, faced with a choice between making innocent automata and making beings who, in acting freely, would sometimes go wrong; there was open to him the obviously better possibility of making beings who would act freely but always go right. Clearly, his failure to avail himself of this possibility is inconsistent with his being both omnipotent and wholly good.[3]

This objection is more serious than Flew's and must be dealt with more fully. The free will defense is an argument for the conclusion that

> (a) God is omnipotent, omniscient, and wholly good, and God creates free men who sometimes perform morally evil actions

is not contradictory or necessarily false.[4] What Mackie says, I think, may best be construed as an argument for the conclusion that (a) *is* necessarily false; in other words, that *God is omnipotent, omniscient, and wholly good* entails *No free men He creates ever perform morally evil actions.* Mackie's argument seems to have the following structure:

> (1) God is omnipotent and omniscient and wholly good.

---

[3] "Evil and Omnipotence," *Mind*, LXIV (1955), p. 209.

[4] And of course if (a) is consistent, then so is the set (a)–(e) (above, p. 116), for (a) entails each member of that set.

(2) If God is omnipotent, He can create or bring about any logically possible state of affairs.

(3) God can create any logically possible state of affairs—(1), (2).

(4) That all free men do what is right on every occasion is a logically possible state of affairs.

(5) God can create free men such that they always do what is right—(4), (3).

(6) If God can create free men such that they always do what is right, and if God is all good, then any free men created by God always do what is right.

(7) Any free men created by God always do what is right—(1), (5), (6).

(8) No free men created by God ever perform morally evil actions—(7).

Doubtless the free will defender will concede the truth of (4). There is a difficulty with (2), however, for

(a) *That there is a state of affairs that is not created by God* is a logically possible state of affairs

is clearly true. But (2) and (a) together entail

(b) If God is omnipotent, God can create a state of affairs that is not created by God.

And (b), of course, is false; (2) must be revised. The obvious way to repair it seems to be something like

(2′) If God is omnipotent, then God can create any state of affairs S such that *God creates S* [5] is consistent.

Similarly, (3) must be revised:

---

[5] And even this is really too strong; certain restrictions must be laid upon the substituend set of "S" (see below, p. 170).

(3') God can create any state of affairs S such that *God creates S* is consistent.

(2') and (3') do not seem to suffer from the faults besetting (2) and (3); but now it is not at all evident that (3') and (4) entail

(5)   God can create free men such that they always do what is right

as the original argument claims. To see this, we must note that (5) is true only if

(5a) God creates free men such that they always do what is right

is consistent. But (5a), one might think, is equivalent to

(5b) God creates free men and brings it about that they always freely do what is right.

And (5b), of course, is *not* consistent; for if God *brings it about* that the men He creates always do what is right, then they do not do what is right *freely*. So if (5a) is taken to express (5b), then (5) is clearly false and clearly not entailed by (3') and (4).

On the other hand, (5a) could conceivably be used to express

(5c) God creates free men and these free men always do what is right,

which is surely consistent; it is indeed logically possible that God create free men and that the free men created by Him always do what is right. And conceivably the objector is using (5) to express this possibility—that is, it may be that (5) is meant to express

The Free Will Defense

(5d) The proposition *God creates free men and the free men created by God always do what is right* is consistent.

If (5) is equivalent to (5d), then (5) is true—in fact, necessarily true (and hence trivially entailed by (3′) and (4)). But now the difficulty crops up with respect to (6), which, given the equivalence of (5) and (5d) is equivalent to

(6′) If God is all good and the proposition *God creates free men and the free men He creates always do what is right* is consistent, then any free men created by God always do what is right.

Mackie's aim is to show that the proposition *God is omnipotent, omniscient, and all good* entails the proposition *No free men created by God ever perform morally evil actions.* His attempt, as I outlined it, is to show this by constructing a valid argument whose premise is the former and whose conclusion is the latter. But then any additional premise appealed to in the deduction must be necessarily true if Mackie's argument is to succeed. And although (6′) is one such additional premise, there seems to be no reason for supposing that (6′) is true at all, let alone necessarily true. Whether the free men created by God would always do what is right would presumably be up to them; for all we know they might sometimes exercise their freedom to do what is wrong. Put in a nutshell the difficulty with the argument is the following. Proposition (5a) (God creates free men such that they always freely do what is right) is susceptible of two interpretations ((5b) and (5c)). Under one of these interpretations (5) turns out to be false and the argument therefore fails. Under the other interpretation (6) turns out to be contingent, and again the argument fails.

So far, then, the free will defense has emerged unscathed from Mackie's objection. One feels, however, that more can be said here, that there is something to Mackie's argument. What more? Well, perhaps something along the following lines. It is logically possible that all men always do only what is right. Now God is said to be omniscient and hence knows, with respect to any person he proposes to create, whether that person would or would not commit morally evil acts. For every person P who in fact performs morally evil actions, there is, evidently, a possible person P' who is exactly like P in every respect except that P' never performs any evil actions. If God is omnipotent, He could have created these possible persons instead of the persons He did in fact create. And if He is also wholly good, He *would*, presumably, have created them, since they differ from the persons He did create only in being morally better than they are.

Can we make coherent sense out of this revised version of Mackie's objection? What, in particular, could the objector mean by "possible person"? and what are we to make of the suggestion that God could have created possible persons? I think these questions can be answered. Let us consider first the set of all those properties it is logically possible for human beings to have. Examples of properties *not* in this set are such properties as *being over a mile long, being a hippopotamus, being a prime number,* and *being divisible by four.* Included in the set are such properties as *having red hair, being present at the Battle of Waterloo, being President of the United States, being born in 1889,* and *being a pipe smoker.* Also included are such moral properties as *being kind to one's maiden aunt, being a scoundrel,* and *performing at least one morally wrong action.* Let us call the properties in this set H properties. The complement $\overline{P}$ of an H property P is the property a thing has just in case it does not have P. And a *consistent set* of H properties is a set of H properties such that it is logically possible that

The Free Will Defense

there be a human being having every property in the set. Now we can define "possible person" in the following way:

> x is a possible person = def. x is a consistent set of H properties such that for every H property P, either P or $\overline{P}$ is a member of x.

To *instantiate* a possible person P is to create a human being having every property in P. And a set S of possible persons is a *co-possible set of possible persons* just in case it is logically possible that every member of S is instantiated.[6]

Given this technical terminology, Mackie's objection can be summarily restated. Everyone grants that there is no absurdity in the claim that some man who is free to do what is wrong never, in fact, performs any wrong action; it follows that there are many possible persons containing the property *is free to do wrong but always does right*. And since it is logically possible that all men always freely do what is right, there are presumably several co-possible sets of possible persons all of whose members contain the property in question. Now God, if He is omnipotent, can instantiate any possible person and any co-possible set of possible persons he chooses. Hence, if He were all good, He would have instantiated one of the sets of co-possible persons all of whose members freely do only what is right.

In spite of its imposing paraphernalia the argument, thus restated, suffers from substantially the same defect that afflicts Mackie's original version. There are *some* possible persons God obviously cannot instantiate—those, for example, containing the property *is not created by God*. Accordingly it is *false* that God can instantiate just any possible person He chooses.

But of course the interesting question is whether

---

[6] The definiens must not be confused with: for every member M of S, it is logically possible that M is instantiated.

(9) God can instantiate possible persons containing the property of always freely doing what is right

is true; for perhaps Mackie could substitute (9) for the premise just shown to be false. Is (9) true? Perhaps we can approach this question in the following way. Let *P* be any possible person containing the property *always freely does what is right*. Then there must be some action A such that *P* contains the property of being free with respect to A (i.e., the property of being free to perform A and free to refrain from performing A). The *instantiation* of a possible person *S*, I shall say, is a person having every property in *S*; and let us suppose that if *P* were instantiated, its instantiation would be doing something morally wrong in performing A. And finally, let us suppose that God wishes to instantiate *P*. Now *P* contains many properties in addition to the ones already mentioned. Among them, for example, we might find *is born in 1910, has red hair, is born in Stuttgart, has feeble-minded ancestors, is six feet tall at the age of fourteen,* and the like. And there is no difficulty in God's creating a person with these properties. Further, there is no difficulty in God's bringing it about that this person (let us call him Smith) is free with respect to A. But if God *also* brings it about that Smith refrains from performing A (as he must to be the instantiation of *P*) then Smith is no longer free with respect to A and is hence not the instantiation of *P* after all. God cannot cause Smith to refrain from performing A, while allowing him to be free with respect to A; and therefore whether or not Smith does A will be entirely up to him; it will be a matter of free choice. Accordingly, whether God can instantiate *P* depends upon what Smith would freely decide to do.

This point may be put more accurately as follows: First, we shall say that an H property *Q* is *indeterminate* if *God creates a person and causes him to have Q* is necessarily false; an H property is *determinate* if it is not indeterminate. Of the properties we ascribed to P, all are determinate except *freely refrains from doing A* and *always freely does what is right*. Now conside P_1, any set of determinate members of P that is maximal with respect to the property of entailing no indeterminate member of P.[7] In order to instantiate P God must instantiate P_1. It is evident that there is at most one instantiation of P_1, for among the members of P_1 will be some such individuating properties as, for example, *is the third son of Richard and Lena Dykstra*. P_1 also contains the property of being free with respect to A; and if P_1 is instantiated, its instantiation will either perform A or refrain from performing A. It is of course possible that P_1 is such that if it is instantiated its instantiation I will perform A. If so, then if God allows I to remain free with respect to A, I will do A; and if God prevents I from doing A, then I is not free with respect to A and hence not the instantiation of P after all. Hence in neither case does God succeed in instantiating P. And accordingly God can instantiate P only if P_1 is *not* such that if it is instantiated, its instantiation will perform A. Hence it is possible that God cannot instantiate P. And evidently it is also possible, further, that *every* possible person containing the property *always freely does what is right* is such that neither God nor anyone else can instantiate it.[8]

It is possible, then, that God cannot instantiate any possible person containing the property *always freely does what is right*. It is also possible, of course, that He *can* instantiate some such possible persons. But *that* He can, if indeed He can, is a contingent truth. And since Mackie's project is to prove an entail-

---

[7] I.e., such that the addition of any member of P yields a set that entails some indeterminate member of P.

[8] For a moderately different version of this argument see my "Pike and Possible Persons," *Journal of Philosophy*, LXIII (1966), 106.

ment, he cannot employ any contingent propositions as added premises. Hence the reconstructed argument fails.

The difficulty with the reconstructed argument is the fact that God cannot instantiate just any possible person He chooses, and the possibility that God cannot instantiate any possible persons containing the property of always freely doing what is right. Perhaps the objector can circumvent this difficulty.

The H properties that make trouble for the objector are the indeterminate properties—those which God cannot cause anyone to have. It is because possible persons contain indeterminate properties that God cannot instantiate just any possible person He chooses. And so perhaps the objector can reformulate his definition of "possible person" in such a way that a possible person is a consistent set S of *determinate* properties such that for any determinate H property P, either P or $\overline{P}$ is a member of S. Unfortunately the following difficulty arises. Where I is any indeterminate H property and D is a determinate H property, D-or-I (the property a person has if he has either D or I) is determinate. And so, of course, is D. The same difficulty, accordingly, arises all over again—there will be some possible persons God cannot instantiate (those containing the properties *is not created by God or has red hair* and *does not have red hair*, for example). We must add, therefore, that no possible person *entails* an indeterminate property.

Even so our difficulties are not at an end. For the definition as now stated entails that there are no *possible free persons*; that is, possible persons containing the property *on some occasions free to do what is right and free to do what is wrong*.[9] We may see this as follows. Let P be any possible free person. P then contains the property of being free with respect to some

---

[9] This was pointed out to me by Lewis Creary. I am also indebted to Mr. Creary for a correction in the next paragraph.

action A. Furthermore, P would contain either the property of performing A (since that is a determinate property) or the property of refraining from performing A. But if P contains the property of performing A and the property of being free with respect to A, then P entails the property of freely performing A, which is an indeterminate property. And the same holds in case P contains the property of refraining from performing A. Hence in either case P entails an indeterminate property and accordingly is not a possible person.

Clearly the objector must revise the definition of "possible person" in such a way that for any action with respect to which a given possible person P is free, P contains neither the property of performing that action nor the property of refraining from performing it. This may be accomplished in the following way. Let us say that a person S is *free with respect to a property* P just in case he can freely choose whether or not to have P.[10] So, for example, if a person is free to leave town and free to stay, then he is free with respect to the properties *leaves town* and *does not leave town*. And let us say that a set of properties is free with respect to a given property P just in case it contains the property *is free with respect to* P. Now we can restate the definition of "possible person" as follows:

> x is a possible person = def. x is a consistent set of determinate H properties such that (1) for every determinate H property P with respect to which x is not free, either P or $\bar{P}$ is a member of x, and (2) x does not entail any indeterminate property.

---

[10] More accurately, S is free with respect to P if and only if (either there is some action A such that S is free with respect to A, and such that if S performs A he has P, or there is an action with respect to which S is free such that if he *refrains* from performing it he has P) and (either there is an action with respect to which S is free such that if he performs it he has $\bar{P}$, or there is an action with respect to which S is free and such that if he refrains from performing it he has $\bar{P}$).

And let us add the following new definition:

Possible person P has indeterminate property I = def. if P were instantiated, P's instantiation would have I.

Under the revised definition of "possible person" it seems apparent that God, if He is omnipotent, can instantiate any possible person, and any co-possible set of possible persons, he chooses. But, the objector continues, if God is also all good, He will, presumably, instantiate only those possible persons that have some such indeterminate H property as that of always freely doing what is right. And here the free will defender can no longer make the objection which held against the previous versions of Mackie's argument. For if God can instantiate any possible person he chooses, he can instantiate any possible free persons he chooses.

The free will defender can, however, raise what is essentially the same difficulty in a new guise: what reason is there for supposing that there are *any* possible persons, in the present sense of "possible person," having the indeterminate property in question? For it is clear that the proposition *Every possible free person has the property of performing at least one morally wrong action* is possibly true. But if every possible free person performs at least one wrong action, then every actual free person also freely performs at least one wrong action; hence if every possible free person performs at least one wrong action, God could create a universe without moral evil only by refusing to create any free persons at all. And, the free will defender adds, a world containing free persons and moral evil (provided that it contained more moral good than moral evil) would be superior to one lacking both free persons and moral good and evil. Once again, then, the objection seems to fail.

The definitions offered during the discussion of Mackie's objection afford the opportunity of stating the free will defense

The Free Will Defense

more formally. I said above (p. 136) that the free will defense is in essence an argument for the conclusion that (a) is consistent:

(a) God is omnipotent, omniscient, and wholly good, and God creates persons who perform morally evil actions.

One way of showing (a) to be consistent is to show that its first conjunct does not entail the negation of its second conjunct; that is, that

(b) God is omnipotent, omniscient, and wholly good

does not entail

(c) God does not create persons who perform morally evil actions.

Now one can show that a given proposition p does not entail another proposition q by producing a third proposition r whose conjunction with p is consistent and entails the denial of q. What we need here, then, is a proposition whose conjunction with (b) is both logically consistent and a logically sufficient condition of the denial of (c).

Consider the following argument:

(b) God is omnipotent, omniscient, and wholly good.
(r_1) God creates some free persons.
(r_2) Every possible free person performs at least one wrong action.
∴ (d) Every actual free person performs at least one wrong action—(r_2).
∴ (e) God creates persons who perform morally evil actions—(r_1), (d).

This argument is valid (and can easily be expanded so that it is formally valid). Furthermore, the conjunction of (b), (r_1), and (r_2) is evidently consistent. And, as the argument shows, (b), (r_1), and (r_2) jointly entail (e). But (e) is the denial of (c); hence (b) and (r) jointly entail the denial of (c). Accordingly (b) does not entail (c); and (a) (*God is omnipotent, omniscient, and wholly good, and God creates persons who perform morally evil acts*) is shown to be consistent. So stated, therefore, the free will defense appears to be successful.

At this juncture it might be objected that even if the free will defense, as explained above, shows that there is no contradiction in the supposition that God, who is wholly good, omnipotent, and omniscient, creates persons who engage in moral evil, it does nothing to show that a wholly good, omnipotent, and omniscient being could create a universe containing as *much* moral evil as this one seems to contain. The objection has a point, although the fact that there seems to be no way of measuring or specifying amounts of moral evil makes it exceedingly hard to state the objection in any way which does not leave it vague and merely suggestive. But let us suppose, for purposes of argument, that there is a way of measuring moral evil (and moral good) and that the moral evil present in the universe amounts to ϕ. The problem then is to show that

(b) God is omnipotent, omniscient, and wholly good

is consistent with

(f) God creates a set of free persons who produce ϕ moral evil.

Here the free will defender can produce an argument to show that (b) is consistent with (f) which exactly parallels the argument for the consistency of (b) with (c):

(b) God is omnipotent, omniscient, and wholly good.
(r_3) God creates a set S of free persons such that there is a

balance of moral good over moral evil with respect to the members of S.

(r_4) There is exactly one co-possible set S' of free possible persons such that there is a balance of moral good over moral evil with respect to its members; and the members of S' produce ϕ moral evil.

Set S is evidently the instantiation of S' (i.e., every member of S is an instantiation of some member of S' and every member of S' is instantiated by some member of S); hence the members of S produce ϕ moral evil. Accordingly, (b), (r_3), and (r_4) jointly entail (f); but the conjunction of (b), (r_3), and (r_4) is consistent; hence (b) is consistent with (f).

III

The preceding discussion enables us to conclude, I believe, that the free will defense succeeds in showing that there is no inconsistency in the assertion that God creates a universe containing as much moral evil as the universe in fact contains. There remains but one objection to be considered. McCloskey, Flew, and others charge that the free will defense, even if it is successful, accounts for only *part* of the evil we find; it accounts only for moral evil, leaving physical evil as intractable as before. The atheologian can therefore restate his position, maintaining that the existence of *physical evil*, evil which cannot be ascribed to the free actions of human beings, is inconsistent with the existence of an omniscient, omnipotent, and all-good deity.

To make this claim, however, is to overlook an important part of traditional theistic belief; it is part of much traditional belief to attribute a good deal of the evil we find to Satan, or to Satan and his cohorts. Satan, so the traditional doctrine goes, is a mighty nonhuman spirit who, along with many other angels, was created long before God created men. Unlike most of his colleagues Satan rebelled against God and has since been creating whatever havoc he could; the result, of course, is physical evil. But now we see that the moves available to the free will defender in the case of moral evil are equally available to him in the case of physical evil. First he provides definitions of "possible nonhuman spirit," "free nonhuman spirit," and so on, which exactly parallel their counterparts where it was moral evil that was at stake. Then he points out that it is logically possible that

> (r_5) God creates a set S of free nonhuman spirits such that the members of S do more good than evil,

and

> (r_6) There is exactly one co-possible set S' of possible free nonhuman spirits such that the members of S' do more good than evil,

and

> (r_7) All of the natural evil in the world is due to the actions of the members of S.

He points out further that (r_5), (r_6), and (r_7) are consistent with each other and that their conjunction is consistent with the proposition that God is omnipotent, omniscient, and all good. But (r_5) through (r_7) jointly entail that God creates a universe containing as much natural evil as the universe in fact contains; it follows then, that the existence of physical evil is not inconsistent with the existence of an omniscient, omnipotent, all-good deity.

Now it must be conceded that views involving devils and other nonhuman spirits do not at present enjoy either the extensive popularity or the high esteem of, say, quantum mechanics. So, for example, Flew:

The Free Will Defense

To make this more than just another desperate *ad hoc* expedient of apologetic it is necessary to produce independent evidence for launching such an hypothesis (if 'hypothesis' is not too flattering a term for it).[11]

But in the present context this claim is surely incorrect; to rebut the charge of contradiction the theist need not hold that the hypothesis in question is probable or even true. He need hold only that it is not inconsistent with the proposition that God exists. Flew suspects that "hypothesis" may be too flattering a term for the sort of view in question. Perhaps this suspicion reflects his doubts as to the meaningfulness of the proposed view. But it is hard to see how one could plausibly argue that the views in question are nonsensical (in the requisite sense) without invoking some version of the verifiability criterion, a doctrine whose harrowing vicissitudes are well known.[12] Furthermore, it is likely that any premises worth considering which yield the conclusion that hypotheses about devils are nonsensical will yield the same conclusion about the hypothesis that God exists. And if *God exists* is nonsensical, then presumably theism is not self-contradictory after all.

We may therefore conclude that the free will defense successfully rebuts the charge of contradiction brought against the theist. The problem of evil (if indeed evil constitutes a problem for the theist) does not lie in any inconsistency in the belief that God, who is omniscient, omnipotent, and all good, has created a world containing moral and physical evil.

IV

But even if there is no contradiction in the assertion that God has created a world containing moral and physical evil, is

---

it not clear that the existence of evil is *evidence against* the existence of God? It is not clear. The view that evil disconfirms theistic belief is not often explicitly stated, but it is widely held. Hume suggests it, Nelson Pike seems to endorse it, and John Wisdom also accepts it.[13]

To facilitate stating the view and its various versions, suppose we say that a proposition *p* *confirms* a proposition *q* just in case *q* is more probable than not on *p*—that is, just in case *q* would be more probable than not on what we knew if *p* were all we knew relevant to *q*. Further, *p* *disconfirms* *q* if *p* confirms the denial of *q*. Now an obvious and attractive interpretation of the atheologian's current claim is that

(E) there is evil

disconfirms

(G) God exists

where we shall take (G) to be equivalent to or entail the proposition that there is a wholly good, omniscient, omnipotent spirit.

But *does* (E) disconfirm (G)? How is this atheological position to be developed—that is, what are the grounds for this claim? Certainly not, for example, that nine out of ten universes created by an omnipotent, omniscient, and perfectly good being contain no evil; our evidence is a bit scanty for that. The argument will have to be indirect in some way; and it is not easy to see how it will go. Waiving that difficulty for the moment, perhaps we may still find an approach to this position. Suppose we state the *free will hypothesis* as follows:

(F₁) A world containing moral good (provided that it con-

---

[13] Hume, *Dialogues Concerning Natural Religion* (London, 1947), p. 211; Pike, "Hume on Evil," *Philosophical Review*, LXXII (1963), 195–197; Wisdom, "God and Evil," *Mind*, XLIV (1935), pp. 1–20.

The Free Will Defense

tains more moral good than moral evil) is better (other relevant factors being equal) than one containing natural good alone; and every co-possible set of possible free persons whose members freely perform substantially more good than evil, has members who perform evil as well as good actions.[14]

Now it is apparent, I think, that (E) does not disconfirm the conjunction of (E) with (F_1); (E) seems to have no direct bearing on (F_1) alone, although the conjunction of (F_1) with the proposition that in fact there exist free persons whose members freely perform substantially more good than evil entails (E). Nor does (E) appear to disconfirm the conjunction of (E) and (F_1) with (G); if (F_1) were true, God could not create a universe containing moral good without permitting evil. It is a generally accepted principle of inductive logic that a proposition confirms the logical consequences of any proposition it confirms—that is, if p confirms q and q entails r, then p confirms r. But it follows from this "consequence condition" that if p disconfirms q, then p disconfirms the conjunction of q with any other proposition. Since, in the present case, (E) does not disconfirm the conjunction of (E) with (F_1) and (G), it follows that it does not disconfirm (G). So stated, therefore, this atheological claim seems to be false.

But if this atheological position fails, perhaps it is only because it fails to take into account the full range of our evidence; it altogether neglects the variety and extent of the evil we find. (E), after all, asserts merely that there is evil in the world, which would be true if the total extent of evil were an insignificant peccadillo on the part of an otherwise admirably disposed angel. Suppose we explicitly recognize, then, that there is both natural and moral evil; and suppose we say that

---

[14] See above, p. 148.

the evil we know to exist amounts to ϕ. We may then rewrite (E) as

(E′) There is both natural and moral evil and the evil in the world amounts to ϕ.

And, it is added, although perhaps (E) does not disconfirm (G), (E′) certainly appears to.[15]

Reflection on the procedure by which I argued that the existence of physical evil is not logically incompatible with the existence of God (above, p. 149) discloses that a similar argument is available here. Let us replace (F_1) by

(F_2) The evil in the world is due to the free actions of personal beings (nonhuman spirits as well as human persons); a world containing a balance of moral good over moral evil is better (other relevant factors being equal) than one containing no moral good; there is a balance of moral good over moral evil in the universe at large; and every co-possible set S of possible free personal beings with respect to the actions of the members of which there is a balance of moral good over moral evil as great as the one that actually obtains, is such that the members of S produce evil amounting to ϕ or more.

(F_2) is an unwieldy item. Nonetheless it is evident, I think, that (E′) alone does not disconfirm it; nor does (E′) disconfirm the conjunction of (E′) with (F_2) and (G). But then (E′) does not disconfirm (G).

There is one more manuever open to the atheologian. We can imagine him rejoining as follows: Although (E′) does not disconfirm (F_2), other things we know do; we know that physical evil (e.g., deaths resulting from the Lisbon earthquake) is not to be attributed to the actions of men; and we have

_____
[15] This is Wisdom's view (*op. cit.*).

every reason to doubt that there are any nonhuman personal beings whose actions could produce natural evil. Hence what we know disconfirms one of the conjuncts of (F₂); hence it disconfirms (F₂) and the conjunction of (F₂) with (E) and (G). Here the atheologian is claiming that our *total evidence,* the set of propositions we (i.e., you and I) know to be true, disconfirms (G)–and–(F₂)–and–(E′), even if (E′) alone does not, on the grounds that our total evidence disconfirms the supposition that nonhuman personal beings (devils, perhaps) cause natural evil. But does it? Do we have evidence for the proposition that the Lisbon earthquake was not caused by the activity of some disaffected fallen angel? I certainly do not know of any such evidence. To be sure, we do not usually think of the Lisbon earthquake as the result of such activity; the idea is perhaps repugnant to "modern" habits of thought. But this is scarcely evidence against it. No doubt the Lisbon earthquake can be explained as the result of purely natural causes; we have no need, it may be said, of the devil hypothesis. But again this is no evidence against it; the fact that we "have no need" of a given hypothesis shows perhaps that we have no evidence for it, but it hardly shows that we do have evidence against it. If there is evidence against this hypothesis, it is not easy to find. Nevertheless there is perhaps an air of paradox about claiming that we have no evidence against the supposition that some devil caused the Lisbon earthquake. Furthermore our total evidence is such a vast and variegated affair that it is never easy to determine what it supports and what it does not. I shall claim, therefore, not that our total evidence does not disconfirm the conjunction of (E′) with (G) and (F₂), but only that it is by no means clear that it does. But then it is by no means clear that our total evidence disconfirms (G); and hence this atheological argument is inconclusive.

Seven

Verificationism and
Other Atheologica

IN this chapter I shall examine a miscellany of atheological arguments, beginning with the claim that the *unverifiability* of religious assertions renders them in some way suspect.

I

"The main danger to theism today comes from people who want to say that 'God exists' and 'God does not exist' are equally absurd." [1] That the most important questions about religious belief, these days, are questions of meaning and significance rather than truth, is repeated often enough.[2] It seems

---

[1] J. J. C. Smart, "The Existence of God," in *New Essays in Philosophical Theology*, ed. A. Flew and A. MacIntyre (London, 1955).

[2] See for example, Ronald Hepburn, *Christianity and Paradox* (London, 1958), pp. 6, 15; R. B. Braithwaite, *An Empiricist's View of the Nature of Religious Belief* (Cambridge, 1955); John Wilson, *Language and*

to be widely believed that certain developments in twentieth-century philosophy (particularly twentieth-century "linguistic" philosophy) have shown that there is something semantically improper about typical religious utterances. Certainly this suspicion is not altogether misplaced; the writings of many theologians are of a granitic opacity designed, it may seem, more to conceal than to reveal their author's thought. And (as the Christian tradition has insisted from the beginning) some of the central concepts and doctrines of Christian theism as found in the Bible and the creeds are difficult to grasp. This much is undeniable. But just how is contemporary philosophy relevant here? How, exactly, have contemporary "linguistic" philosophers raised this ancient problem in a new and acute form?

Most of the discussion has concerned alleged difficulties in *verifying* or *falsifying* typical religious and theological utterances. And here a focal point of discussion has been Antony Flew's "Theology and Falsification." [3] Let us look carefully at what Flew says.

Flew begins the central part of his argument by stating the law of double negation:

Now to assert that such and such is the case is necessarily equivalent to denying that such and such is not the case.[4] Suppose then we are in doubt as to what someone who gives vent to an utterance is asserting, or suppose that, more radically, we are skeptical as to whether he is really asserting anything at all, one way of trying to understand (or perhaps it will be to expose) his utterance is to

---

Christian Belief (London, 1958), Chapter I; W. Blackstone, *The Problem of Religious Knowledge* (Englewood Cliffs, 1953), Introduction. Most of the authors in *New Essays in Philosophical Theology* seem to share this opinion.

[3] *New Essays in Philosophical Theology*, p. 96.

[4] Here Flew helpfully adds (in a footnote): "For those who prefer symbolism: $p \equiv \sim \sim p$."

attempt to find what he would regard as counting against, or as being incompatible with, its truth.[5]

So far, quite unexceptionable. It is doubtless true (if less than exciting) that one way to understand an assertion is to see what is incompatible with it. But Flew goes on to give for this truism an *argument* the first premise of which is again the law of double negation:

For if the utterance is indeed an assertion it will necessarily be equivalent to a denial of the negation of the assertion. And anything which would count against the assertion, or which would induce the speaker to withdraw it and to admit that it had been mistaken, must be part of (or the whole of) the meaning of the negation of that assertion.[6]

If the first premise of the argument is unexceptionable, the second is not nearly so innocent. Although Flew does not explain "count against," what he says suggests that anything *incompatible with* an assertion counts against it. Again, Flew does not explain what it is for something to be *part of the meaning of* an assertion. But presumably anything that is part of the meaning of an assertion is contained in or *entailed* by that assertion. If so, however, certain curious consequences ensue. Consider, for example, the assertion

(A) Feike Vander Horst is in Zeeland.

Now many things are incompatible with (and hence count against) A—for example,

(B) Feike Vander Horst is in Australia

and

(C) Feike Vander Horst is in Paterson, New Jersey.

---

[5] *Loc. cit.*
[6] *Ibid.*

(B) and (C), then, must be part of the meaning of the denial
of (A); hence on this showing, *Feike Vander Horst is not in
Zeeland* entails that Feike is both in Australia and in Paterson,
New Jersey. But then the denial of (A) is logically inconsistent
in that it entails the (inconsistent) conjunction of (B) with
(C)[7] (A), therefore, is necessarily true; it is logically impossible that Feike be anywhere but in Zeeland. But of course by
the very same sort of reasoning it will follow that (A) is logically inconsistent; both

> (D) Feike Vander Horst is in the northern quarter of Zee-
> land

and

> (E) Feike Vander Horst is in the southern quarter of Zee-
> land

are incompatible with (hence count against) the denial of (A);
therefore they are part of the meaning of (and hence entailed
by) the denial of (A)'s denial—that is, by (A); hence (A) is
inconsistent as well as necessary. Flew's second premise, therefore, seems to entail a contradiction.

This is indeed a beguiling spectacle; Flew evidently means
to prove a truistic conclusion by deducing it from a self-contradictory premise. The argument is certainly valid (if a contradiction entails just any proposition) but things do not auger well
for its soundness. Perhaps Flew is not being entirely serious.
Or perhaps I have misunderstood his argument. In any event,
the theist will be happy to accept its conclusion, as well as the
consequence that

if there is nothing which a putative assertion denies, then there

---

[7] The purist who objects that (B) *and* (C) is not, in fact, logically
inconsistent may be mollified if we conjoin the denials of (C) and (B)
to (B) and (C) respectively.

is nothing which it asserts either: and so it is not really an assertion.[8]

A theist who claimed that some of his assertions denied nothing at all—not even their own negations—would be backward and benighted indeed. Even Heidegger, the verificationist's favorite whipping-boy, would no doubt concede that "the not negates itself" is inconsistent with its contradictory.

Having exegeted his text, Flew proceeds to the application:

Now it often seems to people who are not religious as if there was no conceivable event or series of events the occurrence of which would be admitted by sophisticated religious people to be a sufficient reason for conceding 'there wasn't a God after all' or 'God does not really love us then'. . . . Just what would have to happen not merely (morally and wrongly) to tempt us but also (logically and rightly) to entitle us to say 'God does not love us' or even 'God does not exist'? I therefore put to the succeeding symposiasts the simple central questions, 'What would have to occur or to have occurred to constitute for you a disproof of the love of, or of the existence of, God?'[9]

Numberless hosts of writers (including some theologians) have repeated this challenge and found in it a real difficulty for the theist.[10] And several writers, both believers and unbelievers, have suggested that religious beliefs be *reinterpreted* in such a way that they turn out to be verifiable. A. C. MacIntyre in *Metaphysical Beliefs* suggests a way of understanding religious beliefs which, he thinks, shows that one can accept the beliefs and still hold to the view that all significant statements are

---

[8] Flew, *op. cit.*, p. 98.

[9] *Ibid.*

[10] E.g., R. Hepburn, *op. cit.*, p. 11; W. Blackstone, *op. cit.*, p. 53; R. B. Braithwaite, *op. cit.*, p. 6; John Wilson, *op. cit.*, pp. 7–8; and Duff-Forbes, in "Theology and Falsification Again," *Australasian Journal of Philosophy*, XXXIX (1961), 143.

Verificationism and Other Atheologica

verifiable.[11] In *An Empiricist's View of the Nature of Religious Belief* R. B. Braithwaite offers a reinterpretation of Christian beliefs according to which they are consistent with the verificationist thesis. Sometimes these reinterpretations assume truly heroic proportions, as, for example, when David Cox helpfully suggests that Christians resolve henceforth to use the statement "God exists" to mean "some men and women have had, and all may have, experiences called 'meeting God.'"[12] He also suggests that when we say "God created the world from nothing" what we should mean is "everything we call 'material' can be used in such a way that it contributes to the well-being of men." (I might remark here that certain Christian theologians—Bultmann and some of his followers in particular—seem to me to be doing something quite as outrageous.)

But the first thing to note is that the legitimacy of this challenge does not follow from what was previously established. No doubt the assertion that there is a God, if it is meaningful, must deny many other assertions and exclude many states of affairs; but it does not follow that it must exclude some conceivable *happening* or *event* or series of events—unless, indeed, we allow such Pickwickian events as God's going out of existence or his revealing to us that he no longer loves us. (Of course if "event" is to include these, then the challenge is easily answered.) Nonetheless the theist can perhaps meet the challenge head on. My discovering a contradiction in the proposition *God exists* would constitute a disproof of it; and if after death I were to meet Father Abraham, St. Paul, and St. John (I think I could recognize them), who united in declaring they had been duped, perhaps I should have sufficient reason for conceding that God does not love us after all.

But clearly enough this is not at all the sort of event or hap-

[11] London, 1957.
[12] "The Significance of Christianity," *Mind*, LIX (1950), 47.

pening Flew has in mind. What he means is that meaningful assertions must be falsifiable by some *empirical* state of affairs, or some proposition with *empirical content*. What is empirical content and under what conditions does a proposition have it? Duff-Forbes takes Flew to be chiding the religious for trying to make assertions that no *observation statements* count against.[13] It appears, then, that according to Flew a meaningful (contingent) proposition must be falsifiable by observation statements; there must be some finite and consistent set of observation statements that entails its denial. If so, Flew is embracing a version of the famous *verifiability criterion of meaning*.

Oddly enough, a number of theologians have apparently joined forces with Flew. Paul van Buren, for example, declares that

The empiricist in us finds the heart of the difficulty not in what is said about God but in the very talking about God at all. We do not know "what" (*sic*) God is and we cannot understand how the word "God" is being used.

The problem of the Gospel in a secular age is a problem of its apparently meaningless language, and linguistic analysts will give us help in clarifying it.[14]

What sort of help will they give us?

The heart of the method of linguistic analysis lies in the use of the verification principle—that the meaning of a word is its use in its context. The meaning of a statement is to be found in, and is iden-

---

[13] *Op. cit.*, p. 143. An observation statement is "any sentence which—correctly or incorrectly—asserts of one or more specifically named objects that they have, or that they lack, some specified observable characteristic" (cf. Carl Hempel, "Problems and Changes in the Empiricist Criterion of Meaning" in Leonard Linsky, ed., *Semantics and the Philosophy of Language* [Urbana, 1952], p. 165).

[14] *The Secular Meaning of the Gospel* (New York, 1963), p. 84.

tical with, the function of that statement. If a statement has a function, so that it may in principle be verified or falsified, the statement is meaningful, and unless or until a theological statement can be submitted in some way to verification, it cannot be said to have a meaning in our language game.[15]

One might expect a theologian to have about as much sympathy for verificationism as a civil rights worker for the Ku Klux Klan; yet van Buren is by no means the only theologian who believes that "linguistic analysis" has shown that we must accept the verifiability criterion. But in fact the lot of the verificationist has been far from enviable. The many attempts to state the verifiability criterion have met a common fate; each has been so restrictive as to exclude statements the verificationists themselves took to be meaningful, or so liberal as to exclude no statements at all. Here I cannot trace the detailed history of these attempts;[16] but Flew, his numerous epigoni, and their theological allies, seem to have neglected this study altogether. The version Flew apparently accepts was recognized very early to be unsatisfactory. As Hempel remarks in a slightly different connection, one must suppose that if a given statement is meaningful, so is its denial. Flew's criterion does not meet this condition: for (as Hempel remarks) although a universal statement like *All crows are black* passes the test, its existential denial does not. *There is at least one pink unicorn* is consistent with any finite and consistent set of observation statements. (Apparently it is Flew rather than the theologian who is holding that some propositions have no denials.) So we must add—as the second clause of a recursive definition— that if a statement is meaningful, so is its denial. But the result is still far too restrictive; for now, as Hempel points out, statements of mixed quantification (*For every substance there*

---

[15] *Ibid.*, pp. 104–105.
[16] See the Hempel article mentioned above, n. 13.

is a solvent, Every tree is about the same size as some other tree) turn out to be meaningless.

We could repair this difficulty, perhaps, by adding further that the logical consequences of a meaningful statement are meaningful; but then our criterion no longer rules anything out. For consider such a "statement" as *The not regularly nothings itself* and call it N. Its conjunction with any falsifiable statement S will be meaningful (in that any set of observation statements inconsistent with S will be inconsistent with *S and N*); since it will entail N, the latter too is meaningful.

Upon perceiving the futility of some earlier versions (including the one Flew appears to adopt) A. J. Ayer restated the verifiability criterion as follows:

A statement *p* is meaningful if and only if there is a statement *q* such that the conjunction of *p* with *q* entails an observation statement not entailed by *q* alone.[17]

It was quickly pointed out, however, that this confers meaning upon every statement: where N is *The not nothings itself* and S is any observation statement, N and *if N then S* entails S; since *if N then S* alone does not, N is meaningful.

In the introduction to the second edition of *Language, Truth and Logic* Ayer hoped to repair this difficulty as follows:

I propose to say that a statement is directly verifiable if it is either itself an observation-statement, or is such that in conjunction with one or more observation-statements it entails at least one observation-statement which is not deducible from these other premises alone; and I propose to say that a statement is indirectly verifiable if it satisfies the following conditions: first, that in conjunction with certain other premises it entails one or more directly verifiable statements which are not deducible from these other premises alone; and secondly, that these other premises do not in-

---

[17] *Language, Truth and Logic*, 2nd ed. (New York, 1946), p. 39.

clude any statement that is not either analytic, or directly verifiable, or capable of being independently established as indirectly verifiable.[18]

But in a review of the revised edition of *Language, Truth and Logic* Alonzo Church pointed out that this revision is no improvement:

> Let O_1, and O_2, and O_3 be three 'observation-statements' . . . such that no one of the three alone entails any of the others. Then using these we may show of any statement S whatever that either it or its negation is verifiable, as follows: Let $\sim O_1$ and $\sim S$ be the negations of O_1 and of S respectively. Then (under Ayer's definition) $(\sim O_1 \cdot O_2) \vee (O_3 \cdot \sim S)$ is directly verifiable, because with O_1 it entails O_3. Therefore (under Ayer's definition) S is indirectly verifiable—unless it happens that $(\sim O_1 \cdot O_2) \vee (O_3 \cdot \sim S)$ alone entails O_2, in which case $\sim S$ and O_3 together entail O_2, so that $\sim S$ is directly verifiable.[19]

Here the matter rested until 1961, when Professor Peter Nidditch issued a rebuttal of Church's objection:

> Let p, q, and r, be any three specific observation-statements such that no one of them alone entails any of the others, and let s be *any statement whatever*. Church's thesis is that, on Ayer's definition, s, or its negation $\sim s$, is always verifiable. If this is correct, then it obviously completely destroys the point and utility of the Verifiability Principle.
>
> (a) To begin with, Church points out that
>
> $$p \text{ and } (\sim p \cdot q) \vee (r \cdot \sim s) \text{ jointly entail r.} \qquad (A)$$
>
> Since r is not entailed by p alone, it results from the second clause of Ayer's definition of directly verifiable statements that
>
> $$(\sim p \cdot q) \vee (r \cdot \sim s) \text{ is directly verifiable} \qquad (B)$$

---

[18] *Ibid.*, p. 13.
[19] *Journal of Symbolic Logic* (1949), p. 53.

I certainly grant the correctness of (A) and (B).

(b) The next stage of the argument has two parts.

(bi) According to Church, if $(\sim p \cdot q) \vee (r \cdot \sim s)$ does not alone entail q, then

$$s \text{ and } (\sim p \cdot q) \vee (r \cdot \sim s) \text{ jointly entail } q, \tag{C}$$

and from this, together with Ayer's definition, he concludes that

$$s \text{ is indirectly verifiable.} \tag{D}$$

This allegation is easily disposed of. Looking at Ayer's two conditions for indirectly verifiability, we can see that, in view of (B) and (C), s satifies the first condition, while, *unless s is analytic or verifiable,* it cannot satisfy the second condition. (I assume that Ayer's "include" means "include *intra se*" and not "include *inter se*". If it does mean the latter, Church's criticism is very easily sidestepped by amending the original to mean "include *intra se*".) [20]

Now presumably a group of premises contains a proposition *p inter se* if *p* is one of the group; it contains *p intra se* if *p* is one of the group or a component of one of the group (as *s* is a component of $(\sim p \cdot q) \vee (r \cdot \sim s)$. But this suggestion fares no better than its forebears. Where N is *the not nothings itself* and O_1 and O_2 are any observation statements logically independent of each other and of N, N and O_1 is directly verifiable, since in conjunction with O_2 it entails O_1. But then N is indirectly verifiable, for together with O_1 it entails the directly verifiable N *and* O_1. Here the "other premises" mentioned in Ayer's definition obviously include, *inter se*, or *intra se*, or in any other way, only O_1.

It was suggested to me[21] that the definition of direct verifiability be revised as follows:

[20] *Mind* (1961), pp. 88–89.

[21] By Messrs. Michael Slote, Michael Stocker, and Robert Shope.

Verificationism and Other Atheologica

p is directly verifiable if p is an observation statement or there is an observation statement q such that (1) p and q entails an observation statement r that neither p nor q alone entails, and (2) the argument from p and q to r is minimal in the sense that if any conjunct of p or q is deleted, the resulting argument is invalid.

This avoids the preceding difficulty (as well as some difficulties that arise if the second clause is not added) but is still vulnerable: $N \cdot (\sim O_1 \vee \sim N \vee O_2)$ will be directly verifiable, for conjoined with O_1 it entails O_2 in such a way that conditions (1) and (2) of the definition are met. And again N will be indirectly verifiable, for conjoined with O_2 it entails $N \cdot (\sim O_1 \vee \sim N \vee O_2)$.

The fact is that no one has succeeded in stating a version of the verifiability criterion that is even remotely plausible; and by now the project is beginning to look unhopeful.[22]

But suppose the criterion could be stated in a way which satisfied the verificationist. (We could, after all, say simply that the statements of science and "common sense" are meaningful and those of transcendental metaphysics and theology meaningless.) Why should anyone accept it? Why should the theist not retort as follows: "Your criterion is obviously mistaken; for many theological statements are not empirically verifiable; but theological statements are meaningful; hence it is false that all and only verifiable statements are meaningful"? What could the verificationist reply? What sort of argument could he bring forward to show the theologian that he ought to accept the verifiability criterion and stop proclaiming these meaningless theological pseudo-statements? About all he could say here would be that his criterion does fit scientific and common-sense statements and does not fit theological statements. And to this the theologian could agree with equanimity; there are,

---

[22] See James Cornman, "Indirectly Verifiable: Everything or Nothing," *Philosophical Studies* (forthcoming).

no doubt, many properties which distinguish scientific and commonsense statements from theological statements. But of course that does not suffice to show that theological statements are meaningless or logically out of order or anything of the sort.

In the light of this and of the fact that it seems impossible to state the verifiability criterion the question becomes acute: how *are* we to understand Flew's challenge? What exactly is he requiring of theological statements? Is he chiding the theist for ignoring some version of the verifiability criterion? If so, which version? Until these questions are answered it is impossible to determine whether his challenge is legitimate or even what the challenge *is*. If the notion of verifiability cannot so much as be explained, if we cannot so much as say what it is for a statement to be empirically verifiable, then we scarcely need worry about whether religious statements are or are not verifiable. How could we possibly tell? As a piece of natural atheology, verificationism is entirely unsuccessful.[23]

II

J. L. Mackie finds the concept of omnipotence incoherent:

This leads to what I call the Paradox of Omnipotence: can an omnipotent being make things which he cannot control? It is clear that this is a paradox; the question cannot be answered satisfactorily either in the affirmative or in the negative. If we answer "Yes," it follows that if God actually makes things which he cannot control, he is not omnipotent once he has made them: there are *then* things which he cannot do. But if we answer "No," we are immediately asserting that there are things which he cannot do, that is to say that he is already not omnipotent.[24]

---

[23] And this makes the dizzy gyrations of those theologians who accept it more puzzling than ever; perhaps they would do well to *study* it before rushing to embrace it.

[24] "Evil and Omnipotence," *Mind*, LXIV (1955), 210.

Verificationism and Other Atheologica

Perhaps we can set out the alleged paradox in more detail as follows:

(1) Either God can make things He cannot control or God cannot make things He cannot control.
(2) If He can, then if He did, He would not be omnipotent.
(3) If He cannot, then there are things He cannot do and hence He is not omnipotent.

Now (2) as it stands does not contribute its share to the paradox; it says only that if God can make things He cannot control then He could lose his omnipotence—from which it does not obviously follow that He is not *now* omnipotent. Perhaps (2) could be revised as follows:

(2′) If God can make things He cannot control, then it is possible that there be things He cannot control, in which case God is not omnipotent.[25]

(1), (2′), and (3) together entail that God is not omnipotent. But are (2′) and (3) true? One thinks immediately of consulting an appropriate definition of omnipotence. This easy course has an important drawback; no appropriate definition of omnipotence seems to be available.

No one, presumably, expects an omnipotent being to be capable of performing such logically impossible actions as creating a square circle. We might therefore attempt the following definition:

(D₁) x is omnipotent if and only if x is capable of performing any logically possible action.

But *the action of making a table God did not make* is surely a logically possible action; hence by (D₁) God can perform it,

<hr />

[25] See George Mavrodes, "Some Puzzles Concerning Omnipotence," *Philosophical Review*, LXXII (1963), 221.

if He is omnipotent; since He cannot, He is not, under (D_1), omnipotent. This difficulty suggests (D_2):

> (D_2) x is omnipotent if and only if x is capable of performing any action A such that the proposition x *performs* A is logically possible.

(D_2) seems too liberal. Consider the man who is capable only of scratching his ear. For any action A, if the proposition *The man who is capable only of scratching his ear performs* A is consistent, then the man who is capable only of scratching his ear will, presumably, be able to perform A, thus turning out, under (D_2), to be omnipotent. But perhaps this difficulty could be resolved by proposing, not a *definition* of omnipotence, but an explanation of the statement that *God is omnipotent*; even if we cannot give a *general* explanation of omnipotence, we may be able to say what *God is omnipotent* comes to:

> (D_3) God is omnipotent if and only if God is capable of performing any action A such that the proposition *God performs* A is logically possible.

But suppose I am thinking of *the action of creating a square circle*. Then God cannot perform the action I am thinking of, despite the contingency of the proposition *God performs the action I'm thinking of*. Hence by (D_3), once more, God is not omnipotent.

Presumably the solution lies in somehow limiting the substituend set of the variable "A" in (D_3): it ought to include such expression as "the action of creating a square circle" but exclude "the action I am thinking of." Just how this is to be accomplished is not easy to say. And hence, it seems, we cannot test ($2'$) and (3) by resorting to a definition of omnipotence.

Bernard Mayo and George Mavrodes agree that (3) ought to be rejected.[26] Mavrodes puts it as follows:

On the assumption that God is omnipotent, the phrase "a stone too heavy for God to lift" (or "a being God can't control") becomes self-contradictory. For it becomes "a stone which cannot be lifted by Him whose power is sufficient for lifting anything." But the "thing" described by a self contradictory phrase is absolutely impossible and hence has nothing to do with the doctrine of omnipotence.[27]

Hence (3) is false. *The action of making a being God cannot control* is a logically impossible action; hence God's inability to perform it does not entail that he is not omnipotent.

This solution to the paradox involves an assumption that Mayo and Mavrodes do not make explicit: the assumption that the proposition *God is not omnipotent* is necessarily false. The phrase "a stone too heavy for God to lift" is equivalent to "a stone which cannot be lifted by Him whose power is sufficient for lifting anything" *only if* it is *necessarily* true that if God exists, then his power is sufficient for lifting anything; that is, only if the proposition *God is not omnipotent* is necessarily false. *There is a stone that God cannot lift* entails *There is a stone that an omnipotent being cannot lift* only if it is necessarily false that God is not omnipotent. We might put the assumption by saying that God is *necessarily* omnipotent.[28] But is the assumption true?

Fortunately we need not argue that issue: there is another way of resolving the paradox. For consider

---

[26] Mayo, "Mr. Keene on Omnipotence," *Mind*, LXX (1961), 249; Mavrodes, *op. cit.*

[27] *Op. cit.*, p. 222.

[28] See below, pp. 173–183.

(4) It is possible that (God is omnipotent and it is possible that there is a being God cannot control).[29]

(4) asserts that the conjunction of *God is omnipotent* with *It is possible that there is a being God cannot control* is consistent. And (4) is either true or false. If (4) is false, then (3) is utterly groundless and pretty clearly false. We may see this as follows: (3) asserts that

(a) God cannot make things God cannot control

entails

(b) God is not omnipotent.

Now if (4) is false, then if God is omnipotent, the proposition *There is a being God cannot control* is necessarily false. But then the action of creating a being God cannot control is not logically possible. And then, clearly enough, (a) does not entail (b). So if (4) is false, (3) (i.e., the proposition that (a) entails (b)) is true only if it is false that God is omnipotent. So then one who asserts that (3) is true is shamelessly begging the question.

Suppose on the other hand that (4) is true; then (2′) is not. According to (2′),

(c) It is possible that there are things God cannot control

entails

(d) God is not omnipotent.

But the assertion that (c) entails (d) is equivalent to the denial of (4), since what it asserts is that the conjunction of *God is omnipotent* with *It is possible that there is a being God*

---

[29] Here I must thank Thomas Jager, Robert Bush, and Paul Mellema for prodding me to simplify (4).

cannot control is not possible. Hence if (4) is true, (2′) is false.

What we have, then, is a counterdilemma. Either (4) is true or it is false; in either case one of the premises of the paradox is unacceptable; so the paradox fails.[30]

III

In 1948 J. N. Findlay proposed an engagingly original piece of natural atheology that can only be described as an ontological argument for the nonexistence of God. He began by stating two "requirements of the religious attitude":

Religious attitudes presume *superiority* in their objects, and such superiority, moreover, as reduces us, who feel the attitudes, to comparative nothingness. . . . To feel religiously is therefore to presume surpassing greatness in some object. . . . And hence we are led on irresistibly to demand that our religious object should have an *unsurpassable* supremacy along all avenues, that it should tower infinitely above all other objects. . . .

But we are also led on irresistibly to a yet more stringent demand . . . : we can't help feeling that the worthy object of our worship can never be a thing that merely *happens* to exist. . . . His own non-existence must be unthinkable in any circumstances. . . . God must be wholly inescapable, as we remarked previously, whether for thought or for reality. . . .

Not only is it contrary to the demands and claims inherent in religious attitudes that their object should *exist* "accidentally": it is also contrary to these demands that it should *possess its various excellences* in some merely adventitious or contingent manner. . . . And so we are led on irresistibly, by the demands inherent in religious reverence, to hold that an adequate object of our worship must possess its various qualities in *some necessary* manner.[31]

---

[30] In essence this resolution resembles Mavrodes' (see n. 25, above).

[31] "Can God's Existence Be Disproved?" *Mind*, LVII (1948), 176–186. Reprinted in *The Ontological Argument*, ed. Plantinga (New York, 1965), pp. 111–122, and page references are to this volume. The present quotation is from pp. 116–118.

An adequate object of religious worship must exist and possess its qualities necessarily. But the consequences of this requirement are devastating:

> Plainly (for all who share a contemporary outlook) they entail not only that there isn't a God, but that the Divine Existence is either senseless or impossible. . . . Those who believe in necessary truths which aren't merely tautological, think that such truths merely connect the *possible* instances of various characteristics with each other: they don't expect such truths to tell them whether there will be instances of such characteristics. This is the outcome of the whole medieval and Kantian criticism of the Ontological Proof. And, on a yet more modern view of the matter, necessity in propositions merely reflects our use of words, the arbitrary conventions of our language.[32]

As I argued in Chapter Two, the "whole medieval and Kantian criticism of the Ontological Proof" may be taken with a grain of salt. No one has yet succeeded in showing that existential statements are all contingent; indeed, Kant himself pretty clearly thought the existential statements of mathematics to be necessary, if not analytic. There is nothing here, it seems to me, to show that there could be no logically necessary beings. But I wish to turn first to the other demand of the religious attitude —that its object should "possess its various qualities in some necessary manner." Theists have sometimes made this kind of suggestion. How is it to be explained?

At the very least, it supposes the absence of certain kinds of *change* in God. According to St. Augustine, for example, "that is not properly called eternal which undergoes any degree of change." [33] We might reasonably suppose that a being undergoes changes just in case it possesses at one time a property that at another time it lacks. Here the word "property" is so

---

[32] *Ibid.*, p. 119.
[33] *De Trinitate*, IV, ch. 18.

taken that a thing has the property of being (a) ϕ if and only if the proposition that it is (a) ϕ is true; and a thing, x, has the property of being (a) ϕ at a given time t if and only if it is true that at t it is (a) ϕ. But now it is surely clear that God *does* undergo change. For the proposition *God was worshiped by St. Paul in A.D. 40* is true, unlike the proposition *God was worshiped by St. Paul in 100 B.C.*; hence in A.D. 40 God had a property He lacked in 100 B.C. St. Augustine was by no means prepared to deny this obvious fact; in *De Trinitate*, IV, chapter 5, he gives a similar example to show that change can indeed be predicated of God *relatively*, as he puts it. What does he mean, then, when he says that God is changeless? Perhaps we can state his claim as follows. Let us say that a property P is *relational* for a being x just in case the proposition that x has P entails the existence of a (contingent) being distinct from x. So the property of being worshiped by St. Paul would be one of God's relational properties along with the property of loving St. Paul and the property of knowing that St. Paul was converted on the road to Damascus. On the other hand, the properties of loving everyone, being omniscient, and being everlasting are among God's nonrelational properties. And to say that God is changeless is to say that any property God has at one time but lacks at another is one of his relational properties.

But Augustine goes further than this. He maintains a view that entails and presumably explains the position just stated; this is the view that an eternal being is not merely changeless, but unchangeable, not subject to or capable of change. It is not merely true, but in some way *necessarily* true, that God does not change with respect to his nonrelational properties. God's nonrelational properties are, we might say, loss-proof. Augustine construes or explains this in terms of the distinction between essential and accidental properties, a traditional distinction that very many contemporary philosophers reject out of hand. We might state Augustine's view by saying that all of God's non-relational properties are essential; that God has no property that is both accidental and nonrelational. But this brings us to Findlay's question. What are we to make of this distinction between essential and accidental properties? This is a difficult and very large topic and what I shall say will be, I am afraid, both sketchy and merely suggestive.

But perhaps we may make a beginning by saying that an object x has a property P essentially if and only if it is false that x might not have had P, or impossible or inconceivable that x should have lacked P. Goebbels, for example, might have been, had things turned out differently, a fair-minded man; but it is inconceivable that he should have been (all along) an alligator. Green might not have been my favorite color; but it is impossible that it should have lacked the property of being a color. The property of being odd is essential to the number seven; the property of having been referred to by me is accidental to it. And while *being married to Xantippe* is an accidental property of Socrates, *not being an eighteenth-century Irish washerwoman*, perhaps, is not.

Findlay is certainly right in claiming that many contemporary philosophers reject this distinction. Some philosophers, for example, construe the traditional doctrine as amounting to the claim that

(1) An object x has a property P *essentially* if and only if x has P and the statement x *lacks* P is necessarily false,

adding, of course, that an object has a property accidentally if it has that property but does not have it essentially. On this account the property of being an American seems to be essential to the oldest American in Paris, in that the statement *The oldest American in Paris is not an American* seems necessarily

false. These philosophers then note a certain peculiar consequence of (1)—namely that a single object may appear to have
the same property both essentially and accidentally. The tallest
conqueror of Mount Everest, for example, has the property of
having conquered Mount Everest necessarily; the most famous
resident of Redlands, Washington, does not; and yet the first is
the very same person as the second. Which of an object's properties are essential and which accidental seems to depend upon
the way in which the object is referred to; consequently these
philosophers reject the distinction as incoherent.

But clearly enough (1) is not an adequate account of the
traditional distinction. It is not impossible or inconceivable, in
the requisite sense, that the tallest conqueror of Mount Everest
should have failed to reach the top; nor is being the husband of
Xantippe an essential property of the husband of Xantippe.
On the traditional doctrine, the necessary falsehood of *a lacks
P* (where "*a*" is standing in for any singular referring expression) does not entail that *a* has P essentially. Nor does the
contingency of *a lacks P* entail that P is not an essential property of *a*; if I am thinking of the number seven, then what I
am thinking of has the property of being prime essentially despite the contingency of *What I am thinking of is not prime*.
But perhaps a property P is an essential property of *Socrates*
just in case Socrates has P and the proposition *Socrates lacks
P* is necessarily false. Difficulties arise if we generalize to (1);
but the instantiation of (1) for Socrates may seem harmless
enough, as it will in any case where a proper name replaces
the variable "*x*" in (1). So suppose we adopt the following
definition:

(2) *x* has P necessarily if and only if *x* has P and the proposition *x lacks P* is necessarily false (where the domain
of the variable "*x*" is unlimited but the set of its substituends contains only proper names).

Socrates, then, has the property of being a person essentially if and only if Socrates is a person and the proposition *Socrates lacks the property of being a person* is necessarily false. But the same sort of difficulty seems to arise again. For consider Socrates' least significant property. No doubt we may suppose that it will not be essential to him. And yet

(A) Socrates lacks Socrates' least significant property

seems to be necessarily false: it seems to entail that there is a property Socrates both has and lacks. Or suppose I am thinking of the property of not being a prime number. Then the property I am thinking of is essential to Socrates, despite the apparent contingency of *Socrates lacks the property I am thinking of*.

This difficulty is an obvious analogue of the one besetting (1). There the difficulty arose because there were pairs of substituends for the variable "x" that denoted the same object but had differing logical properties. Here the difficulty arises because there are similar pairs of substituends for the variable "P." "Snub-nosedness" and "Socrates' least important property" are expressions denoting the same property (let us suppose); but "Socrates lacks Socrates' least important property," unlike "Socrates lacks snub-nosedness," expresses a necessary falsehood. The difficulty concerning the substituends for "x" was resolved by limiting the substituend set of "x" to proper names, thereby excluding definite descriptions. Can we do the same thing here? Unfortunately it is not apparent that "snub-nosedness" is a proper name of the property *snub-nosedness*, nor even that properties have proper names at all. Still, expressions like "whiteness," "masculinity," "mean temperedness," and the like, differ from expressions like "Socrates' least important property," "the property I'm thinking of," "the property mentioned on page 37," and so on, in pretty much the way that proper names of individuals differ from definite descriptions of them.

And so perhaps we can resolve the difficulty by rejecting (2) in favor of

(3) x has P necessarily if and only if x has P and the proposition x *lacks* P is necessarily false (where the domain of the variable "x" is unlimited but its substituend set contains only proper names, and where the domain of of the variable "P" is the set of properties and its substituend set contains no definite description or expressions definitionally equivalent to definite descriptions).

But what about individuals that have no proper names, and properties denoted only by definite descriptions? (3) offers us no way of telling with respect to such an individual and such a property, whether the individual has the property necessarily. Here we must recognize that the domains of the variables "x" and "P" are not really unlimited; they must contain only objects for which there are proper names, and properties denoted by expressions other than definite descriptions. But of course this limitation really comes to very little; for it is always open to us to *name* individuals and to furnish the appropriate sort of denoting expressions for properties.

Given the appropriate revision of (3), then, many of Socrates' properties will be clearly contingent and others clearly necessary. There are other properties—for example, *being a Greek, having been born, having a body*—that will be neither clearly contingent nor clearly necessary properties of Socrates; but this, I take it, is by no means fatal to the distinction. Thus (3) is perhaps satisfactory as far as it goes. And now we can ⁻tate the traditional distinction in such a way that the restrictions on the substituend sets of its variables may be dropped:

(4) P is an *essential property* of x if and only if x has P and there is a being y identical with x and a property P' iden-

tical with P such that y has P' necessarily (in the sense of (3)).[34]

According to Augustine and much of the theistic tradition, then, all (or almost all)[35] of God's nonrelational properties— omnipotence, omniscience, benevolence and the like—are essential to him. And conceivably Findlay is right in holding that this or something very like it is a requirement of the attitude of worship. But what have "modern views of necessity" to do with it? Many contemporary philosophers reject the distinction between essential and accidental properties (partly, perhaps, because they fail to understand it), but others accept it. There is no "view of necessity" accepted by all who "share a contemporary outlook" that precludes the existence of a being having the properties in question essentially.

Findlay is mistaken, then, in supposing that "modern views of necessity" make it absurd to suppose that there is a being that possesses some of its qualities essentially. (The fact is, it seems to me, that *every* being has some essential properties.) But what about the other requirement of the religious attitude —the requirement, namely, that its object exist in some necessary manner? Is the theist really obliged, as Findlay suggests, to hold that the proposition *God exists* is logically necessary? Must he hold that God is a *logically* necessary being? No doubt it is part of theism to describe God as noncontingent and neces-

---

[34] Here I am indebted for a correction to Nicholas Wolterstorff.

[35] On this characterization of Augustine's view *existence* would be an essential property of God, since it is one of His nonrelational qualities. Augustine does not clearly accept the view that the proposition *God does not exist* is logically false, and perhaps it would be best not to saddle him with it. This can easily be accomplished, either by modifying (3) slightly or by appropriately reducing the claim that *all* of God's nonrelational properties are essential to Him.

sary; but must the necessity be *logical* necessity? How are we to understand the claim that God is a necessary being?

Suppose someone, struck by the fact that his desk might not have existed, asks, "Why is it that this desk exists?" Perhaps there are several sorts of reply we could give him. One answer might be that the desk exists because a certain carpenter made it. But suppose our questioner is still puzzled; the carpenter, he says, also might not have existed, so why did *he* exist? We could answer again by referring to some other beings or states of affairs which were causally sufficient for the existence of the carpenter; but of course, the same question will arise about these beings, and about the causes of these beings, and so on indefinitely. No matter how far back we push this series of questions and answers, our questioner may remain dissatisfied. It may appear to us that he is looking for a *final* answer, one which puts an end to the indefinitely long series of questions and answers where the answer to each question mentions a being or state of affairs about which precisely the same question again may be asked. In seeking a *final* answer, he is seeking a statement which puts an end to this series of questions and answers and allows no further question of the same sort. So perhaps a necessary being may be characterized as (a) a being such that some statement referring to it can properly serve as a final answer in this sort of question and answer series, an answer which puts an end to the series. But a final answer in the series would refer to a being of an unusual sort; such a being must be one about which the question "Why does it exist?" *does not arise* or cannot sensibly be asked. A necessary being, therefore, may be further characterized as (b) a being about which one cannot sensibly ask why it exists. When the theist, therefore, asserts that God is the necessary being, we may construe his remark in the following way. He is pointing

out that we cannot sensibly ask, "Why is it that God exists?"
And he is holding that some assertion about God is the final
answer in the series of questions and answers we have been
considering.

Next, we should note that the question "Why does God
exist?" never does, in fact, arise. Those who do not believe
that God exists will not, of course, ask *why* He exists. But
neither do believers ask that question. Outside of theism, so
to speak, the question is nonsensical, and inside of theism, the
question is never asked. But it is not that the religious person
fails to ask why God exists through inadvertence or because
of lack of interest. If a believer were asked why God exists, he
might take it as a request for his reasons for believing in God;
but if it is agreed that God exists, then it is less than sensible
to ask why He does. And the explanation is not hard to find.
Essential to theism is an assertion to the effect that there is
a connection between God and all other (logically contingent)
beings, a connection in virtue of which these others are causally
dependent upon God. It is part of the Hebraic-Christian conception of God that He is "Maker of heaven and earth." But
it is also a necessary truth that God is uncreated and in no way
causally dependent upon anything else.

And so it is clear that it is absurd to ask why God exists. To
ask that question is to presuppose that God does exist; but it
is a necessary truth that if He does, He has no cause; hence
there is no answer to a question asking for His causal conditions. The question "Why does God exist?" (so construed) is
therefore an absurdity. A person who seriously asks it betrays
misapprehension of the concept of God.

Let us suppose, then, that God is a necessary being in the
sense characterized above.[36] Does not such necessity satisfy the

---

[36] For a fuller (and somewhat confused) discussion of divine necessity,

requirements of the attitude of worship? It has seemed so to many worshipers; most have not thought that God must be a logically necessary being in order to be worthy of our worship. And Findlay has given us not the slightest reason to think them mistaken.

These atheological arguments are as unsuccessful as the arguments from natural theology we considered in Part I; natural atheology seems no better than natural theology as an answer to the question "Are religious beliefs rationally justified?" In Part III I shall try a different approach to this question.

---

see my "Necessary Being," in *Faith and Philosophy*, ed. A. Plantinga (Grand Rapids, 1963), pp. 97–108.

Part III

GOD AND OTHER MINDS

Eight

Other Minds and Analogy

IN Parts I and II we examined two traditional answers to the question with which this study began: Is it rational to believe in the existence of God? And since neither natural theology nor natural atheology seems to provide a successful answer to this question, we have made little enough progress. But how, exactly, does this question arise? Presumably as follows. If a man believes that the star Sirius has a planetary system containing a planet with mountains over 40,000 feet tall, then if his belief is to be rational or reasonable he must have some reason or evidence for it. Similarly, it may be said, with the existence of God: the theist must be able to answer the question "How do you know or why do you believe?" if his belief is to be rational; or at any rate there must *be* a good answer to this question. He needs evidence of some sort or other; he needs some reason for believing.

Obviously this raises many questions. What is evidence? What relation holds between a person and a proposition when the person has evidence for the proposition? Must a rational person have evidence or reasons for all of his beliefs? Presumably not. But then what properties must a belief have for a person to be justified in accepting it *without* evidence? Is a person justified in believing a proposition only if it can be inferred inductively or deductively from (roughly) incorrigible[1] sensory beliefs? Or propositions that are obvious to common sense and accepted by everyone?

These are obviously some of the most difficult and persistent problems of epistemology. A direct assault on them would be bold indeed, not to say foolhardy. What I propose is to examine the problem before us by exploring its connections with an analogous problem—the so-called problem of other minds. Perhaps this problem may be put as follows: each of us believes that he is not alone in the universe—that there are other beings who think and reason, hold beliefs, have sensations and feelings. And while a person can observe another's behavior and circumstances, he cannot perceive another's mental states. "The thoughts and passions of the mind are invisible" says Thomas Reid.[2] "Intangible, odorless, and inaudible," we might add; and they cannot be tasted either. Hence we cannot come to know that another is in pain in the way in which we can learn that he has red hair; unlike his hair, his pain cannot be perceived. And, on the other hand, although some propositions ascribing pain to a person are incorrigible for *him*, no such proposition is incorrigible for anyone else. We cannot observe the thoughts and feelings of another; so we cannot *determine by observation* that another is in pain. How then do we ever know that another is in pain? What is our evidence?

But can we not sometimes *see that* a man is in pain? Can we

---

[1] Proposition *p* is incorrigible for S if and only if S *believes p* entails *p* and S *believes not-p* entails *not-p*.

[2] Reid, *Works* (Edinburgh, 1858) p. 450.

not sometimes see that someone is thinking, depressed, or exuberant? And if *anything* would be "determining by observation" that another is in pain, surely *seeing* that he is would be. So where is the problem? It must be conceded that in a perfectly ordinary use of "see that" one may properly claim to see that someone else is in pain. In the same or a similar use, one can see that a child has measles, that a pipe will give a sweet smoke, and that electrons of a certain sort are sporting in the cloud chamber. One can even see (if one reads the newspapers) that John Buchanan of the House Un-American Activities Committee referred (no doubt mistakenly) to the Imperial Wizard of the Ku Klux Klan as the "Inferior Lizard." In a similar use of the term the theist, impressed by the harmony and beauty of the universe or the profundity of the Scriptures, may justifiably (even if mistakenly) claim to see that God exists.

And so of course our use of "determine by observation" will have to be a technical use. How is it to be explained? Perhaps we cannot explain it fully; perhaps we must give examples and hope for the best. One can determine by observation that Johnny's face is flushed and covered with red spots; one cannot determine by observation that his blood contains measle germs. One can determine by observation that today's newspaper contains the sentence "Mr. Buchanan referred to the Imperial Wizard as the 'Inferior Lizard' "; but if one is not present at the hearings one cannot determine by observation that Mr. Buchanan thus misspoke himself. Furthermore, in the technical (but not the ordinary) use of the term sentences of the form "S determines by observation that S' is in pain only if S is the same person as S'" expresses a necessary truth; similarly for "S determines by observation that a bodily area contains a pain only if he feels a pain in that area."

Now suppose we use "determines$_1$" for the narrower technical sense, and "determines$_2$" for the broader sense in which one determines by observation (by seeing) that someone else is in pain. Then a man can determine$_2$ that Mr. Buchanan referred to the Wizard as a Lizard only if he determines$_1$ the truth of some *other* proposition, and knows or believes a proposition connecting it with Mr. Buchanan's thus referring to the Wizard. Furthermore, the theist can see that (i.e., determine$_2$ that) God created the world only if in addition to determining$_1$ that the world is beautiful and orderly he knows some proposition connecting the existence of a beautiful and orderly world with the existence of God. In the same way I can determine$_2$ that Jones is in pain only if I know or believe some proposition connecting what I determine$_1$ with his being in pain; and the problem is: do I know any such proposition? If so, *how?* What is my reason or evidence for supposing it true?

So there is an initial symmetry here. Some of the very bad poetry read at Kiwanis club travelogues calls our attention to the beauty and majesty of the mountains and concludes that one can simply see that the world was created by God. Here it is appropriate to ask what the connection is between God and the mountains, and how one knows that if the latter are beautiful and majestic, they were created by the former. But similarly for the suggestion that one simply sees that someone is in pain (in seeing that his behavior and circumstances are such and such); we must ask what the connection is between pain-behavior[3] and pain, and how one knows that the former is usually accompanied by the latter.

How *do* we know these things? Baron von Hügel suggested that we know the mind of another (on at least some occasions) directly, in the same way we know our own minds. He appar-

---

[3] Where the term "pain-behavior" is simply a label for a recognizable pattern of behavior (and is not short for any such description as "behavior accompanied by pain").

ently believed that just as a man has "direct access" to his own mind, so he may on some occasions have direct access to someone else's. It is not easy to understand the suggestion, but presumably it comes to supposing that some propositions ascribing mental states to others are incorrigible for me—and this seems to be just false.

Another answer I shall merely salute and dismiss is that of the behaviorist, who claims that every mental-state-ascribing proposition is logically equivalent to some proposition about behavior and circumstances. There is an initial difficulty here: how are we to take the term "about"? Is any proposition whose subject is Jones's behavior (or which is equivalent to such a proposition) *about* Jones's behavior? If so, there is absolutely no doubt that propositions about Jones's behavior entail propositions ascribing mental states to him: consider, for example, *Jones's irritating behavior is caused by a persistent backache.* If we take "about" in this way then logical behaviorism becomes a truism. But if we cannot take it in this very broad sense, how is it to be narrowed? Several possibilities present themselves but none seems very satisfactory.

Nonetheless I suppose we really do have an idea of what the intended sense of "about" is, even if we cannot say just what it is. But in that sense of the term, no one has produced even one example of a mental-state-ascribing proposition that is equivalent to some behavior-*cum*-circumstances proposition; nor has anyone suggested even the ghost of a reason for supposing that there are such examples. Hence in what follows I take it for granted that behaviorism is false.

Historically, perhaps the most important answer to the question of other minds is the analogical position.[4] According to

---

[4] The analogical argument for other minds was suggested by Descartes (*Discourse on Method*, Pt. V) and Locke (*Essay Concerning Human Understanding*, Bk. IV, ch. iii, par. 27). It was explicitly stated by Hume

this position one cannot determine by observation that some-one else is in some mental state or other; neither are proposi-tions ascribing mental states to others incorrigible for anyone. Nevertheless, it holds, each of us has or can easily acquire evi-dence for such beliefs. Each of us can construct a sound in-ductive argument for the conclusion that he is not the only being that thinks and reasons, has sensations and feelings— an argument whose premises state certain facts about his own mental life and about physical objects (including human bodies), but do not entail the existence of minds or mental states that are not his own. In this chapter and the next I shall argue that the analogical position is as good an answer as we have to the question "do we know and how do we know the thoughts and feelings of another?" [5]

The analogical position has come under heavy and sustained attack during the last few years. The most powerful of these attacks are associated with the work of Wittgenstein, as are the most viable contemporary alternatives to the analogical posi-tion. In what follows I shall argue that these objections and alternatives are (so far as they are intelligible) unsound. Since Wittgenstein's writings present substantial problems of inter-pretation, however, I shall consider the objections and alterna-

(*Treatise of Human Nature*, Bk. I, Pt. III, sec. xvi) and by J. S. Mill (*An Examination of Sir William Hamilton's Philosophy* [London, 1889], pp. 243–244). More recently it has been tentatively endorsed by C. I. Lewis (*An Analysis of Knowledge and Valuation* [La Salle, Ill., 1946], p. 143). It has been restated and reaffirmed by A. J. Ayer (*The Problem of Knowledge* [London, 1956], pp. 214–221); by C. D. Broad (*Mind and Its Place in Nature* [London, 1925], pp. 335–347); by Stuart Hampshire ("Analogy of Feeling," *Mind*, LXI [1952], 1–12); by H. H. Price ("Our Evidence for Other Minds," *Philosophy*, XIII [1938], 425–436); by Bertrand Russell (*Human Knowledge: Its Scope and Limits* [New York, 1948], pp. 483–486); and by Walter Stace (*The Theory of Knowledge and Existence* [Oxford, 1932], pp. 186–192).

[5] John Wisdom, *Other Minds* (London, 1956), p. 192.

tives as they appear in the writings of philosophers who have tried to clarify and explain them.

I

First, an objection having to do with the learning of words for mental processes and the acquiring of the concepts of these processes. Norman Malcolm believes that according to the analogical position one can learn what pain is only "from his own case" (i.e., by having pain),[6] but this, he thinks, is a mistake:

If I were to learn what pain is from perceiving my own pain then I should, necessarily, have learned that pain is something that exists only when *I* feel pain. For the pain that serves as my paradigm of pain (i.e., my own) has the property of existing only when I feel it. That property is essential, not accidental; it is nonsense to suppose that the pain I feel could exist when I did not feel it. So if I obtain my *conception* of pain from pain that I experience, then it will be part of my conception of pain that *I* am the only being that can experience it. For me it will be a *contradiction* to speak of *another's* pain.[7]

---

[6] "Knowledge of Other Minds" (KOM), *Journal of Philosophy* (1958). Reprinted in *The Philosophy of Mind*, ed. V. C. Chappell (Englewood Cliffs, 1962), pp. 151–160. Page references will be to this volume.

[7] "Wittgenstein's *Philosophical Investigation*" (WPI), *Philosophical Review*, 1954. Reprinted in Chappell, *op. cit.*, pp. 81–101. Page references are to this volume. This argument is really directed against the possibility of a private language; but Malcolm holds that the idea of a private language is intimately tied to the idea that one can learn what pain is from his own case (i.e., by experiencing pain); indeed, he believes that the latter is a "typical expression of the idea of a private language" (WPI, p. 75). He also holds that "the fundamental error of the argument from analogy" is "the mistaken assumption that *one learns from one's own case* what thinking, feeling, sensation are" (KOM, p. 156; Malcolm's italics). In *Knowledge and Certainty* (Englewood Cliffs, 1963), p. 105, Malcolm rejects this argument on the grounds that it incorrectly presupposes that the distinction between qualitative and numerical identity holds for pains. It is not clear to me, however, what giving up this distinction in the case

Taken as an objection to the analogical position, this argument seems to be an *ignoratio*. For what the analogical position entails is not that one could learn what pain is "from his own case" but only that a person could (logically) know what pain was even if he were the only sentient creature with a human body. Hence it is not even clear that the analogical position entails that a person must *learn* what pain is; there is no contradiction in the proposition that Jones knows what pain is but never learned what it was, either because he has known what it was all his life, or because he acquired the concept all right, but not by *learning*.[8] Strictly speaking, the analogical position need say nothing at all about the conditions under which a person can or must learn what pain is.

One who merely sidestepped an argument as intriguing as this one, however, would be churlish indeed. And perhaps it could be maintained that even if the analogical position is consistent with the proposition that one cannot learn what pain is from his own case, it would be a good deal less attractive if that proposition were true. Malcolm's argument clearly requires, as an added premise, something like the following principle:

(P₁) If I get my conception of C by experiencing objects and all the objects from which I get my conception have a property P necessarily, then my conception of C is such that the proposition *Whatever is an instance of C has P* is necessarily true.

---

of pains comes to, nor how, exactly, giving it up affects the argument; what follows seems to me, in any case, to be a stronger reason for mistrusting the argument, in that it does not depend upon giving up that distinction.

[8] "It is logically possible that someone should have been born with a knowledge of the use of an expression or that it should have been produced in him by a drug; that his knowledge came to him by the way of the normal process of teaching is not necessary" (Malcolm, WPI, p. 86).

Is (P_1) true? To find out, we must know what it is for an object to have a property necessarily. What Malcolm says suggests

(D_1) x has P necessarily if and only if x has P and the proposition x *does not have* P is necessarily false.

And the suggestion is that if I get my conception of pain by experiencing pain, then each of my paradigms (i.e., the pains from which I get the conception) has the property of *existing only when I feel it* necessarily, in the sense explained above. Nevertheless, there are peculiarities involved here. One is the fact that an object x may have a property P necessarily while y which is identical with x, does not.[9] The first American to reach the summit of Mount Everest, for example, has the properties of being an American and being a conqueror of Mount Everest *necessarily*; Jim Whittaker has these properties contingently. And this fact is fatal to (D_1). For given (D_1) it will not be true that each of my paradigms of pain has the property of *existing only when I feel it* necessarily. For suppose that the headache I am thinking of is one of my paradigms of pain: since *The headache I am presently thinking of exists when I do not feel it* is a contingent proposition, the headache I am presently thinking of does not have the property of *existing only when I feel it* necessarily. It is of course *identical with* something that has the property in question necessarily; but under (D_1) the headache I am presently thinking of has it contingently. Hence it is false that all of my paradigms of pain have that property necessarily.

Taking our cue from that fact, we might try to rectify matters by embracing (D_2):

(D_2) x has P necessarily if and only if there is something

---

[9] See above, pp. 175–180.

y such that (1) *x* is identical with *y* and (2) *y* has P
necessarily in the sense of (D₁).

No heir to the ills of (D₁), (D₂) has its own troubles. For if
ostensive definition is possible at all, (P₁), given (D₂), will be
false. Suppose Alexander the Great acquires his conception of
redness from some toys all of which were given him by his
father Philip. Then each of his paradigms of redness has the
property of being a gift from Philip. And each of them is identical with something that has that property necessarily in the
sense of (D₁): his red toy horse, for example, is identical with
the toy horse given him by Philip. Hence all of his paradigms
of red have the property of being gifts from Philip necessarily
in the sense of (D₂). But then, by (P₁), Alexander's conception of red must be such that *All red things are gifts of Philip*
is necessarily true; hence (D₂) will not do either.

Given (D₁), (P₁) is equivalent to

(P₂) If every one of the objects from which I get my conception of C is such that every description of it entails
that it has P, then my conception of C will be such
that the proposition *Whatever is an instance of C has
P* is logically necessary.[10]

And given (D₂), (P₁) is equivalent to

(P₃) If, for every one of the objects from which I get my
conception of C, there is a description of it entailing
that it has P, then my conception of C is such that the
proposition *Whatever is an instance of C has P* is necessarily true.

---

[10] Where a *description* is any name or definite description of an object
and where a description D of an object entails that the object has a property P just in case it is necessarily true that anything to which D applies
has P.

And of course both (P_2) and (P_3) turned out unsatisfactory. Following their lead, however, we might think (P_4) more promising:

> (P_4) If every one of the objects from which I get my conception of C is such that every description of it entailing that it is one of my paradigms of C also entails that it has P, then my conception of C is such that the proposition *Whatever is an instance of C has P* is necessarily true.

Perhaps (P_4) entails that no one can learn what pain is from his own case; for any description of a pain entailing that it is one of my paradigms also entails, it might be said, that it has the property of existing only when I feel it. (P_4), however, is really a wholesale assault upon ostensive definition generally; it has no special bearing upon learning what pain is from one's own case. For no matter what concept C is, any description of a thing *x* entailing that *x* is one of my paradigms of C also entails that I have *perceived or experienced x*; hence (P_4) entails that any concept I get by experiencing objects applies (necessarily) only to objects I have perceived or experienced.[11]

But perhaps Malcolm has the following in mind. Sometimes an object might not have had a property it in fact has, although the proposition that it lacks that property is necessarily false. The man standing on the corner might not have been on the corner, and that despite the necessary falsity of *The man standing on the corner is not on the corner.* Your yacht might have been shorter than it is, again despite the necessary falsity of *Your yacht is shorter than it is.* This is the distinction between essential and accidental properties I developed in Chapter Seven; and while it may leave some questions, there are many cases in which it clearly applies. So consider

---

[11] I owe this point to Robert C. Sleigh, Jr.

(D₄) x has P necessarily if and only if x has P and it is false that x might not have had P.

The suggestion, of course, is that if I learned what pain is from my own case, then each of my paradigms of pain has the property of *existing only when I feel it* necessarily.

I said that in some cases there is no difficulty in determining whether a given object has a certain property necessarily in the sense of (D₄). Unfortunately, this is not one of those cases. Wittgenstein suggests the possibility that I feel a pain in your arm; if you feel a pain there too, and feel one of the same duration, intensity, and so on as the one I feel, then perhaps you and I are feeling the very same pain. Suppose, then, that this is possible and that both of us have a pain—the very same pain—in your left arm. Presumably that pain might have existed even if you had not felt it (provided I had); and it certainly might have existed even if I had not felt it. So is it true that my pains necessarily exist only when I feel them? That question apparently turns on whether it is possible for two persons to have the very same pain. Perhaps that is possible; it is at any rate not clearly impossible. And hence it is by no means clear that (P₁) and (D₄) entail that one could not learn what pain is from his own case.

And in any event (P₁), given (D₄), appears to be too strong. For consider sneezes. Presumably one can learn what sneezes (along with coughs and, perhaps, grunts) are by ostensive definition, by perceiving them. Yet it is false, I take it, that some of my sneezes might have been sneezed by someone other than myself. Any sneeze of mine has the property of being one of my sneezes *necessarily*. Now suppose Alexander the Great learns what sneezes are by perceiving his own and his father's sneezes —that is, suppose that all of his paradigms of sneezing are sneezed either by himself or by Philip. By (P₅), Alexander's conception of sneezing would be such that the proposition

Other Minds and Analogy

All sneezes are sneezed by Alexander or Philip is necessarily true. If (P_5) is true, therefore, Alexander cannot learn what sneezes are by perceiving his own and his father's sneezes— but surely he can.

This intriguing suggestion, therefore, turns out to be unsuccessful as an objection to the analogical position.

II

Next, a more nebulous objection, more often encountered in the oral tradition than in the published writings of Wittgenstein's followers. According to this objection, "The idea of a private language is presupposed by every program of inferring or constructing the 'external world' and 'other minds.' " [12] And, of course, private languages are allegedly logically impossible. Now the issues surrounding the question of the possibility of a logically private language are complex and difficult, and the arguments by which Wittgenstein and his followers purport to show its impossibility are not easy to follow.[13] I shall here examine the other premise of the objection—the claim that the analogical position entails or presupposes the possibility of such a private language.

But first we must try to get a reasonably clear idea of what it is that is supposedly entailed by the analogical position. How are we to understand the claim that a given language is a *private* language? "By a 'private language' is meant one that not merely is not but *cannot* be understood by anyone other than the speaker." [14] So a language is a private language if and

---

[12] Malcolm, WPI, p. 75.

[13] Cf. Hector Castañeda, "The Private Language Argument," in *Knowledge and Experience*, ed. C. D. Rollins. See also the comments on Castañeda's paper and Castañeda's reply, all in the same volume; and see Judith Jarvis Thomson, "Private Languages," in *American Philosophical Quarterly*, I, 20–32.

[14] *Ibid.*, p. 74.

only if someone speaks and understands it, and only one person *can* understand it. The word "can" here, presumably, does not mean the same as in "I cannot read Arabic"; it signifies, presumably, logical or conceptual necessity. We might, therefore, be inclined to define a private language as follows:

(a) L is a private language if and only if (1) (some of) the terms in L are understood by only one person and (2) the proposition *More than one person understands all of the terms in L* is necessarily false.

But of course this characterization will be defective in the same way as D_1 (above, page 195): suppose Friday's tribe is annihilated by a natural disaster while he is visiting Robinson Crusoe; suppose Friday alone now speaks and understands the language of his tribe. We might define "Fritish" as "the language Friday alone speaks"; and Fritish would then be a private language in the sense of (a). But surely no one means to deny that a language like Fritish is possible. It is *not* impossible, in the requisite sense, that more than one person understand the language which Friday alone understands, just as it is not impossible that more than one person drive the automobile that I alone drive. (It is, of course, impossible that there be an automobile which I alone drive and which is driven by more than one person.) Friday alone understands Fritish; but someone else—indeed, any number of persons—*might have* understood it. So I shall characterize a private language as one such that (1) only one person understands it, and (2) it is false that someone else might have understood it. And it is a private language in this sense the possibility of which, according to the claim under discussion, is entailed by the analogical position.

But why should anyone think that the analogical position *does* entail the possibility of such a private language? "By a 'private' language is meant one that not merely is not but *can-*

not be understood by anyone other than the speaker. The reason for this is that the words of this language are supposed to 'refer to what can only be known to the person speaking; to his immediate private sensations.' " [15] Now part of what is suggested here, I take it, is that

(b) If some of the words of a language referred to what can only be known to its speaker, that language would be a private language.

I think Malcolm (and perhaps Wittgenstein too) means to endorse (b). But the passage also suggests for consideration the proposition

(c) A person's immediate sensations can be known only to him.

While it is not altogether clear what is meant by the suggestion that a man's sensations are *known* to him, and can be known *only* to him, if a man's pains can be known only to him then presumably he alone can know that he is in pain. And certainly neither Malcolm nor Wittgenstein means to endorse (c). But neither, of course, is it any part of the analogical position to assert that a man's sensations can be known only to him; the whole point of the position is the claim that a man can know that someone else is in pain, for instance, *via* the analogical argument. So (2) surely cannot be used in an attempt to show that one who accepts the analogical position is committed to the possibility of a private language, unless it can be demonstrated that (2) follows from propositions explicitly acknowledged as part of that position.

Here it might be maintained that

(d) A man's immediate sensations are *private*

---

[15] WPI, p. 74. The passage Malcolm quotes is from the *Philosophical Investigations* (New York, 1953), par. 243.

is part of the analogical position; and from (d) alone or together with some other proposition characteristic of the analogical position it follows that a man's immediate sensations can be known only to him.[16] But what does it mean to say that sensations are private? A recurring suggestion is that although it is possible for two persons to share a sensation in the sense of having *similar* sensations, it is logically impossible that two persons have *numerically the same* sensation.[17] You could discover that your pain is identical with mine, is the identical pain, just as your wife might discover that her dress is identical with my wife's. But just as in the latter case there are two dresses, so in the former there are two pains—yours and mine. We might therefore define "privacy" as follows: Sensations are private just in case it is logically impossible that two persons have numerically the same sensation.

What Wittgenstein says in the *Investigations* (par. 253) might suggest that sensations are *not* private, that you and I could feel the same pain, numerically the same pain. Whether this is or is not a possibility is not easy to tell. But why suppose that the analogical position is committed to the privacy of sensations? Why can't one who accepts the analogical argument simply let the chips fall where they may with respect to that question? Why need he take a position at all? It might be thought that if sensations were not private, the analogical argument would be superfluous and unnecessary. If you and I can feel the same pain, have the same pain, presumably I would not need the analogical argument to establish

---

[16] "It is a convention that any feeling one has is an experience which is private to oneself. And so it becomes a necessary truth that one person cannot have, and therefore cannot strictly know, the experiences of another" (A. J. Ayer, "One's Knowledge of Other Minds," in *Philosophical Essays* [London, 1954], p. 195).

[17] See, for instance, Ayer, *Foundations of Empirical Knowledge* (London, 1940), pp. 137–139.

the fact that you are in pain. But of course this would be a mistake. For from the fact that I am feeling a pain which you also feel (and which is hence *your* pain) it does not follow that I know or believe that you are in pain. I should need the analogical argument, or something like it, presumably, as evidence for the belief that the pain which I feel is also felt by *you*. Whether or not pains are private, in the above sense, is quite irrelevant to the analogical position. And hence the fact (if it is a fact) that *Pains are private* entails that a man's pains are known only to him, shows that the analogical position entails the possibility of a private language only if *Pains are private* is necessarily true and hence trivially entailed by the analogical position—in which case every proposition would entail the possibility of a private language.

The analogical position does, of course, entail that a man has *privileged* or *direct access* to some of his own sensations but not to the sensations of anyone else. So on the analogical position a man's sensations are private to him in the sense that he alone has privileged access to them; someone might argue, therefore, that if a man's sensations are private to him in this sense then they are known only to him. Now what does the analogical arguer mean to assert when he claims that a man has privileged access to his own sensations and only to them? Perhaps we may define this notion as follows: a person S has privileged access to a mental state M of a person S' just in case S *believes S' has* (or *is in*) M entails S' *has* (or *is in*) M. It is then clear that a person does have privileged access to at least some of his own sensations. A man cannot mistakenly believe, for example, that he is in pain. But if so, then it is necessarily true that any man who believes that he is in pain, is in pain. It is equally obvious, however, that no one has direct access to the mental states of another.

One who accepts the analogical position, therefore, may wish to say that a man's knowledge of his own sensations is *better founded* or *more certain* than his knowledge of someone else's; he might be inclined to accept the principle that if S_1 and S_2 have knowledge of S_3's mental states, and S_1 but not S_2 has direct access to S_3's mental states, then S_1's knowledge is better founded than is S_2's.[18] He might say correspondingly that one knows his own sensations in a different way from the way in which he knows someone else's. He might therefore hold both that his knowledge of his own mental states was more certain than his knowledge of another's, and that he knows his own sensations in a different way from the way in which he knows the mental states of another, and he might hold that these things follow from the fact that he has direct access only to his own mental states. But it certainly does not follow that no one can know the mental states of another.

In characterizing the idea of a private language, Malcolm suggests that "at bottom it is the idea that there is only a contingent and not an *essential* connection between a sensation and its outward expression." [19] Now of course it *is* part of the analogical position to hold that the connection between a sensation and its outward expression is logically contingent. No proposition about[20] a man's behavior, on that view, entails or is entailed by any proposition ascribing a sensation to him. Relative to any proposition about Jones's behavior, the proposition *Jones is in pain* and its denial are both logically possible. But how does it follow from this that a private language is possible? Surely an argument is needed here. And in fact Malcolm suggests that if the connection between pain and behavior is merely contingent, then a man's sensations can be known

---

[18] Or he might say (see n. 16, above) that S *strictly knows* S_1's sensations only if S has privileged access to them.

[19] WPI, p. 75

[20] Bear in mind my earlier *caveat* about "about."

only to him: "For the behavior that is, for me, contingently associated with 'the sensation of pain' may be for you, contingently associated with 'the sensation of tickling'; the piece of matter that produces in you what you call 'a metallic taste' may produce in me what, if you could experience it, you would call 'the taste of onions'; my 'sensation of red' may be your 'sensation of blue'; we do not know and cannot know whether we are talking about the same things." [21] If a man's sensations are known only to him and one can, as the analogical arguer avers, talk about his sensations, then a private language is possible. So if pain and behavior are contingently connected, a private language would be possible.

But of course this argument does not come to much as an objection to the analogical position. The latter holds both that pain and behavior are contingently connected and that, *via* the analogical argument, one person can know that another is in pain. An argument, therefore, that employs as a premise the proposition that if the connection between pain and behavior is contingent, no one could know that another was in pain, cannot be taken seriously as an objection to the analogical position. What would be required here is some argument for that premise. And of course such an argument would be quite independent of the whole private language controversy; its conclusion would entail that the analogical position is false regardless of the outcome of the controversy.

This argument, then, like the preceding one, must be deemed inconclusive. It seems to give us no reason at all for rejecting the analogical position.

III

P. F. Strawson develops an interesting objection to what he calls "the Cartesian analysis of a person"—an objection that

---

[21] WPI, p. 96

would, if sound, refute the analogical position.[22] The Cartesian analysis, as depicted by Strawson, represents a person as the union of two things—a body and mind. These two things are of different logical types: no property significantly predicable of one is significantly predicable of the other. What Strawson is rejecting, then, is the view that a person is really a composite of two substances such that to one of them mental predicates alone are ascribable while to the other only physical or bodily properties can be ascribed. Why does Strawson reject this view? His reasoning begins with the claim that "it is a necessary condition of ascribing states of consciousness, experiences, to oneself, in the way one does, that one should also ascribe them, or be prepared to ascribe them, to others who are not oneself." [23] Secondly, a necessary condition of the ability to ascribe states of consciousness to others is the ability to identify, "referringly think about," those things other than oneself to which states of consciousness are to be ascribed. And thirdly, "if the things one ascribes states of consciousness to, in ascribing them to others, are thought of as a set of Cartesian egos to which only private experiences can, in correct logical grammar, be ascribed . . . then there is no question of telling that a private experience is another's." [24] The point here is that unless I have a way of distinguishing one particular of a given type from other particulars of that type, I am unable to ascribe any attribute to any member of that type. But if the particulars in question are "inaccessible" to me (in just the fashion that, on the Cartesian and analogical view, other selves are inaccessible) and if the attributes to be ascribed are likewise inaccessible in that same way, I have no way of distinguishing, in thought, one particular of that type from others of the same type. And if I

---

[22] *Individuals: An Essay in Descriptive Metaphysics* (London, 1959).
[23] *Ibid.*, p. 99.
[24] *Ibid.*, p. 100.

am unable to identify other subjects of experience, I am unable to predicate states of consciousness of others; hence I am unable to predicate them of myself. This position, therefore, entails that no one is able to predicate states of consciousness of anything whatever.

The Cartesian is likely to reply that the argument is an *ignoratio*. For he does not, of course, assert that only "private experiences can, in correct logical grammar" be predicated of selves or mental substances. After all, Descartes held that there is a large class of selves such that to each of the members of this class a causal relationship to a physical body can correctly be ascribed; and according to the analogical position each of us can discover that many states of consciousness are accompanied by distinctive behavioral states. Further, the Cartesian might continue, one could identify another subject of experience as "the subject of experience which stands to *that* body in the same relation that the subject of my experiences stands to *this* body." Bodies other than my own are certainly not inaccessible to me in the way in which another's states of consciousness are. Strawson takes account of this objection to his argument in the following words:

But this suggestion is useless. It requires me to have noted that my experiences stand in a special relation to body M, when it is just the right to speak of *my* experience that is in question. That is to say, it requires me to have noted that *my* experiences stand in a special relation to body M; but it requires me to have noted this as a condition of being able to identify other subjects of experiences, i.e., as a condition of my having the idea of myself as a subject of experience, i.e., as a condition of thinking of any experience as *mine*.[25]

Now if this were correct, the analogical position would be futile. But exactly why is the "right to speak of my experience"

---

[25] *Ibid.*, p. 101.

in question for the Cartesian? To find out, we shall have to formulate the argument against the Cartesian more precisely.

The first premise is explained in a long footnote.[26] As stated in the text and explained in that footnote it is susceptible of several interpretations. I shall suggest an interpretation which seems to me likely both because Strawson's words suggest that he would accept it and because the premise so interpreted is fairly plausible in its own right; I shall not argue that my interpretation is in fact Strawson's meaning. Since the premise is a specification of a *general* principle governing predication, I shall state it without specific reference to mental substances and states of consciousness:

(1) A necessary condition of a person N's ascribing a predicate P to an individual a is that N have a conception of the appropriate occasions for ascribing P to individuals other than a.

(2) N's being able to identify individuals other than a is a necessary condition of N's having a conception of the appropriate occasions for ascribing P to individuals other than a.

The crucial word here is "identify." Strawson states the following general requirement for identification:

(3) "N can identify a particular only if N knows some individuating fact about that particular." [27]

We are now in a position to try to understand why Strawson believes that the Cartesian cannot identify other subjects of experience by means of some such locution as "the subject of experience that stands in the same relation to that body as the

[26] *Ibid.*, p. 99.
[27] *Ibid.*, pp. 23, 181–183.

subject of my experiences stands to this body." One is immediately struck by the thought that perhaps Strawson is here using "necessary condition" in such a fashion that "*N*'s doing *a* is a necessary condition of *N*'s doing *b*" entails that *N* must do *a before* he can do *b*. At any rate on this interpretation Strawson's argument against the Cartesian would be valid. For premises (1) and (2) interpreted in this way entail that one must be able to identify other subjects of experience *before* one can predicate experiences of himself—that is, before one can think of or refer to his own experiences at all. And one can identify, referringly think about, other subjects of experience in the way the analogical position suggests only if one *is already able* to predicate experiences of himself—that is, already able to recognize certain experiences as his own. But this is not, presumably, Strawson's meaning. For (1) and (2) state *general conditions* of predication. And under the present interpretation these conditions are logically incapable of fulfillment, not merely with respect to discourse in the Cartesian mode about other minds, but with respect to any predication of any property of any individual whatever. For under the interpretation in question, the above three principles come to the following: before I can predicate any property of any individual I must have a conception of the appropriate occasions for predicating that property of other individuals (1). Before I can have a conception of the appropriate occasions for predicating that property of other individuals I must be able to *identify* other individuals (2). And being able to identify an individual entails knowing some individuating fact about that individual (3). But if I know an individuating fact about an individual I am already able to predicate a property of that individual, the property, namely, which distinguishes it from other individuals. Hence before I am able to predicate any property

of any individual I must be able to predicate some property
of some individual; and it is accordingly logically impossible
for me to predicate any property of any individual.[28]

If this is correct, we do well to look for a different interpretation of Strawson's objection. And a natural suggestion is that
Strawson means, not that N's ability to identify other subjects
of experience must be temporally prior to his ability to predicate experiences of them, but only that at any time at which
N is able to predicate experiences of others, he must be able
to identify them. The crucial premises then turn out as follows:

> If N can predicate states of consciousness of himself at time
> *t*, N has, at *t*, a conception of the appropriate occasions for
> predicating states of consciousness of others.

> If N has a conception of the appropriate occasions for pred-
> icating states of consciousness of others, at *t*, N is able, at
> *t*, to identify other subjects of experience.

The discussion so far has centered about Strawson's claim
that one who held a Cartesian position could not make a certain suggestion about the identification of other subjects of experience—the suggestion that another subject of experience
could be identified as for example, "the subject of experience
that stands in the same causal relation to *that* body as the subject of my experiences stands to *this* one." But now the question becomes acute: why *can't* the Cartesian stick with this
suggestion? I should think he could comfortably agree to (1)
and (2) while maintaining the thesis about identification
Strawson denies him. With respect to (1), for example, he
might hold the following: if N can predicate mental states of
himself at time *t*, then, at *t*, N knows (or believes, thinks, etc.)
that for any mental state *M* he predicates of himself, if he were

---

[28] For a fuller statement of this argument, see my "Things and Persons,"
Review of Metaphysics, XIV (1961), 510.

to observe a correlation between a state *B* of his body and the presence of *M*, then any occasion on which he observes a body similar to his in state *B* is an appropriate occasion for predicating *M* of another subject of experience. And with respect to (2) he might claim to be able to identify the subject of experience in question in just the way Strawson prohibits. I quoted above (p. 207) the argument Strawson produces at this point; but under the present interpretation of "necessary condition" that argument turns out to be nothing more than a restatement of principles (1) and (2).

We might be tempted to object that if the Cartesian or analogical view were right *no one could ever know for sure* that there were subjects of experience connected with bodies other than his own. But that would be to change the subject altogether; Strawson has maintained not merely that on these views no one could know for sure that there were other subjects of experience (with that the Cartesian might possibly agree), but that no one could so much as predicate experiences, states of consciousness, either of others or of *himself*. And if I have interpreted his argument aright, it does not substantiate this claim. We seem to be left with the bare assertion that on the Cartesian or analogical view it is impossible to see how anyone could come by the concept of selfhood at all, or how anyone could form the idea of a subject of experience. These objections, then, are inconclusive.

Nine

Alternatives to the
Analogical Position

IN Chapter Eight, I began the comparison of our alleged knowledge of God with our alleged knowledge of other minds by arguing that the analogical position is the best answer any of us has to what I shall call the "epistemological question": "How do I know that there are other beings that think and feel, reason and believe?" By way of supporting this claim I considered and rejected several alternatives to the analogical position, as well as a set of Wittgensteinian objections to it. In this chapter I shall consider a pair of contentions that are at once objections to and alternatives to the analogical position.

I

A number of contemporary philosophers follow Wittgenstein in believing that the epistemological question is not to be answered by any tenuous analogical reasoning; its answer is to be found in the fact that "inward processes stand in need of outward criteria." In "Knowledge of Other Minds," for example, Norman Malcolm expresses his belief that the argument from analogy for other minds "still enjoys more credit than it deserves," quotes a statement of that argument by J. S. Mill, and then delivers the following counter:

> More interesting is the following point: suppose this reasoning could yield a conclusion of the sort "it is probable that that human figure (pointing at some person other than oneself) has thoughts and feelings." Then there is a question as to whether this conclusion can *mean* anything to the philosopher who draws it, because there is a question as to whether the sentence "That human figure has thoughts and feelings" can mean anything to him. Why should this be a question? Because the assumption from which Mill starts is that he has no criterion for determining whether another "walking and speaking figure" does or does not have thoughts and feelings. If he had a criterion he could apply it, establishing with certainty that this or that human figure does or does not have feelings (for the only plausible criterion would lie in behavior and circumstances that are open to view), and there would be no call to resort to tenuous analogical reasoning that yields at best a probability. If Mill has no criterion for the existence of feelings other than his own, then in that sense he does not understand the sentence "That human figure has feelings" and therefore does not understand the sentence "*It is probable* that that human figure has feelings." [1]

So the analogical argument is either superfluous or impossible: either we do not need it to answer Mill's question, or if we do need it we do not have a criterion for its conclusion and "in that sense" cannot understand it. But *is* there such a sense of "understand"? (One can, of course, *invent* such a sense for

---

[1] *Journal of Philosophy*, LX (1958), 969–78. Reprinted in *The Philosophy of Mind*, ed. Vere Chappell (Englewood Cliffs, 1962), pp. 151–160, and page references are to this volume. The quotation is from p. 152.

it.) To answer we must know what it is to have a *criterion* for *p*, or for determining that *p*. Here Malcolm gives the following hints as to what this technical term means: if Mill has a criterion he can "establish with certainty" that Smith is (or is not) in pain. This criterion, further, will apparently be some observable state of affairs ("the only plausible criterion would lie in behavior and circumstances that are open to view"). And the suggestion, apparently, is that if a man cannot establish with certainty that Jones is in pain, then he does not understand the sentence "Jones is in pain." Why not? Because "he has no idea what would count for or against it"?[2] But here either "count for or against" is being used in a technical and unexplained fashion or else the remark is false. For Mill certainly has some idea of what would count for or against Jones's being in pain. His engaging in the sort of behavior in which *Mill* engages when in pain, for example, would count *for* Jones's being in pain; his behaving in some other way would count against it. So Mill does have an idea of what would count for Jones's being in pain. Why then must he also have a criterion for *Jones is in pain* in order to understand the sentence "Jones is in pain"? And is it true that if Mill has a criterion for that proposition, then he can establish its truth or falsity without resorting to the analogical argument? To answer these questions we must learn more about criteria.

In "Wittgenstein's *Philosophical Investigations*" Malcolm explains further:

What makes something into a symptom of *y* is that experience teaches that it is always or usually associated with *y*; that so-and-so is the criterion of *y* is a matter, not of experience, but of "definition". (354) The satisfaction of the criterion of *y* establishes the existence of *y* beyond question; it repeats the kind of case in which we were taught to say '*y*'. The occurrence of a symptom

---

[2] *Ibid.*, p. 156.

of *y* may also establish the existence of *y* 'beyond question'—but in a different sense. The observation of a brain process may make it certain that a man is in pain—but not in the same way that his pain behavior makes it certain. Even if physiology has established that a specific event in the brain accompanies bodily pain, still it *could* happen (it makes sense to suppose) that a man might be in pain without that brain event occurring. But if the criterion of being in pain is satisfied, then he *must* be in pain.[3]

Consider the proposition *Jones is in pain*, and call it *P*. What this passage clearly asserts is that it is impossible that *P* be false when the criterion for *P* is satisfied. The impossibility in question, furthermore, is not merely causal or empirical; it is a matter of definition. Hence it is a *necessary* truth that if the criterion for *P* is satisfied, then *P* is true; the proposition that the criterion for *P* is satisfied *entails P*.

The very next passage, however, seems to complicate matters:

The preceding remarks point up the following question: Do the propositions that describe the criterion of his being in pain *logically* imply the proposition "He is in pain"? Wittgenstein's answer is clearly in the negative. Pain-behavior is a criterion of pain only in certain circumstances. If we come upon a man exhibiting violent pain-behavior couldn't something show that he is not in pain? Of course. For example, he is rehearsing for a play; or he has been hypnotized and told, 'You will act as if you are in pain, although you won't be in pain,' and when he is released from the hypnotic state he has no recollection of having been in pain; or his pain-behavior suddenly ceases and he reports in apparent bewilderment that it was as if his body had been possessed—for his movements had been entirely involuntary, and during the 'seizure' he had felt no pain; or he has been narrowly missed by a car and as soon as a sum for damages has been

---

[3] *Philosophical Review*, LXIII (1954), 530–559. Reprinted in Chappell, *op. cit.*, pp. 81–101, and page references are to this volume. The quotation is from p. 87.

pressed into his hand, his pain-behavior ceases and he laughs at the hoax, or . . . etc. The expressions of pain are a criterion of pain in *certain* "surroundings," not in others. (cf. 584)

How can we understand this in such a way that it does not conflict with the clear teaching of the preceding passage? Perhaps as follows. In the appropriate circumstances, certain kinds of behavior are the criterion for P. Let b be some kind of behavior which in the relevant circumstances is the criterion for P; and let B be the proposition that Jones is manifesting b. Suppose further that c is a circumstance in which Jones's manifesting b is the criterion for P; and let C be the proposition that c obtains. Now Malcolm is clearly asserting that B does not entail P; for b is the criterion for P only in certain circumstances.[4] Nor, therefore, does B entail that the criterion for P is satisfied. But the conjunction of B and C with the proposition that in c, b is the criterion for P does entail that the criterion for P is satisfied; and hence it entails P as well. This gives us a consistent interpretation of what Malcolm says. Although the proposition that the criterion for P is satisfied entails P, the proposition that Jones is engaging in the sort of behavior which, in the appropriate circumstances, constitutes the criterion for P, does not.

An interesting question here is whether the conjunction of B with C entails P—that is, does the proposition that c obtains conjoined with the proposition that Jones is engaging in pain-behavior entail that Jones is in pain? Suppose that B *and* C does entail P. Then apparently some proposition about[5] behavior and circumstances entails a mental-state-ascribing proposition. And of course no such propositions *do* entail mental-

---

[4] Is the suggestion that if C is true then B entails P? Presumably not; for if p is consistent, then it entails that q entails r only if q entails r (i.e., whether or not p is true).

[5] See above, p. 191.

state-ascribing propositions; nor does Malcolm believe that they do.[6] *B and C*, accordingly, does not entail *P*.

On the other hand, *B and C* conjoined with

D In *c* Jones's manifesting *b* is the criterion for *P*

does entail *P*. Hence *D* must be a contingent proposition.[7]

But if it is, how is Mill supposed to know that it is *true?* Mill can observe, of course, that Jones is engaging in *b* and that *c* obtains; but before he could use his criterion, if he had one, to establish that *P* is the case, he would have to establish the fact that in *c*, Jones's manifesting *b* is indeed the criterion for *P*. And how could be establish that? What would be evidence for it? Here he would need the analogical argument, presumably, or something very like it. Or perhaps something else. At any rate it is clear, I believe, that Malcolm has not told us enough about the nature of criteria for us to determine whether or not his original argument against Mill is sound. For under the present understanding of "criteria" there is no reason to think that if Mill has a criterion for *P* then he can establish that *P* is true without resorting to the analogical argument or something like it. So far, therefore, we have no reason for supposing that argument otiose, or that the "criteriological position" offers a genuine alternative to the analogical position.

Some further remarks in the same article suggest a different sense for "criterion":

" 'But, if you are *certain*, isn't it that you are shutting your eyes in face of doubt?'—They are shut". (224) This striking remark suggests that what we sometimes do is draw a boundary around *this* behavior in *these* circumstances and say, 'Any additional circumstances that might come to light will be irrelevant to whether this man is in pain.' . . . If your friend is struck by a car and

---

[6] Cf. "Wittgenstein's *Philosophical Investigations*," p. 89.

[7] If *p and q and r* entails *s*, and *r* is necessary, then *p and q* entails *s*.

writhes with a broken leg, you do not think: Perhaps it was
prearranged in order to alarm me; possibly his leg was anesthetized
just before the 'accident' and he isn't suffering at all. Someone
could have such doubts whenever another person was ostensibly
in pain. Similarly: "I can easily imagine someone always doubting
before he opened his front door whether an abyss did not yawn
behind it; and making sure about it before he went through the
door (and he might on occasion prove to be right)—but that
does not make me doubt in the same case." (84)[8]

These remarks may suggest that all or almost all of us do in
fact take pain-behavior as an expression of pain. It is simply
a fact of human nature that upon observing a human being
behaving in the relevant way (and in the relevant circumstances) we are certain that he is in pain. And to take pain-
behavior as a criterion of pain is simply to react in this way:
to be certain, on an occasion when a person is displaying pain
behavior, that he is in pain. To say that pain-behavior is the
criterion of pain is not to say that there is some logical or evidential connection between statements describing pain-behavior
and statements ascribing pain to someone; it is just to say that
on most occasions when one human being observes another
manifesting pain-behavior (in the relevant circumstances), he
is certain that the other is in pain.

In this sense of "criterion," of course, the man who accepts
the analogical position may very well have a criterion for pain.
Doubtless Mill had one. A person who accepts the analogical
argument need not employ it in order to convince himself that
there are other people or that others are sometimes in pain.
Aquinas and Anselm believed in God and also presented certain proofs of God's existence. Their acceptance of the latter,
however, was not a necessary condition of their faith in God;

---

[8] "Wittgenstein's *Philosophical Investigations*," p. 90. The passages
Malcolm quotes are from the *Investigations* (New York, 1953).

in the same way a man can be certain that one who displays typical pain behavior is indeed in pain, while appearing to the analogical argument as a justification, or partial justification, for his certainty.

Thus far we have not discovered a sense for "criterion" in which Malcolm's argument against Mill is sound. In "Wittgenstein's Use of 'Criterion' " Rogers Albritton explains Wittgenstein's use of that term as follows:

That a man behaves in a certain manner, under certain circumstances, cannot entail that he has a toothache. But it can entail something else, which there is no short way of stating exactly, so far as I can find. *Roughly*, then: it can entail that anyone who is aware that the man is behaving in this manner, under these circumstances, is *justified in saying* that the man has a toothache, in the absence of any special reason to say something more guarded (as, for example, that there is an overwhelming probability that the man has a toothache).[9]

What Albritton says suggests the following:

> C₁ Where p and q are states of affairs, p is a criterion for q if and only if it is necessary that anyone who knows that p obtains and has no reason for supposing that q does not, is justified in believing that q obtains.

So stated, this explanation has the consequence, I think, that Jones's exhibiting typical pain behavior is not a criterion of his being in pain. For it is not a necessary truth that anyone who (a) knows that Jones is exhibiting typical pain behavior, and (b) has no reason for supposing that he is not in pain, is justified in believing that Jones is in pain. Consider the man who satisfies (a) and (b) but believes that Jones's behavior is altogether irrelevant to his being in pain. He believes that Jones

---

[9] *Journal of Philosophy*, LVI (1958) 845–857. The quotation is from p. 856.

is in pain, all right—not, however, because (a) is true but because it's Thursday and it is his belief that on Thursdays everyone is in pain. Even if p is a first-rate reason for q, indeed, entails q, a man may know that p and unjustifiably believe that q—if, for example, he does not believe that p entails q and accepts q just because he has found a slip of paper on which it was written. C_1 must therefore be revised:

> C_2 p is a criterion of q if and only if it is necessary that anyone who knows that p obtains, has no reason for supposing that q does not, and believes that q obtains *on the basis of* his belief that p does, is justified in believing that q obtains.

Albritton is disinclined to believe that pain-behavior is a criterion of pain in the sense he has explained. And it does indeed seem that knowing that Jones is engaging in pain behavior (and meeting the other conditions) is not sufficient for believing justifiably that Jones is in pain; one must also know, or justifiably believe, that *when a man exhibits pain-behavior he is usually in pain.* Be that as it may, C_2 certainly suffers from an opposite defect: for now the state of affairs which obtains just in case *most Dutchmen are ambidextrous and Dykstra is a Dutchman* could be my criterion for Dykstra's being ambidextrous. More relevantly, Mill will now claim as his criterion for *Jones's being in pain* the state of affairs which obtains just in case the proposition *There is a correlation between pain and pain-behavior in Mill's case, and Jones is exhibiting pain-behavior* is true. For the burden of his position is that the correlation he observes between pain and pain-behavior in his own case inductively justifies his belief that whenever a man exhibits pain-behavior he is in pain; but the latter together with the fact that Jones is exhibiting pain-behavior entails that Jones is in pain. On this version of "criterion" one who accepts the

Alternatives to the Analogical Position

analogical position may indeed have a criterion for *that human figure's having feelings*; part of the position just is that pain-behavior is (or can be) a criterion, in the current sense, for someone's being in pain. And so we still have not found a sense of the term "criterion" which will be of use in Malcolm's argument against the analogical position.

Sydney Shoemaker suggests the following as an explanation of "the sense of 'criterion' which has become current through the influence of Wittgenstein's later work":

A test of whether something is one of the criteria for the truth of judgments of a certain kind is whether it is conceivable that he might discover empirically that it is not, or has ceased to be, evidence in favor of the truth of such judgments. If it is evidence, and it is not conceivable that it could be discovered not to be (or no longer to be) evidence, then it is one of the criteria. If so and so's being the case is a criterion for the truth of a judgment of identity, the assertion that it is evidence in favor of the truth of the judgment is necessarily (logically) rather than contingently (empirically) true. We know that it is evidence, not by having observed correlations and discovered empirical generalization, but by understanding the concept of a ϕ. . . . The search for the criteria for the truth of a judgment is the search for necessarily true propositions asserting that the existence of certain phenomena or states of affairs is evidence of the truth of that judgment.[10]

Although Shoemaker is talking in part about the criteria for the identity of certain kinds of objects, he obviously means his remarks to apply to criteria generally. His suggestion seems to be something like the following: suppose we know that eight

---

[10] *Self-Knowledge and Self-Identity* (Ithaca, 1963), pp. 3–4. (Shoemaker explicitly disclaims any intention of dealing directly "with the doubts and difficulties that have been raised concerning this notion in recent philosophical discussion." Nonetheless his suggestion is interesting and worth considering.)

out of ten nine-year-old Chevrolets have defective wiring; then

A   George's car is a nine-year-old Chevrolet

is inductive evidence for

B   George's car has defective wiring.

That A is evidence for B, however, is a contingent truth; it is conceivable that we should discover its falsity. We might do this, for example, by discovering

C   George's car has just been rewired by a competent mechanic (and almost no such cars have defective wiring)

or possibly

D   Nine out of ten nine-year-old Chevrolets have impeccable wiring.

More generally, where p is inductive evidence for q, the proposition that p is evidence for q is only contingently true; on the other hand, p is *a criterion* for q if and only if the proposition that p is evidence for q is logically necessary.

Shoemaker says nothing further here about the conditions under which one proposition is evidence for another (and in the present context that omission is surely no grounds for complaint). One naturally supposes that p is evidence for q just in case q is more probable than not on p—that is, just in case q would be more probable than not with respect to what we knew if p were all we knew relevant to q. (And, of course, p would be evidence *against* q if p were evidence for q's denial.) If this is Shoemaker's intention, however, then his explanation of the distinction between criteria and symptoms seems to me to embody a confusion. Let me explain why. In the first place, A *by itself* is not inductive evidence for B. For A alone does not disconfirm (is not evidence against)

Alternatives to the Analogical Position

E All nine-year-old Chevrolets have magnificent wiring.

But then A does not disconfirm the conjunction of A with E,[11] which entails

F George's car has splendid wiring.

Hence A does not disconfirm F.[12] But if so, A does not confirm B, since B entails the denial of F.[13] Of course A conjoined with

G Eight out of ten nine-year-old Chevrolets have defective wiring

is evidence for B; but A alone is not. The conjunction of A with G is inductive evidence for B; but how could we possibly discover that it is *not* evidence for B? We could, indeed, discover C (George's car has just been rewired). To do so, however, would not be to discover that A *and* G is not evidence for B; it would be to discover the truth of a proposition whose conjunction with A *and* G is evidence for the falsity of B. Indeed, there is no way of discovering that A *and* G does not confirm B; for the proposition that it does is itself necessarily true.

Taking Shoemaker's suggestion this way, then, I think we get the result that no proposition is ever merely inductive evidence for any other proposition; and the equally unlikely result that such a proposition as A *and* G is a criterion for the truth of B. And, of course, under this understanding of "criterion"

---

[11] By the principle that if p is not evidence against q, then it is not evidence against its conjunction with q.

[12] By the principle that if p does not disconfirm q, then p does not disconfirm any proposition entailed by q. (This follows from the principle that if p is evidence for q, then p is evidence for any logical consequence of q.)

[13] By the principle that if p does not disconfirm q and r entails the denial of q, then p is not evidence for r. (This also follows from the principle mentioned in the previous footnote.)

Mill would indeed have a criterion for *Jones is in pain*; his criterion would be the conjunction of the premises of the analogical argument whose conclusion was that proposition.

Now Shoemaker clearly believes that a proposition p may be evidence at one time but not at another for a proposition q. So·no doubt he is not using the locution "evidence for" in what I said was the natural way to use it. How then does he mean to use it? The following is a possibility: in assessing the evidential relevance of one proposition to another what we consider is the probability of the first on the second *together with* our background information, or that part of it relevant to the case in question. Where e is our background information, then, p is evidence for q just in case (1) q is more probable than not on the conjunction of p with e, and (2) the probability of q on the conjunction of p with e is greater than its probability on e alone. Given then this explanation of "evidence for," A above would indeed be evidence for B; for presumably G would be part of our relevant background information. Furthermore, we could discover that A was *not* evidence for B by making a discovery effecting the right sort of change in our background information. We might conceivably discover D, for example; if D became a part of our background information then presumably B would no longer be more probable than not on the conjunction of the latter with A. Given this conception of evidence, how can we state Shoemaker's distinction between criteria and inductive evidence? The essence of the distinction, of course, is that p is *criterial* evidence for q only if it is necessarily true that p is evidence for q; but merely inductive evidence if the latter is only contingently true. So perhaps we can put this as follows:

> C_3 Where e is our relevant background information, p is
> a criterion for q if and only if there is no proposition

r consistent with p and with q[14] such that when e' is formed from e by conjoining r with e (and deleting any conjunct of e inconsistent with r,[15] q is not more probable than not on the conjunction of p with e'.

On C_3, however, it appears that no behavioral proposition is (or states) a criterion for Jones's being in pain. For any such proposition would say, of Jones, that he is displaying behavior of a certain specified sort S. But now consider

H Jones is almost never in pain when he displays behavior of sort S.

This will be consistent with the proposition that Jones is in pain as well as the proposition that Jones is displaying behavior of sort S. And our background information is of such a sort that when we add H to it, its conjunction with *Jones is displaying behavior of sort S* will not be evidence for *Jones is in pain*. Hence on C_3 the former will not be a criterion for the latter; hence C_3 is unsuccessful.

There remains but one more possibility I wish to examine. Consider what we may call the *myriokranic syllogism*, where (1) the major premise is a proposition of the form *most* (almost all, the vast majority of, etc.) A's are B; (2) the minor asserts of some particular x that is an A; (3) the conclusion states of that same x that it is a B, and (4) the minor premise does not entail the conclusion. Suppose we say further that the minor premise of a myriokranic syllogism is evidence for its conclusion in just those cases where our background information contains the major. We may say still further, then, that where (and only where) the major premise is necessarily true,

---

[14] This qualification serves to eliminate some trivial counterexamples.

[15] This must be stated with greater care to be fully accurate; but the gain would not be worth the price in complication.

the minor is necessarily evidence for the conclusion. Now perhaps Shoemaker's suggestion may be put as follows:

C_4 Where p is a criterion for q and p and q each predicate a property of the same individual, there is a myriokranic syllogism whose minor premise is p, whose conclusion is q, and whose major premise is necessarily true.

Of course this would not constitute a perfectly general explanation of the nature of criteria; for no doubt it is false that wherever p is a criterion for q, p and q predicate a property of the same individual. Nonetheless, it may hold for the cases relevant to the present discussion; for it might be argued that *Jones is displaying pain-behavior* is a criterion (in the sense just explained) for *Jones is in pain* in that

M   On most occasions when a person displays pain-behavior he is in pain

is necessarily true.

I think Shoemaker believes that M is necessarily true; and Albritton tentatively attributes the view that it is to Wittgenstein.[16] Is it? It certainly does not appear to be. It has the look of a fact of common experience, as Albritton remarks. Of course other propositions which at first blush do not seem to be necessary have been shown to be so; *Some properties have no associated sets* does not look necessary at first glance either. But at any rate, we need an argument, and a substantial one, for the claim that M is necessarily true.

Shoemaker appears to suggest such an argument.[17] He apparently means to argue that (1) if M is contingent, its denial is conceivable. And (2) if its denial is conceivable, one could

---

[16] Albritton, *op. cit.*, p. 856.

[17] *Op. cit.*, pp. 188–190. I *think* Shoemaker is arguing for the necessity of M in this passage; but that he is doing so is not altogether clear.

Alternatives to the Analogical Position

"imagine what it would be like" for the usual correlation between pain-behavior and pain to fail in one's own case. But, he argues, in fact no one can imagine this. Curiously enough, however, Shoemaker employs as a premise the proposition that one can imagine what it would be like for a certain state of affairs to obtain only if one could *establish* or *prove* that it obtained:

The claim that one can imagine what it would be like for the state of affairs S (the failure of the usual correlations between pain-behavior and pain) to become, in one's own case, the rule rather than the exception is, I think, equivalent to the claim that one could *establish* that this had occurred in one's own case; one could express this claim by saying that there is something one can imagine occurring that would *show* one that this had happened in one's own case.[18]

Now premise (2) above is true (and relevant to the argument) only if "one can imagine what it would be like if p" is equivalent to something like "one can see that p is contingent." But if so, Shoemaker is espousing the peculiar principle that if one can see that p is contingent, then one can or could establish or discover that p is true. And this seems obviously false. *That I am alive or am conscious* is contingent and so is its denial; yet it is scarcely possible for me to establish the latter. *That there are beings capable of making discoveries* is also contingent; but surely its denial cannot be discovered or established.

Once more, then, we have not been able to find a sense of "criterion" under which Malcolm's argument against Mill is plausible.

Like Malcolm and Shoemaker, P. F. Strawson accepts the view that there are behavioral criteria for mental states. And if he has no very clear explanation of the criteriological rela-

---

[18] *Ibid.*, pp. 189–190.

tionship, what he seeks to establish is not merely that it does in fact connect behavior and mental states, but that its connecting them is a necessary condition of our being able to predicate mental states either of ourselves or of others; he offers a "transcendental deduction" of the criteriological relation. I quote the argument in full:

Clearly there is no sense in talking of identifiable individuals of a special type, a type namely, such that they possess both M-predicates and P-predicates, unless there is in principle some way of telling, with regard to any individual of that type, and any P-predicate, whether that individual possesses that P-predicate. And in the case of at least some P-predicates, the ways of telling must constitute in some sense logically adequate kinds of criteria for the ascription of P-predicates. For suppose in no case did these ways of telling constitute logically adequate kinds of criteria. Then we should have to think of the relation between the ways of telling and what the P-predicate ascribes, or a part of what it ascribes, always in the following way: we should have to think of the ways of telling as *signs* of the presence, in the individual concerned, of this different thing, viz., the state of consciousness. But then we could only know that the way of telling was a sign of the presence of the different thing ascribed by the P-predicate, by the observation of correlations between the two. But this observation we could each make only in one case, viz., our own. And now we are back in the position of the defender of Cartesianism who thought our way with it was too short. For what, now, does 'our own case' mean? There is no sense in the idea of ascribing states of consciousness to oneself, or at all, unless the ascriber already knows how to ascribe at least some states of consciousness to others. So he cannot argue in general 'from his own case' to conclusions about how to do this; for unless he already knows how to do this, he has no conception of *his own case*, or any *case*, i.e., any subject of experiences.[19]

---

[19] *Individuals* (London, 1959), pp. 105–106.

Alternatives to the Analogical Position

Let me try to state this argument a bit more precisely. In order to simplify matters I shall specify the argument with respect to a certain kind of mental state, pain, and the "ways of telling" appropriate to that state which I shall call P-behavior. Strawson's argument may then be outlined as follows:

(1) If P-behavior is not a logically adequate criterion for the ascription of pain, P-behavior is a *sign* of pain.

(2) If a person N knows at time t that P-behavior is a sign of pain, then at some prior time t_{-1} N observed a correlation between P-behavior and pain in his own case.

(3) If at t_{-1} N noted a correlation between pain and P-behavior in his own case, then N was able to predicate pain of himself at t_{-1}.

(4) If at t_{-1} N was able to predicate pain of himself, then at t_{-1} N knew how to predicate pain of others.

(5) If at t_{-1} N knew how to predicate pain of others, then at t_{-1} N knew that P-behavor is a sign of pain.

Step (6) would be a repetition of (2) with "t_{-1}" substituted for "t" and "t_{-2}" for "t_{-1}." Steps (7), (8), and (9) would parallel (3), (4), and (5); step (10) would again parallel (2) with the substitution of "t_{-2}" for "t" and "t_{-3}" for "t_{-1}"; and so on. The conclusion Strawson draws, of course, is that if P-behavior were not a logically adequate criterion for the ascription of pain, no one could ascribe pain to anyone else; and hence no one could ascribe pain to himself either.

There is an ambiguity in the phrase "knows how to predicate pain of others" as it occurs here. Step (4) of this argument is clearly intended to be identical with the central premise of Strawson's argument against the Cartesian[20]—the premise that "it is a necessary condition of ascribing states of consciousness, experiences, to oneself, in the way one does, that one should

---

[20] See above, p. 205.

also ascribe them, or be prepared to ascribe them, to others who are not oneself." [21] (I shall call that premise "the predication principle.") Accordingly (4) ought to be taken as

(4a) If at t–1 N was able to predicate pain of himself, then at t–1 N had a conception of the appropriate occasions for predicating pain of others,

and (5) ought to be rewritten as

(5a) If at t–1 N had a conception of the occasions appropriate for ascribing pain to others, then at t–1 N knew that P-behavior is a sign of pain.

But it is not at all clear that (5a) ought to be accepted. Suppose that in accordance with step (2) N could know that P-behavior is a sign of pain only if he had observed a correlation between P-behavior and pain. At time t–2, *before* he has observed any such correlation, N might make the following declaration: If I observe a connection between my pain and P-behavior on my part at t–1, then any occasion after t–1 on which I observe P-behavior which is not mine will be an appropriate occasion for predicating pain of someone else. If he were to make such a declaration, he would "have a conception of the circumstances appropriate for predicating pain of someone else," although he would not then know that P-behavior is a sign of pain, for he would not have made the requisite observation. Hence it seems that step (5) cannot be accepted.

Now for a couple of objections to my refutation. First, we should note that Strawson distinguishes a weaker and a stronger version of the predication principle.[22] He claims that his arguments require only the weaker version, which is the one I have been ascribing to him and under which in fact the arguments

[21] Strawson, *op. cit.*, p. 99.
[22] *Ibid.*

are not sound. The stronger version of that principle asserts
that a necessary condition of one's being able to predicate mental states of himself is that one *in fact* predicate mental states
of others (as opposed to merely having a conception of the appropriate occasions for so predicating them). And someone
might say that Strawson's argument can be rescued by employing the stronger version of the predication principle. Here we
must again remember the two possible interpretations of "necessary condition": the stronger principle *may* be asserting that
before N can ascribe pain to himself he must have ascribed it
to someone else. So taken, the principle has little to recommend it, for it is supposed to be a specification of a *general*
principle about predication; but that general principle would
then be the absurd assertion that before I can predicate any
property of any one thing I must have predicated that property
of something else. The other sense of "necessary condition" is
not easy to apply to the predication principle in its stronger
formulation, but presumably it would come to something like
this: I cannot have predicated pain of myself before I have
predicated it of others—that is, any time at which I predicate
a mental state of myself is a time before which or at which I
predicate that state of someone else. And the general principle
of which this is a specification would be: any time at which N
predicates a property P of individual a is a time at which or
before which N predicates that property of some other individual. This in turn entails that the first occasion on which
anyone predicates a property of anything is one on which he
predicates that property *of at least two things*. I take it that the
principle so stated is utterly gratuitous. But a little reflection will
satisfy anyone who is interested that the declaration I ascribed
to N at t–2 can be reformulated so as to be consistent even
with that peculiar version of the predication principle.

So Strawson does not succeed in showing, it seems to me,

that if we are able to predicate mental states of ourselves, there must be criteria for the predication of these states of others. There seems to be no explanation of the criteriological position which enables us to see that it furnishes either a valid objection or a genuine alternative to the analogical position.

II

Wittgenstein remarks: "My attitude towards him is an attitude towards a soul. I am not of the *opinion* that he has a soul." [23] Shoemaker explains and develops this aphorism:

It is, I should like to say, part of our "form of life" that we accept what other persons say at face value, without normally raising or even considering the question whether they understand the meanings of the expressions they utter, or whether their apparent testimony is really testimony. Normally there is no inference, and certainly not an inductive inference, from "He uttered the sounds 'I went for a walk yesterday'" to "He said that he went for a walk yesterday." We regard a person who is talking, not as making sounds, from which, knowing the circumstances under which such sounds have been uttered in the past, we can make certain inductive inferences, but as *saying something.* . . . It would be misleading to describe this as a *belief* on our part, the belief that people who use the words we use generally mean by them what we mean by them. It is rather a matter of attitude, of the way in which we respond to a person who is talking.[24]

I shall use . . . the term "human being" in a technical sense, to mean "something that looks like, and has the physical characteristics (anatomical structure, chemical composition and so forth) of a person." What might be regarded as essential attributes of persons, e.g., being able to remember some of their past actions, being capable of learning the use of language, and so forth, I shall regard as only contingent properties of human

---

[23] *Op. cit.*, p. 178.
[24] *Op. cit.*, p. 249.

beings. My distinction between persons and human beings is similar to Locke's distinction between a person and a man.[25]

In Section 6 I introduced a technical use of the term "human being" and insisted on a conceptual distinction between human beings, things that look like and have the physical characteristics of persons, and persons. The "attitude" referred to above can be further described by saying, this distinction notwithstanding, that we regard human beings as persons without having evidence that they are persons. Involved in being a person is having a memory, and this involves having the ability to make, without evidence, true statements about one's own past. It is part of our attitude that we do not normally demand that particular human beings have this ability, though there could be human beings who do not have it.[26]

These passages express an objection to the analogical position—an objection that I shall inelegantly call "the attitudinal objection." But how, exactly, is it opposed to the analogical position? At what points does it differ from it? To see this we must characterize the analogical position more fully. Let us say that a man's *total evidence* is a set of propositions meeting the following conditions: (1) he knows every member of it, and (2) every member of it is either necessarily true or merely about physical objects or merely about his own mental state or a logical consequence of such propositions. According to the analogical position, there is a large class K of propositions that are about other persons and their mental states and are more probable than not on my total evidence. I believe many of these propositions, furthermore, and my justification for doing so is just the fact that they *are* more probable than not on my total evidence. And finally, these propositions can be shown to be probable on my total evidence by inductive or analogical argu-

---

[25] *Ibid.*, p. 237.
[26] *Ibid.*, p. 250.

ments. Now among the members of K we should find, for example, the following:

(a) I am not the only person.

(b) On most occasions when a person displays pain-behavior, he is in pain.

(c) Jones is a person.

(d) On most occasions when a human being (in what Shoemaker calls his "technical sense") displays pain-behavior, some person is in pain.

(e) All human beings (in the technical sense) are persons.

(f) On most occasions when a human being (in the technical sense) emits sounds that, in some language, constitute a sentence expressing a memory or perceptual judgment, that memory or perceptual judgment is true.

(g) On most occasions when a person emits sounds that, in some language or other, constitute a sentence expressing a memory or perceptual judgment, that memory or perceptual judgment is true.

(h) Jones is in pain.

So much for my brief statement of the analogical position. Now the attitudinal objection (as I understand Shoemaker's development of it) would begin by claiming that the members of K fall into three groups. Some of them (for example (b) and (g)) are necessarily true.[27] A second group (group II) in-

---

[27] Shoemaker argues for the necessity of (b) on pages 168–178 (and elsewhere); on pages 229–236 he argues for the necessity of (g). It is doubtful, I think, that sentences (b) and (g) ordinarily express necessary propositions; I am inclined to believe that what Shoemaker takes as a technical sense of "human being" is in fact the usual sense both of "person" and "human being." But even if this is so, we can take it that the term "person" is used technically in (b) and (g), in such a fashion that they do express necessary propositions. Then sentences (b), (d), (f) and (g) would express the propositions that Shoemaker takes them to, but it would be (b) and (g) rather than (d) and (f) that involve technical

cludes (c) and (e). These are not believed at all; our stance with respect to them is a matter of attitude. I do not believe (or know, assume, take for granted) that Jones is a person; instead I *regard* him as a person; my attitude toward him is an attitude toward a person. The analogical position errs doubly, then: it supposes that the propositions in the second group are believed and it supposes them more probable than not with respect to my total evidence. The rejection of the analogical position goes even deeper than this, however; so far one who accepted it could concede the above claims and continue to hold his former views with respect to the remaining members of K, including, for example, (h). As the third tenet of the attitudinal objection, then, we add the claim that the remaining members of K (including (h)) constitute a group (group III) that are more probable than not on the conjunction of my total evidence with the members of group II; they are not, however, more probable than not on my total evidence alone.

According to the attitudinal objection, then, no (contingent) member of K is more probable than not on my total evidence alone; and some of them (i.e., the members of group II) are not even believed. Many questions arise here. What, for example, is meant by saying that my stance with respect to the members of group II is a matter of *attitude*? Can I regard Jones as a person without believing (or taking it for granted, or knowing) that he is a person? Fundamentally, however, the questions that arise here are two: What reason is there for supposing that I do *not* believe the members of group II? And what is the reason for supposing (contrary to the analogical position) that none of the (contingent) members of K are more probable than not on my total evidence? I shall deal with each of these questions in turn.

---

uses. Which of these uses is technical and which ordinary is not, in the present context, of much moment.

Shoemaker nowhere explicitly argues that we do not or cannot believe such propositions as that Jones is a person. But he does say the following:

> If this attitude were one of belief, we could inquire into the grounds of the belief. But this is just what we do not do. It is part of the expression of this attitude that the question of what justifies us in regarding what others say as testimony does not arise.[28]

What Shoemaker says here and elsewhere suggests the following argument. First of all, we do know many of the propositions in group III; on many occasions we know the truth of such propositions as *Jones is in pain*. But our evidence for any proposition in group III always includes members of group II; that is, any set of propositions constituting evidence, for us, for some proposition in group III, includes one or more members of group II. Furthermore, we have no evidence for any of the members of group II, and hence if we *believed* them, our belief would be unfounded. But if any evidence we have for the members of group III included unfounded beliefs, we would not know these propositions either; hence we do not believe the members of group II. But then it is pretty hard to say what our position with respect to these propositions *is*, and it seems as appropriate as anything else to say that it is a matter of attitude (toward, presumably, the subjects of the propositions in question).

A crucial premise of this argument is that we have no evidence for the members of group II and that to believe a member of this group for which one has no evidence is to hold an unfounded belief. More specifically: (1) the members of group II are not more probable than not on my total evidence (as defined above); and (2) if someone believes a member of group

---

[28] *Op. cit.*, p. 250.

II that is not more probable than not on his total evidence, his belief is unfounded. What does it mean to say that a belief is unfounded? Here the word is so taken that the following sentences express necessary propositions:

(1) If S's belief that p is unfounded, S does not know p.
(2) If every set of propositions constituting evidence for q for S contains an unfounded belief, then S does not know q.

The following, then, seems to be the idea behind this argument. If you believe a member of group II which is not more probable than not on your total evidence, you do not know that proposition or any other proposition for which it is an essential part of your evidence. On the other hand, if you adopt the appropriate attitude toward this member of group II (or toward its subject) but refrain from believing it, then, though you cannot know *it*, you *can* know its evidential consequences. So if you have the appropriate attitudes you can know the members of group III, despite their being evidentially based on members of group II whose truth you do *not* know.

Now there is certainly something peculiar about this suggestion. Why does the fact that I *believe* a proposition render me epistemologically less favored, with respect to those propositions for which it is an essential part of my evidence, than I would be if I *did not* believe it? Would it not be just as plausible to hold that my having the appropriate attitudes *justifies me in believing* the members of group II *themselves* as well as their evidential consequences? And of course it is very hard to see how the fact that I have the attitudes in question enables me to know propositions which are contingent, corrigible, and require evidence, but for which my best evidence includes propositions I do not know to be true.

The crux of the position, considered as an objection to the

analogical position, however, is the claim that no member of group II is more probable than not on my total evidence; Shoemaker's argument for it has a Wittgensteinian ring:

Let us consider whether it would be possible for me to question whether there is anyone at all (other than myself) who speaks the language I speak, and then to discover empirically, by observing correlations between the uttering of sounds and the past histories of those who utter them, that those around me do speak the language I speak and that certain of their utterances are memory claims and can generally be relied upon. In carrying on such an investigation, I would of course have to rely on my own memory. But one's memory can be mistaken. It is essential to the very notion of memory, as knowledge of an objective past, that there be a distinction between remembering something and merely seeming to remember something. And for there to be such a distinction there must be such a thing as checking up on one's memory and finding that one does, or does not, remember what one seems to remember. As Wittgenstein has pointed out, there are and must be circumstances in which we would accept other sorts of evidence concerning the past as more authoritative than our own memories. An important way of checking up on one's own memory is by reference to the testimony of other persons. But this sort of check would not be available to me if I could not even regard the utterances of other human beings as testimony (e.g., as memory claims) until I had completed my investigation and established the required set of correlations. And the possibility of my checking up on my memories in any other way presupposes the possibility of checking them in this way.[29]

Shoemaker's argument here, I think, is for the conclusion that no person S could produce an argument meeting the following two conditions: (1) its conclusion is that there is someone other than S who uses the language he uses, and (2) neither the premises nor S's evidence for the premises nor the fact that S

---

[29] *Ibid.*, p. 252.

knows the premises presupposes or entails that there are persons other than S. If successful, of course, Shoemaker's objection will show that no analogical argument for other minds can be acceptable. Now the argument appears to be a *reductio*: suppose that

(a) S has produced an argument A of the sort under consideration.

If so, then

(b) S has come to know the truth of the premises of A.

From (a) and (b) (together with some unmentioned premise specifying the possible ways of coming to know the truth of a proposition) it follows that

(c) S must have relied upon his memory in coming to know the truth of the premises of A.

From (a), presumably, it is to follow that

(d) S cannot check up on the alleged memories in question by appealing to the testimony of others.

But

(e) S can check up on his memory in some other way, only if he can check up on them by appealing to the testimony of others.

Hence

(f) S cannot check up on his alleged memories at all.

Shoemaker points out that "it is essential to the very notion of memory that there be a distinction between remembering something and merely seeming to remember something." I think he means to assert here that S *seems* (at some time or other) *to remember that p* does not entail S *remembers that p*; and also that a person has the concept of memory, knows what memory is, only if he does not believe that his seeming to remember that p entails that he does remember that p (or better, believes the former does not entail the latter). Hence we have as another premise

(g) If S has the concept of memory, S knows that S *seems to remember* p does not entail S *remembers* p.

But, Shoemaker adds, there can be a distinction between seeming to remember and remembering only if there is "such a thing as checking up on one's memory and finding that one does, or does not, remember what one seems to remember." I take it here that he means to suggest, not merely that there *is* such a distinction (and hence such a thing as checking up on one's memories), but also that a person can be aware of this distinction only if there is some way in which *he* can check up on *his* memories. So we get another premise:

(h) If S knows that S *seems to remember that p* does not entail S *remembers that p* then S can check up on his memories.

But then it follows from (f) and (h) that

(i) S does not make a distinction between his remembering that p and his seeming to remember that p.

And hence, of course, S does not have the concept of memory.

I am not sure how the argument is meant to proceed from this point. Perhaps the suggestion is that (i) and (c) are inconsistent; this would properly complete the *reductio* and for all I know it may be true. The difficulty with the argument, it seems to me, comes earlier. Its premises entail that

(j) If S produces an argument which (1) is for the conclusion that there is someone other than S who speaks the same language that S does, and (2) has premises such that none of them nor S's evidence for them nor the fact that S knows them presuppose that there are other persons, then S cannot make a distinction between remembering that p and merely seeming to remember that p.

Proposition (j) asserts, therefore, that under the mentioned conditions S could not know that S *seems to remember that p* does not entail S *remembers that p*. And this seems to me to be false. For surely it could happen that at a given time t S seems to remember both that p, and that at t_1 he seemed to remember that *not-p*. But then S could engage in the following reasoning: if *I seem to remember that p* entails *I remember that p*, then I remember that p and that at t_1 I seemed to remember that *not-p*. By another application of the same principle it follows that at t_1 I remembered that *not-p*. But then both p and *not-p* would be the case; hence it is false that *I seem to remember that p* entails *I remember that p*. And then S would surely have a distinction, know the difference, between remembering and merely seeming to remember. Step (j) therefore is false; hence the premises of the argument are not all true.

Where, exactly, does the difficulty arise? Step (h) asserts that if a man has the concept of memory, then he can check up on (at least some of) his memories. Now I am not clear as to whether Shoemaker would construe a person's discovering that he has had at least one false memory belief as a case of checking up on his memory. If he would, however, then it is clear that premise (3) is false and the analogical arguer might perfectly well be able to check up on some of his memories. On the other hand, if he would not regard this as a case of such checking up, then it becomes clear that premise (h) is false and being able to check up on one's memories is not a necessary condition of knowing that there is a difference between seeming to remember something and really remembering it.

Premise (g) of Shoemaker's argument asserts that a person S does not have the concept of memory unless he recognizes that there is a difference between seeming to remember something and remembering it; unless, that is, he knows that S *seems to remember that p* does not entail S *remembers that p*. Now perhaps the argument can be restated by replacing (g) with a slightly stronger premise:

(m) S has the concept of memory only if he can discover that some of his memory beliefs are false without appealing to other memory beliefs.

But why can the analogical arguer not check his memory, by, for example, consulting his notebook? Perhaps he keeps a journal in which he records the results of his self-observation. The answer, of course, will be that if he did, he would be obliged to rely on his memory for such facts as that when he made the entry in question he used "1" as the numeral corresponding to the number one; he must also rely upon his memory for such facts as that he is the person who made the entry in question. What he appeals to in checking his memory belief presupposes that some *other* memory belief is true; he therefore has no *independent* check on his memory beliefs; he is treating what he seems to remember as the "highest court of appeal":

Imagine that you were supposed to paint a particular color "C", which was the color that appeared when chemical substances X and Y were combined. Suppose that the color struck you as brighter on one day than on another; would you not sometimes say: "I must be wrong, the color is certainly the same as yesterday"? This shows that we do not always resort to what memory tells us as the verdict of the highest court of appeal.[30]

---

[30] Wittgenstein, *op. cit.*, par. 56.

Alternatives to the Analogical Position

Commenting on this passage Malcolm says:

There is, indeed, such a thing as checking one memory against another, e.g., I check my recollection of the time of departure of a train by calling up a memory image of how a page of the time-table looked—but "this process has got to produce a memory which is actually *correct*. If the mental image of the time-table could not itself be *tested* for correctness, how could it confirm the correctness of the first memory?" (265)[31]

This passage suggests that (m) must give way to something like

(n) S has the concept of memory only if S can discover that some of his memory beliefs are false without appealing to other memory beliefs or propositions he could know to be true only if he knew that some of his memory beliefs were true,

or (in view of Shoemaker's claim that any other way of checking one's memory beliefs presupposes checking them by appealing to the testimony of others)

(o) S has the concept of memory only if S can discover that some of his memory beliefs are false by appealing to the testimony of others.

But these premises appear to be too strong. Before Friday showed up, Robinson Crusoe could not appeal to the testimony of others in order to check his memory beliefs; yet surely it would be foolish to infer that he could not learn anything he did not already know, or no longer knew what he had once learned, or no longer possessed the concept of memory. Crusoe did have the testimony of others prior to shipwreck; but once he was shipwrecked he had only his own memory to rely on, even for such facts as that the testimony of others with respect

---

[31] WPI, p. 77. The passage Malcolm quotes is from the *Investigations*.

to a given matter was, for example, *p*. Shoemaker presumably takes it, therefore, that there is some significant difference between the situation of the analogical arguer and Crusoe's situation. Yet it is very hard to see what that difference would be. Is the difference that while it is merely physically impossible that Crusoe appeal to the testimony of others, it is logically impossible that the analogical arguer do so? No. For of course it is not logically impossible for the analogical arguer to appeal to the testimony of others. What is impossible is that he both do that and produce a worth-while analogical argument. And it is similarly impossible that Crusoe both be out of contact with others and accept the testimony of others. So what exactly is the relevant difference? Steps (n) and (o) must be so amended that they function in Shoemaker's argument but do not entail that Crusoe lacks the concept of memory; and it is certainly not easy to see how to do this. But pending such amendment, I think we must conclude that Shoemaker's argument, and with it the attitudinal objection, is inconclusive. Once more, then, we have found neither a valid objection nor a viable alternative to the analogical position.

Ten

God and Analogy

IN the last two chapters I defended the analogical position against several objections and argued that it was more successful than any current alternative to it.[1] We should note, furthermore, that the analogical argument for other minds strongly resembles the teleological argument for the existence of God. They answer similar questions; both are inductive or analogical arguments; each is perhaps the most successful answer to the question it addresses. In this chapter I shall argue that the analogical position finally falls prey to the very objection that, in Chapter Four, I urged against the teleological argument.

I

Perhaps we may begin by considering A. J. Ayer's statement of the analogical position: "On the basis of my own experience

---

[1] Of course I did not consider every alternative that has been proposed: see below, p. 269.

God and Other Minds

I form a general hypothesis to the effect that certain physical phenomena are accompanied by certain feelings. When I observe that some other person is in the appropriate physical state, I am thereby enabled to infer that he is having these feelings; feelings which are similar to those that in similar circumstances I have myself." [2] Noting that this formulation seems open to the "one case alone" objection, Ayer suggests that

the objection that one is generalizing from a single instance can perhaps be countered by maintaining that it is not a matter of extending to all other persons a conclusion which has been found to hold for only one, but rather of proceeding from the fact that certain properties have been found to be conjoined in various circumstances. . . . So the question that I put is not: Am I justified in assuming that what I have found to be true only of myself is also true of others? but: Having found that in various circumstances the possession of certain properties is united with the possession of a certain feeling, does this union continue to obtain when the circumstances are still further varied? The basis of the argument is broadened by absorbing the difference of persons into the difference of the situations in which the psycho-physical connections are supposed to hold.[3]

This version of the analogical argument may bear fuller statement. Initially it is pointed out that while a person can observe another's behavior and circumstances, he cannot perceive another's mental states. Hence we cannot come to know that another is in pain, for example, by perceiving his pain. And, on the other hand, although some propositions ascribing pain to a person are incorrigible for *him*, no proposition ascribing pain to him is incorrigible for anyone else. We might put these things technically by saying that no one can *determine by observation* that another is in pain.[4]

---

[2] *The Problem of Knowledge* (Edinburgh, 1956), p. 249.

[3] *Ibid.*, pp. 250–251.

[4] See Chapter Eight, p. 188.

God and Analogy

According to the analogical position, I nevertheless have or can easily acquire evidence for such propositions as that some other person is in pain and that some person is feeling pain in a bodily area in which I feel nothing. Let us say that S's *total evidence* is a set of propositions such that p is a member of it if and only if (1) p is either necessarily true or solely about[5] S's mental states or solely about physical objects, or a consequence of such propositions, and (2) S knows p to be true. According to the analogical position, my total evidence yields an argument for each of the above conclusions. For

(1) Every case of pain-behavior such that I have determined by observation whether or not it was accompanied by pain in the body displaying it, *was* accompanied by pain in that body.[6]

Applying the so-called straight rule of induction, I conclude that

(2) Probably every case of pain-behavior is accompanied by pain in the body displaying it.

But then on a certain occasion I observe that

(3) B over there (a body other than my own) is displaying pain-behavior.

From (2) it follows that B is pained; since I do not feel a pain there, I conclude that

---

[5] Where a necessary (but not sufficient) condition of a proposition's being solely about my own mind or physical objects is that it not entail the existence of mental states that are not mine.

[6] Where, of course, I determine by observation that pain-behavior on the part of a given body is accompanied by pain in that body only if I feel pain in it; and where the term "pain-behavior" is simply a label for a recognizable pattern of behavior (and hence from the fact that a man displays pain-behavior it does not follow that he is in pain). For a comment on the form of (1) see Chapter Four, note 7.

(4) Some other sentient creature has a pain.

And so I am not the only sentient creature.

But here an objection arises. Consider how I establish (4): I observe that B is displaying pain-behavior. But no matter how intensely I concentrate, no matter how carefully I canvass my feelings, my attempt to feel a pain in B is futile. I feel no pain there. Doesn't this state of affairs provide me with a *disconfirming instance* of (2)? Should I not reject the suggestion that B contains a pain in favor of the conclusion that (2) is false? Consider the following analogy. Justice Douglas is walking through Racehorse Canyon, idly inspecting his surroundings. It occurs to him suddenly that every maple in the Canyon of which he has determined by observation whether it has leaves, has indeed had leaves. (Peculiar things occur to Justice Douglas.) So, he concludes, probably all maples in Racehorse Canyon have leaves. Walking a bit farther, he encounters another maple. Carefully inspecting this one, he fails to see any sign of leaves. He concludes that the maple has invisible leaves.

This procedure on Justice Douglas' part is surely perverse and absurd. What he should have concluded is not that there are leaves that cannot be seen, but that some of the maples in Racehorse Canyon lack leaves. And, by analogy, should I not take my failure to observe pain in B to provide me with a counterinstance to the generalization that every case of pain-behavior is accompanied by pain in the body displaying it?

One who accepts the analogical position, of course, will be quick to reject this suggestion. And perhaps his answer could proceed along the following lines. There is a difference, in general, between failing to observe the presence of A's and observing the absence of A's (observing that no A's are present).[7]

---

[7] I owe this way of putting the distinction to Robert C. Sleigh, Jr.

God and Analogy

A man may fail to see the mountain goats on a distant crag without thereby seeing that no mountain goats are there. But just as there are circumstances in which killing someone constitutes murdering him, so there are circumstances in which failing to perceive a thing constitutes observing its absence. Suppose, for example, that a person with good eyesight is looking at a maple ten feet away to see if it has leaves; the light is ample, his view of the tree is unobstructed, etc. If he sees no leaves, then in failing to see leaves he sees that the tree has no leaves. We might call any set of conditions in which failing to observe leaves on a tree constitutes observing that it has no leaves, an *optimal* set of conditions for observing the presence or absence of leaves. And though it may be difficult, perhaps, to specify the members of such an optimal set, there is no doubt that we are sometimes in circumstances of just that sort. Now if a man justifiably believes that he is in an optimal set of conditions for observing whether or not a tree has leaves, and fails to observe that it does, then he can justifiably believe that he is observing the absence of leaves there; perhaps, indeed, he is *rationally obliged*, in these circumstances, to take it that there are no leaves on the tree.

On the other hand, of course, if he knew that he was *not* in a position to observe whether leaves were present or absent, then his failure to observe leaves would scarcely oblige him to believe that he has a counterinstance to the generalization that all maples have leaves. More generally, under what conditions is a man obliged to take his observing an A and failing to observe that it is[8] B as providing him with a counterinstance to all A's are B? Consider the following three conditions:

---

[8] Since "B" is presumably a variable whose substituends are singular referring expressions, the verb here, strictly speaking, should be "has." For stylistic reasons I shall continue to use "is" except where genuine ambiguity results.

(5) There are no possible circumstances in which failing to observe that an A is B constitutes observing that it is not B.

(6) No one can ever be in a position to observe that an A is not B.

(7) It is not possible to observe that an A is not B.

These three conditions hold with respect to observing whether or not a given bodily area is pained. There are no circumstances in which failing to feel pain in a body other than my own, for example, constitutes observing that that body is free from pain; I cannot observe the absence of pain in a body other than mine. But of course the same really holds for my own body as well; as Wittgenstein says, it is logically possible that someone else feel a pain in my body;[9] I can never tell by observation that my body is free from pain (although of course I can tell that *I* do not feel a pain there). And surely a man who *knows* that one cannot tell by observation that a given bodily area contains no pain is not obliged to conclude that he has a counterinstance to (2). Hence we may assert

(8) A person S is obliged to take his observing that something is A and failing to observe that it is B as providing him with a counterinstance to *All A's are B* only if (a) he does not know that it is impossible to observe that an A is not B, and (b) he does not know that there are no circumstances in which failing to observe that an A is B constitutes observing that it is not B, and (c) he does not know that he cannot be in a position to observe that an A is not B.

Since, of course, I might very well know any or all of these things, I am not obliged, in discovering that (4) is true, to take

---

[9] *Philosophical Investigations*, par. 302.

it that I have a counterinstance to (2); and hence this objection to the analogical position fails.

The fact that one cannot observe the absence of pain delivers the analogical position from the above objection; that fact, nevertheless, is the rock upon which it founders. To see this we must characterize more fully the sort of argument which, on the analogical position, is available to each of us. Let us say that *a simple inductive argument for S* is an argument of the following form:

> Every A such that S has determined by observation whether or not A is B is such that S has determined by observation that A is B.[10] Therefore, probably every A is a B.

And let us say that *a direct inductive argument for S* is an ordered pair of arguments of which the first member is a simple inductive argument *a* for S, and the second a valid deductive argument one premise of which is the conclusion of *a*, the other premises being drawn from S's total evidence.

The contention of the analogical position, then, is that for any person S (or at least for most persons) there is a direct inductive argument for S, for such conclusions as that at a given time *t* someone other than S is in pain. But this is not all that the analogical position holds. For it is of course possible that there be for a person S a direct argument for *p* although *p* is improbable on S's total evidence. What the analogical position must hold here is that for any person S there are direct arguments for the propositions in question and no comparable evidence against them; they must be *more probable than not* on his total evidence.

---

[10] This account would be complicated but not essentially modified if it were so generalized as to take account of the sort of argument where, of his sample of A's, S determines by observation that m/n of them are B and concludes that probably m/n A's are B.

Finally, according to the analogical position, the bulk of my commonsense beliefs[11] about minds and mental states must be more probable than not on my total evidence. It is not sufficient that my total evidence confirm the proposition that there are other sentient beings; it must also confirm, in one way or another, the whole range of commonsense beliefs about the behavioral accompaniments or aspects of anger, joy, depression, and pain, as well as beliefs about the connections between body and mind generally. It need be no part of the analogical position to maintain that for *each* of these propositions there is, for me, a direct argument. For some of them, perhaps, my only evidence is the fact that they are probable with respect to *other* propositions for which I do have direct arguments. But each (or most) of us must have a basic set K of such propositions for each member of which he has a direct argument; and perhaps the remainder of his relevant commonsense beliefs can be shown to be confirmed by the conjunction of the members of K. Furthermore, then, not only must each member of K be more probable than not on my total evidence; their *conjunction* must be. This, of course, is a much stronger claim; it is possible that $p_1 \ldots p_n$ are individually more probable than not on q while their conjunction is not.[12] And among the members of K we should certainly find such propositions as the following:

(a) I am not the only being that feels pain.

(b) There are some pains that I do not feel.

---

[11] The term "belief" is here so used that "Jones believes p" is not inconsistent with (and indeed is entailed by) "Jones knows p."

[12] Let q be *a fair die is about to be thrown*; let p_1 through p_5 be, respectively, *face one will not come up, face two will not come up, face three will not come up, face four will not come up,* and *face five will not come up*. Each of p_1 through p_5 is then more probable than not on q; but their conjunction is not.

(c) Sometimes certain areas of my body are free from pain.

(d) There are some pains that are not in my body.

(e) There are some cases of pain that are not accompanied by pain-behavior on the part of my body.

(f) I am the only person who feels pain in my body.

(g) Sometimes someone feels pain when I do not.

Propositions (a)–(g), of course, are stated for *me*; but there is for any person an analogue, in an obvious sense, of each of those propositions. Now, perhaps, we can summarily restate the analogical position as follows:

(9) For any (or almost any) person S there is a set of propositions K such that the appropriate analogues of (a)–(g) are members of K; and S's total evidence *directly supports* each member of K (i.e., for any member *m* of K there is a direct argument for S supporting *m* but no direct argument for S against *m*); and the conjunction of the members of K is more probable than not on S's total evidence.

So stated, this position is dubious at best. The conjunction of (a)–(g) is not more probable than not on the sort of evidence to which the analogical position directs our attention; nor (with one exception) does the analogical position give us any reason for supposing that (a)–(g) are individually more probable than not on that evidence.

II

Suppose we begin with propositions (a) and (b). Recall that my argument for (a) involves a simple inductive argument from

(1) Every case of pain-behavior such that I have determined by observation whether or not it was accompanied by

> pain in the body displaying it, *was* accompanied by pain in that body

to

> (2) Probably every case of pain-behavior is accompanied by pain in the body displaying it.

But

> (3) B over there (a body other than mine) is displaying pain-behavior,

hence

> (10) Probably B contains a pain.

And since I feel no pain in B, I conclude that

> (b) I do not feel every pain.

Of course if B contains a pain, then some sentient creature or other is feeling a pain in B; hence

> (a) I am not the only being that feels pain.

Such is my evidence, on the analogical position, for (a) and (b). There is a peculiarity about the inference of (2) from (1), however, that ought not to pass unmentioned. As we have noted, I determine by observation that a given body or bodily area contains a pain just in case I feel a pain there. Further, I cannot determine by observation that a bodily area does *not* contain a pain—not even if the area in question is part of my own body. The best I can do along these lines is to determine that *I* do not feel a pain there; but of course it does not follow that *no one* does. So, for any bodily area, I determine by observation whether or not that area is pained *only if* what I determine is that it *is* pained. And consequently no counter-instance to (2) (the argument's conclusion) can possibly turn up in my sample. There are other arguments of this same sort and most of them deserve to be regarded with the gravest suspicion. Consider, for example, the inductive argument for epistemological idealism:

(11) Every physical object of which it has been determined whether or not it has ever been conceived (i.e., perceived or thought of) *has* been conceived.

Therefore,

(12) Probably every physical object is conceived; so there are no unconceived physical objects.

Now it might be said that an alleged inductive argument of this sort clearly proves nothing at all. For if there were any counterinstances to the conclusion, it would be logically impossible for one of them ever to turn up in the sample; and hence we know, in any instance of this sort, that there is no reason to suppose that our sample is a random or fair one. Suppose we are drawing colored marbles from an inexhaustible urn and know that Descartes' evil genius is so guiding our hands that we draw only red ones; ought we then to take the fact that all the marbles we have so far drawn have been red as evidence for the view that all the marbles in the urn are red? If it is impossible for a counterinstance to the conclusion of a simple inductive argument to turn up in its sample (where the conclusion is not itself necessarily true), then the argument is unacceptable. Perhaps we do well, therefore, to accept some such principle as the following:

(A) A simple inductive argument is acceptable only if it is logically possible that its sample class contain a counterinstance to its conclusion.

Now (A) appears to be inadequate[13] on the grounds that it

---

[13] As I was reminded by Lawrence Powers.

fails to eliminate certain arguments that such a principle ought to eliminate. Consider, for example, the following argument for the conclusion that I am not the only human person. Let us say that *x* is *crowman* just in case *x* is either a crow or a human body and that a thing is *minded* if it is the (human) body of a human person. Then

> (13) Every crowman such that I have determined by observation whether or not it was either black or minded, *was* either black or minded.

So probably

> (14) Every crowman is either black or minded.

But

> (15) *B* over there (a human body other than my own) is a crowman and is not black.

Hence *B* is probably minded; hence there is at least one other human person.

This argument will not meet with instant approval. And yet its premise will be true for any of us. For any crow in my sample will have the sample property (i.e., the property of being black or minded); my own body will be in my sample and will have the sample property; and of no human body will I be able to determine that it lacks the sample property. Furthermore, the inference of (14) from (13) does not violate (A); clearly it is *possible* (though it will not happen) that my sample class contain a counter-instance (a white crow, for example) to (14).

An interesting peculiarity of this argument is that it will not serve to establish that *Negroes* are minded or are human persons; the analogue of (15) will not be true for a Negro. Emboldened by this unexpected turn of events a Southern white segregationist (call him Jim Clarke) might go on to argue that for each of us whites, there is an argument of the following kind for the conclusion that no Negroes have minds:

Where x is a *swaneg*, if x is either a Negro or a swan,

(16) Every swaneg such that I have determined by observation whether or not it was either white or nonminded *was* either white or nonminded.

So probably

(17) Every swaneg is white or nonminded.

But

(18) S over there (a Negro) is a swaneg and S is not white.

So probably

(19) S is nonminded.

Jim Clarke's argument clearly has a true premise. Furthermore, it does not run afoul of (A). But Jim Clarke probably fails to anticipate the reply that we might call "the Black Muslim retort"; any Negro can argue as follows: Where x is a *croite*, just in case x is either a crow or a white human body,

(20) Every croite such that I have determined by observation whether or not it was either black or nonminded, *was* black or nonminded.

So probably

(21) Every croite is either black or nonminded.

But

(22) Jim Clarke over there is a croite and Jim Clarke is not black.

So probably

(23) Jim Clarke is nonminded.

God and Other Minds

None of these arguments violates (A); and this is best construed as a deficiency of (A). Perhaps, therefore, we can restate (A). Let us suppose for the moment that we know what it is for a property to have a disjunct or conjunct: the property *being black or minded*, for example, has as one disjunct the property *being black*. And let us say that a property *P* is a *part of* a property *P'* just in case *P* is the same property as *P'* or *P* is a disjunct, conjunct, antecedent, or consequent of *P'* or of a part of *P'*. Then

> (A′) Where α, β, is a simple inductive argument for *S*, β is of the form *All A's have B*, and where *C* is any part of β, α, β is acceptable for *S* only if the propositions *S has examined an A and determined by observation that it lacks C* and *S has examined an A and determined by observation that it has C* are both logically possible.

I am by no means certain that (A′) rules out all of the sorts of arguments it is designed to rule out. With sufficient patience and ingenuity we could perhaps construct an argument that does not violate (A′) but is nonetheless preposterous in pretty much the same way as the above arguments. But at any rate (A′) seems to be *true*. And if it is, the argument from (1) to (2) must be rejected, so that we are left without a direct argument for (a) or (b).

The following (merely suggestive) argument indicates that *any* direct argument for (a) will run afoul of (A′). To get a direct argument for (a) we must first, presumably, get a direct argument for (b) (there are some pains I do not feel). Presumably (b) will follow from some proposition of the form

> (24) Every case of ϕ is accompanied by pain meeting condition ψ

together with a premise asserting that I have observed a case of ϕ but feel no pain meeting condition ψ. The proposition (call it (24′)) of the form exhibited by (24) will not, of course, be necessarily true; it will require inductive support. But any simple inductive argument for (24′) will run afoul of (A′), since its premise will be of the form

(25) Every case of ϕ such that I have determined by observation whether or not it was accompanied by pain meeting condition ψ was so accompanied.

Of course, (24′) need not be the conclusion of a simple inductive argument; perhaps it follows from propositions of the forms

(26) Every case of ϕ is a case of β

and

(27) Every case of β is accompanied by pain meeting condition ψ.

But then obviously the same problem will arise with the proposition of the form depicted in (27) (which is of course the same form as depicted in (13)). It looks as if any direct argument from my total evidence for (a) will involve a simple inductive argument for a proposition like (24′); but in that case we will find that no such direct argument for (a) is palatable if we accept (A′). The fact that one cannot observe the absence of pain appeared earlier to deliver the analogical position from disaster; here it returns to wreak destruction upon it.

But perhaps we should ask at this juncture whether the argument I gave above for (A′) is conclusive. (It *does* seem a bit harsh to insist that my observing that *some* cases of pain-behavior are accompanied by pain gives me no reason at all for supposing that all such cases are so accompanied.) I think the argument is indeed conclusive; but on the other side it might be urged that we never have good reason to suppose that the sample of an inductive argument is a fair sample. This last is a large and complex question. Fortunately we need not enter it at present. For we cannot succor the analogical position by rejecting (A'); if we reject (A') (and adopt no similar principle) we then open the gates to direct argument from my total evidence *against* (a) and (b):

(28) Every pain which is such that I have determined by observation whether or not it was felt by me, was felt by me.

So probably

(29) Every pain is felt by me,

which is the denial of (b), and of an essential premise in our argument for (a). This, no doubt, is a preposterous argument. And yet its peculiarity consists just in the fact that it violates (A'); if we reject (A') we must accept this argument as of equal weight with the argument *for* (b). But then so far as direct arguments are concerned, the *denials* of (a) and (b) are as probable on my total evidence as (a) and (b) themselves, in which case my total evidence does not directly support the latter. Whether or not (A') is to be accepted, therefore, my total evidence does not support (a) and (b).

III

Next, let us consider

(c) Sometimes certain areas of my body are free from pain.

Each of us takes a proposition like (c) to be evidently and obviously true. What sort of evidence, according to the analogical position, do I have for (c)? I cannot, of course, *observe* the absence of pain in my body any more than I can observe its absence in some other body; it is logically possible that when I feel no pain in my arm, someone else does.

However, it does not follow from this (contrary to what one might be tempted to suppose) that I can never, on the analogical position, get evidence for the proposition that a certain area of my body is at a certain time free from pain. For evidence of the following sort is available to me:

> (30) Every pain which is such that I have determined by observation whether or not it was accompanied by pain-behavior on the part of the body in which it was located, has been so accompanied.

So probably

> (31) Every pain is accompanied by pain-behavior on the part of the body in which it is located.

(And of course this inference does not violate (A').) But

> (32) At present my body is not displaying pain-behavior.

Hence probably

> (33) No area of my body is presently pained.

From which, of course, (c) follows. Accordingly my total evidence provides me with a direct argument for (c). We might be tempted to think that it also provides me with a direct argument against (c). Consider those ordered pairs (a, t) whose first members are areas of my body and whose second members are times:

> (34) Every ordered pair (a, t) which is such that I have determined by observation whether or not a was pained at t, has been such that a *was* pained at t.

So probably

(35) Every ordered pair (a, t) is such that a is pained at t.

But then

(36) Probably every area of my body always contains a pain.

But the inference of (35) from (34) runs afoul of (A′), along with, apparently, any other direct argument from my total evidence against (c). If we accept (A′), therefore, we get a direct argument for (c) but none against it; hence on (A′) the analogical position with respect to (c) appears to be vindicated.

We might note parenthetically that if (A′) is to be rejected, my total evidence provides me with direct arguments for propositions even more preposterous than (36); if we let "a" range over human bodies generally, the analogue of (34) will remain true and we get the conclusion that probably every area of every human body is always pained. If we let "a" range over areas of physical objects generally the analogue of (34) still remains true and we get the outrageous result that probably every area of every physical object is always pained. Leibniz and Whitehead apparently overlooked this fertile source of evidence for certain of their conclusions.

IV

The propositions

(d) There are some pains that are not in my body

and

(e) There are some cases of pain that are not accompanied by pain-behavior on the part of my body

may be considered together. What presents itself as the direct argument for (d) is the following:

(1) Every case of pain-behavior such that I have determined by observation whether or not it was accom-

panied by pain in the body displaying it, *was* accompanied by pain in that body.

Hence

(2) Probably every case of pain-behavior is accompanied by pain in the body displaying it.

But

(3) *B* over there (a body other than mine) is displaying pain-behavior,

hence

(10) Probably *B* has a pain.

Hence

(d) There are some pains that are not in my body.

The argument for (e) shares steps (1), (2), (3), and (10) with the above argument. If, in addition,

(37) My body is not now displaying pain-behavior

is part of my total evidence, (e) follows.

The inference from (1) to (2), again, is ruled out by (A′). And, as in the case of (a) and (b), if we accept (A′) we appear to have no direct argument at all for either (d) or (e). On the other hand, my total evidence appears to provide me with direct arguments *against* both (d) and (e):

(38) Every pain which is such that I have determined by observation whether or not it was in my body, *was* in my body.

Hence probably,

(39) All pains are in my body.

This argument does not violate (A′). But is it an acceptable inductive argument? It might be objected that it is causally *impossible* for a person to feel pain anywhere but in his own body, and that, where it is impossible to observe an A which is B (although possibly some A's are B), it is illegitimate to conclude that no A's are B from a premise reporting that no observed A's are B. If a man *knows* that it is impossible to observe an A which is B, then indeed he cannot reasonably conclude that no A's are B from the fact that every A which is such that he has determined by observation whether or not it is B, has turned out not to be B. But things are quite different if he does not know this; ignorant of the fact that one cannot see mountain goats on a glacier at 800 yards, a tenderfoot might sensibly conclude, after futilely inspecting Kulshun Glacier from that distance several weeks running, that no mountain goats frequent it. And, of course, as an analogical arguer I do not initially know that one can feel pain only in his own body; it is just this sort of belief that the analogical argument is supposed to ground and justify. This argument, therefore, is apparently successful.

A similar direct argument holds against (e). Every case of pain which is such that I have determined by observation whether or not it was accompanied by pain-behavior on the part of my body *was* so accompanied; probably, therefore, every case of pain is accompanied by pain-behavior on the part of my body, in which case (e) is false.

If we accept (A'), therefore, we get direct arguments against (d) and (e) but no direct arguments for them. If we reject (A'), of course, we get direct arguments both for and against them; hence in neither case does my total evidence directly support either (d) or (e).

V

This brings us to

(f)   I am the only person who feels pain in my body

and

(g) Sometimes someone feels pain when I do not.

Does my total evidence provide me with a direct argument for
(f)? Apparently not.

(40) Every pain in my body which is such that I have determined by observation whether or not it is felt by me,
has been felt by me

presents itself as the relevant premise; but of course the argument from (40) to (f) flatly conflicts with (A'). Nor, on the
other hand, does my total evidence seem to provide me with
a direct argument against (f). To get such an argument we
should need a direct argument for

(41) Sometimes my body contains a pain I do not feel.

And in order to do that we should need to employ some such
premise as

(34) Every ordered pair (a, t) such that I have determined
by observation whether a was pained at t is such that
a *was* pained at t.

But as we have already seen any simple argument with (34)
as its premise will violate (A').

Now suppose (as seems to be the case) that my total evidence yields no direct argument for (f) but does yield a direct
argument for p and for q, where p and q are logically independent of each other, of (f), and of my total evidence; and
where the conjunction of p with q entails (f). (In such a case,
let us say that my total evidence provides an *indirect* argument
for (f).) Would it then follow that my total evidence supports
(f)? No. It is of course true that if p is more probable than not
on q, and p entails r, then r is more probable than not on q.
But from the fact that p is more probable than not on q, and

r is more probable than not on q, it does not follow that p *and* r is more probable than not on q. And of course where p, q, and r are logically independent and q supports p and q supports r, q supports the conjunction of p with r to a lesser degree than it supports either p or r. So even if my total evidence yielded an indirect argument for (f), it would not follow that my total evidence supports (f). But the fact is that we seem to be unable to find even an indirect argument from my total evidence. That evidence, as we have seen, yields a direct argument for

(42) Whenever my body is pained, it displays pain-behavior

and for

(43) Whenever my body displays pain-behavior, I feel pain.

But (42) and (43) do not entail that I feel every pain in my body or that I alone feel pain in my body; they entail only that whenever *anyone* feels pain there, I do. We seem, therefore, to be able to find neither a direct nor an indirect argument for (f) if we accept (A'); if we reject (A'), of course, we will find direct arguments both for and against (f).

(g)   Sometimes someone feels pain when I do not

resembles (f) in that there seems to be no direct argument from my total evidence either for or against it. It differs from (f) in that there seems to be an indirect argument *against* it. My total evidence directly supports

(44) Every case of pain is accompanied by pain-behavior on the part of my body.

It also yields an argument for

(45) Whenever my body displays pain-behavior, I feel pain.

But (44) and (45) entail

God and Analogy

(46) Whenever any sentient being feels pain, I feel pain, which is the denial of (g).

The upshot of the above is clear. If we reject (A'), we find that a person's total evidence provides direct arguments both for and against each of those commonsense beliefs which, on the analogical position, it is alleged to support. But if we accept (A') (as I believe we should) we still find that a man's total evidence does not support the conjunction of those common-sense beliefs. It does not even support the conjunction of the members of K. Indeed, it does not so much as support the members of K individually; (c) alone appears more probable then not on my total evidence while (d), (e), and perhaps (f) appear to be improbable on it. What the analogical arguer should conclude is that every pain occurs in his own body and is accompanied by pain-behavior on the part of his body (and so, perhaps, he could perform a splendid humanitarian service by *destroying* that wretched body).[14]

The objection to which the analogical position falls victim is clearly an analogue of the objection urged in Chapter Four against the teleological argument for the existence of God. For according to each of these, a certain set of propositions—(a)–(g) in the present case, and (a)–(f) in the case of the teleological argument (see above, p. 109)—is supported by evidence

---

[14] But what about the following version of the analogical argument:

Every human body of which I have determined by observation whether or not it has a human mind connected with it (in a certain complicated way) *has* had a mind connected with it (in that way). Therefore probably every human body has a human mind connected with it in that way.

This formulation is explicitly open to the charge that its sample class consists in just one member—my own body. Hence the argument is a hasty generalization. Furthermore, a little reflection reveals that it suffers from the very same defect as the version considered above.

of a certain kind. The objection, in each case, is that the evidence to which our attention is called supports only *some* of these propositions; but then, of course, the conjunction of these propositions is not, in either case, more probable than not on that evidence.

VI

We began this study by asking whether belief in the existence of God is rational. The natural theologian's answer, we found, is of dubious worth at best. The teleological argument is perhaps his most powerful weapon; and yet it suffers from a crucial and crippling deficiency. But if the answer of the natural theologian does not carry conviction, that of the natural atheologian is even less satisfactory. I then proposed to explore an analogous question in the philosophy of mind: the question how I know, what my reasons are for believing, that I am not the only creature that thinks and feels, reasons and believes. Here I argued that while the analogical position is as good an answer as we have to this question, it nonetheless shares the crippling defect of the teleological argument. And my final query is this: exactly what bearing do these conclusions have on the question with which we began—the question whether it is rational to accept theistic belief?

The answer is not easy, and what I have to say is merely tentative. I think it must be conceded that the theist has no very good answer to the request that he explain his reasons for believing in the existence of God; at any rate he has no answer that need convince the skeptic. But must he have or must there be an answer to this question if his belief in God is reasonable, rationally justifiable: must there be, for any proposition p that I rationally believe (and that is, let us say, contingent and corrigible), a good answer to the "epistemological question": "How do you know that p; what are your reasons for supposing that p is true?" Presumably not. If I am right, the analogical position is the best answer I have to the relevant epistemological question; but even if it is unsatisfactory my belief in (a)–(g) is by no means irrational. Of course there may be other answers; it may be, for example, that some version of what I called the "attitudinal position" (above, p. 233) can be made out with respect to propositions (a)–(g). But clearly the theist could hold the same sort of view with respect to the central tenets of theism; they too could be said to be matters of attitude rather than belief.[15] Again, it is sometimes said that propositions (a)–(g) constitute, for each of us, parts of a well-confirmed scientific hypothesis.[16] But this is really a case of *obscuram per obscuras*: the relationship between a scientific theory and the grounds for accepting it is still a black and boundless mystery. Does each of us have grounds for accepting the proposition that he is not the only being that thinks and reasons, senses and feels, *as a scientific theory?* The question can hardly be considered until we have a clearer understanding of the nature of scientific theories and how they are confirmed; its answer is pretty much anyone's guess. Our understanding of scientific theory is too meager to make it more than a shot in the dark. Still, if it is on target with respect to propositions (a)–(g) of this chapter there seems no reason why it should be wide of the mark for (a)–(f) of Chapter Four.

But let us suppose, as seems to me to be true, that there are no viable alternatives to the analogical position. Then we must conclude, I believe, that a man may rationally hold a contingent, corrigible belief even if there is no answer to the relevant

---

[15] Cf. Norman Malcolm, "Is It a Religious Belief That God Exists?" in *Faith and the Philosophers*, ed. John Hick (New York, 1964), pp. 103–110.

[16] Cf. Paul Ziff, "The Simplicity of Other Minds," *Journal of Philosophy*, LXII (Oct. 1965), 575–585. See also an abstract of my reply to Ziff's paper (*ibid.*, pp. 585–587).

epistemological question. Of course it follows only that *some* such beliefs may be held rationally under the indicated conditions; it does not follow that a man can rationally hold *just any* such belief without a reason or evidence. And, it might be held, although rational belief in other minds does not require an answer to the epistemological question, rational belief in God does. In this connection it is important and relevant that the body of evidence with respect to which we considered (a)–(f) of Chapter Four (the "teleological hypothesis") is different from the relevant evidence in the case of the analogical argument (above, p. 247). I referred to this latter as a man's "total evidence." To avoid confusion, let us call it the "analogical evidence"; and let us refer to the former body of evidence as the "teleological evidence." Now the fact is these bodies of evidence do not coincide. For in scrutinizing the teleological argument we take it for granted that we know a great many facts about minds—for example, that there are *several* of them—that are not to be found in the analogical evidence. The teleological evidence obviously contains the analogical evidence and a great deal more. And hence what has been shown is that (a)–(f) of Chapter Four is as probable, relative to *one* body of evidence, as (a)–(g) of the present chapter is to *another*; and this goes no way at all, it might be said, toward showing that the two are on a par.

That the two bodies of evidence differ in the way suggested must, of course, be conceded. Nonetheless it is true, I think, that if (a)–(f) of Chapter Four is as probable on the first evidence as (a)–(g) of the present chapter on the second, then there is nothing to choose from between them so far as evidence or reasons go; the teleological evidence is the evidence appropriate to the teleological argument. I shall not argue that here, however; instead, let me point out, first, that the conjunction of

God and Analogy

(a)–(f) of Chapter Four is about as probable on the analogical evidence as it is on the teleological. Recall that

(b) The universe was designed by exactly one person

of (a)–(f) was not confirmed by the relevant evidence in that we knew of many cases where things exhibiting the degree of unity characterizing the universe had been the work of *several* persons.[17] But of course if my evidence is limited to the analogical evidence this objection falls by the wayside; my analogical evidence contains no such cases. On the other side, (a), which was supported by the teleological evidence, is not apparently confirmed by the analogical evidence; the latter seems to yield no direct argument for it that does not violate (A′). So (a)–(f) of Chapter Four is about as probable on the analogical evidence as it is on the teleological. But then it follows that (a)–(f) of Chapter Four is as probable on the analogical evidence as is (a)–(g) of the present chapter. For if (a)–(f) is as probable on the teleological evidence as (a)–(g) is on the analogical evidence, and (a)–(f) is as probable on the analogical evidence as on the teleological evidence, then (a)–(f) is as probable on the analogical evidence as (a)–(g).

Of course there may be other reasons for supposing that although rational belief in other minds does not require an answer to the epistemological question, rational belief in the existence of God does. But it is certainly hard to see what these reasons might be. Hence my tentative conclusion: if my belief in other minds is rational, so is my belief in God. But obviously the former is rational; so, therefore, is the latter.

---

[17] See above, p. 109.

INDEX

Index

Index

Index